# DISCOVERING QUALITATIVE METHODS

## *Field Research, Interviews, and Analysis*

**Carol A. B. Warren**
*University of Kansas*

**Tracy X. Karner**
*University of Houston*

An *Instructor's Resource Guide* is available. It provides essay exam questions and suggested projects for each chapter. Also included are suggested sample learning assignments and a series of PowerPoint lectures to accompany the book.

Roxbury Publishing Company
Los Angeles, California

**Library of Congress Cataloging-in-Publication Data**

Warren, Carol A. B., 1944–
Discovering qualitative methods: field research, interviews, and analysis / by Carol A. B. Warren, Tracy X. Karner
p. cm.
Includes bibliographical references and index.
ISBN 1-931719-24-1
  1. Social sciences—Research—Methodology. I. Karner, Tracy X., 1959– II. Title

H62.W2833 2005
001.4'3—dc22                                         2004003494  CIP

Publisher: Claude Teweles
Managing Editor: Dawn VanDercreek
Production Editor: Monica K. Gomez
Cover Photo: Tracy X. Karner
Cover Design: Marnie Kenney
Typography: Jeremiah Lenihan

Printed on acid-free paper in the United States of America. This book meets the standards for recycling of the Environmental Protection Agency.

ISBN 1-931719-24-1

**ROXBURY PUBLISHING COMPANY**
P.O. Box 491044
Los Angeles, California 90049-9044
Voice: (310) 473-3312 • Fax: (310) 473-4490
E-mail: roxbury@roxbury.net
Website: www.roxbury.net

*For Bob Emerson, with love and gratitude.*

# Contents

# Preface

# Welcome to the Study of Qualitative Methods

This book is for students who want to learn about, and perhaps do, research using qualitative methods. Although it is designed primarily for sociology undergraduates, it might also be a useful reference text for graduate students, or students in fields other than sociology. Qualitative methods have a rich and lengthy history in anthropology. Though now a strong and vital component in the discipline of sociology, it wasn't until the early twentieth century that our colleagues began to fully acknowledge the utility and insight of qualitative inquiry. During the last few decades, qualitative methods have also become more commonplace in fields as diverse as business, education, and communications.

The past few decades have seen increasing interest in research and teaching not limited to one discipline. Sociologists who use qualitative methods often have research interests that overlap with other disciplines, including the humanities as well as the other social sciences. Although the main focus of this book is sociological research, we are also concerned to some extent with cultural studies, postmodernism, journalism, and other interdisciplinary interests. Although most of the examples we use to illustrate our points are from qualitative sociological research, we also draw examples from these other fields from time to time.

Today, we are living in a global and globalizing society. Students who want to understand the impact of American industrialism and media on other economies and cultures can use qualitative methods locally to further this understanding. Many qualitative studies focus on the global through the lens of the local; for example, research on Hispanic immigrant groups in California, Vietnamese workers in meat processing plants in Kansas, and Laotian churches in rural Missouri.

Throughout this text, we will focus on just what qualitative research *is* and what unique insights and opportunities this approach offers the investigator. Qualitative methods have a rich history and well-developed epistemology. A qualitative approach to research seeks to explore the social construction of reality—how groups and individuals define situations and give meaning to their experiences and surroundings. Qualitative researchers recognize that research "findings" are not independent of the methods used to produce those findings, or of the standpoints and perspectives of the researcher. Qualitative methods include field research or ethnography, interviewing, and the use of images and documents as data.

Although the steps toward or stages of qualitative research overlap, the process follows a certain sequence: conceptualizing the study; designing the study; preparations, human subjects, and Institutional Review Board (IRB) issues; beginning the study; recording data; completing the interviewing or leaving the field; and—eventually—finalizing the study by writing a research report, article, or book. Along with the similarities, some differences exist between field research and interviewing, both epistemologically and in the conduct of the research. Ethnographic research focuses on behavior and interaction as well as talk, in the present, while interviews focus on talk, or accounts, that may include the past or future as well as the present. Both, however, focus on the lived experience of individuals and their meaning worlds. As Ruth Behar notes:

> I came to ethnography because I wanted to be a storyteller who told stories about real people in real places. I was seduced by the notion of fieldwork, the idea of going some place to find a story I wasn't looking for. . . . the beauty and mystery of the ethnographer's quest is to find the unexpected stories, the stories that challenge our theories. Isn't that the reason why we still go to the field? . . . We go to find the stories we didn't know we were looking for in the first place. (Behar 2003, 16)

The methods of qualitative inquiry that we will be exploring are uniquely suited to the task of finding and telling stories. But more on all this later; for now, what will you find within these pages?

## Plan of the Book

Part I (Chapters 1 and 2) of the book is introductory. Part II discusses doing qualitative research: Chapters 3, 4, and 5 are on field research, Chapters 6 and 7 concern interview studies, and Chapter 8 discusses the textual and the visual. Part III focuses on the analysis (Chapter 9) and writing up (Chapter 10) of qualitative research. And finally, the Epilogue considers the future of qualitative social research in the first decade of the twenty-first century.

Chapters 1 and 2 introduce the reader to what qualitative research is in sociology today, and to the ethics and politics of conducting qualitative research studies. All research is embedded in a particular society at a particular time and place, and reflects that society's ethical, political, economic, scholarly, and practical concerns. Field research and interviewing are specific methods of social research that have been used at least since the early nineteenth century in America and other countries, but the ways in which they were conceptualized and used were different in the 1920s, 1960s, or 2000s.

Chapter 1 examines the epistemology—knowledge foundations—of qualitative methods, and the various approaches to field research and interviewing. In this chapter we discuss the history of qualitative methods in sociology from the Chicago School of the early 1900s to the current debates over postmodernism. The outcomes and purposes of qualitative research are also presented in this chapter, from the student papers written by undergraduates in sociology classes to the final reports provided by applied researchers who have obtained federal grant money to conduct their research.

Among the most important issues in doing qualitative research discussed in Chapter 2 are the politics and ethics of dealing with human subjects. When qualitative sociologists do field research and interviewing, they interact with, talk to, and perhaps develop relationships of various kinds with people, individually and in groups. This interactive basis of qualitative research brings with it a good deal of personal and social responsibility, as well as various bureaucratic and legal issues. In the process of conducting qualitative research, both students and professionals are functioning not only as researchers but also as concerned citizens and individuals, and as representatives of the colleges or universities sponsoring the research.

Part II begins with Chapter 3 on settings for and entrée to field research. In this chapter we talk about the kinds of settings that might be useful and interesting for both individual and team student researchers in terms of feasibility, do-ability, cost, and IRB issues. The various advantages and disadvantages of being a member or not being a member of the setting, and of being open or secretive about one's research purposes (overt vs. covert research), are discussed in this chapter. Issues of entrée into different kinds of settings by different individuals (and the relevancies of gender, age, social status, and other researcher characteristics) are also covered.

As fieldwork continues over time, roles and relationships are offered, formed, and reformed; this is the topic of Chapter 4. A researcher may intend a particular kind of role within the setting, but the people in the setting may incorporate her or him in a way that reflects their own interests and relevancies. Research over time often involves research bargains between the setting members and the field researchers, including emotional, practical, and financial involvements. And since field research is based on personal knowing, various kinds of relationships may be formed in the field, including at times the emotional and the sexual. But in the end, the researcher must (generally) leave the field.

The important business of writing fieldnotes is discussed in Chapter 5. In field research, fieldnotes are the data—what has been recorded about the interaction and talk within the setting. The writing of fieldnotes must be consistent and systematic, so a commitment to this part of the task is vital. We urge student researchers to use computers for their research, because of the flexibility of this particular technology. Student researchers' fieldnotes will probably be supervised by instructors and may be read by fellow students; themes for analysis in these fieldnotes can come from both the readers and the writers. Fieldnotes must be read and reread thoroughly in order to form the basis for qualitative analysis.

In Chapter 6, the first steps toward interview research are discussed. Qualitative research involves a particular type of interview, known by various names; the one we have chosen is qualitative interview. The qualitative interview involves an interviewer (or perhaps more than one), an interviewee (or perhaps more than one), and a topic. This chapter begins with a consideration of the interview topic, since it is with a topic in mind that students generally begin to think of interview research. Armed with a subject matter that is of interest to the researcher and, it is hoped, to the interview respondents too, the researcher develops specific interview questions and begins the process of locating and selecting respondents.

Chapter 7 takes up the premise of the interview as social interaction and as speech event. An interview has elements similar to any other bounded social interaction, including greeting and leaving rituals and question-and-answer sequences. It also takes place in a particular language, evoking specific linguistic meanings for respondent and interviewer. Qualitative interviews are typically tape-recorded, and may (more rarely) be video-recorded. After the interview, the taped interview should be transcribed in its entirety either by the researcher or by someone else involved in the research.

In Chapter 8, we turn our attention to other useful forms of data: the textual and the visual, and how to do qualitative research using texts, images, or documents. One contemporary site for data is the Internet, particularly those places where individuals interact textually, such as chat rooms and support groups. Another site both contemporary and historical is mass media. In this chapter, we discuss the analysis of magazines and advertisements in qualitative research on gender both by sociologists and others involved in cultural studies. We also explore visual sociology, and the various uses of photographic, video, and other imagery in the field. The chapter includes a discussion of the use of historical documents as sources of data: voices from the past and present brought alive by the sociological researcher.

The focus of Part III is on the analysis and presentation of qualitative data. By now, all your data from fieldwork, interviews, and documents are in the form of text as fieldnotes, interview transcripts, and copies or summaries of visual or textual material. All along you, the researcher, will have been reading and rereading, thinking and rethinking these materials, beginning to identify analytic themes and patterns in your data. Once you have left the field or completed the interviews, it is time to focus fully on the analysis of qualitative data, which is discussed in Chapter 9. We outline the various stages and processes that one goes through in developing a full and thickly analytic description. It is a time-consuming, yet vital part of producing competent and compelling research.

In Chapter 10, we talk about writing up qualitative studies, which—unless you are an ethnographic documentary filmmaker—is the most common endpoint of qualitative methods in sociology. We discuss various potential audiences for your written paper, report, or book (probably limited to your instructor at this point) and how to write the paper. The various sections of the paper are discussed in this chapter, using examples from published qualitative research papers. Steps to the finished paper include constructing the abstract, introduction, background material, and review of the substantive literature, the theoretical or conceptual literature, the method section, findings from the data, and a discussion or conclusions.

Finally, in the Epilogue, we explore the future of qualitative sociology in the context of various debates over the political meaning of ethnography and interviewing in a diverse and global society. Qualitative methods have gained legitimacy within sociology, and we think this trend will continue in both applied and more theoretical work. We believe that there has been an expansion of interdisciplinary research using qualitative methods in recent years, in applied, funded team studies, in education research, and in cultural studies using the tools of historians and philosophers as well as sociologists.

Throughout the book we rely heavily on our own work for examples, including fieldnotes, interview transcripts, published papers, and historical analysis. This reliance on our own work is not because we regard it as more exemplary than others'. Rather, we use examples from our own work, such as Warren's fieldnotes in Chapter 5, because we know them—how they were inscribed, stored, analyzed, used—and because in sociology fieldnotes are often private documents. We use interview transcripts that we have worked with extensively because we are deeply familiar with the material in them.

We hope that you will enjoy this book, and that it will be helpful to you as you begin to conduct qualitative sociological research. You are at the beginning of a journey that may be short—one quarter or one semester—or long, the beginning of a career that involves doing qualitative methods. Whichever it is, we wish you luck, success, and the joy of immersing yourself in the worlds of meaning of others, in finding the unexpected stories you did not know you were looking for, and of learning, doing, and being as you take this journey. Welcome to the study of qualitative research.  ❖

# Acknowledgments

First, both of us are thankful to have had each other in this endeavor, together with the support of Claude Teweles, Phong Ho, and Monica Gomez of Roxbury Publishing. We are grateful especially to Bob Emerson, Joe Kotarba, Anne Vittoria, and the many reviewers who read all or part of this manuscript and generously provided insights and enthusiasm for our efforts: Kristine De Welde (University of Colorado), Carol Gardner (Indiana University–Purdue University Indianapolis), Jennifer Hunt (Montclair State University), Rebecca Plante (Wittenberg University), Marybeth C. Stalp (University of Northern Iowa), Jim Thomas (Northern Illinois University), Leslie Wasson (University of South Florida), Judith Wittner (Loyola University), and Alfred A. Young (University of Michigan). Thanks also to those qualitative researchers whose cutting-edge contributions we borrowed, especially Bob Emerson, Jack Katz, Lizette Peter, Cathy Greenblat, Doug Harper, Eric Margolis, Jerome Krase, D. Angus Vail, Mima Cataldo, and Viktoria Gotting. We relied on the work of many other gifted qualitative researchers—far too numerous to mention—without which this book (and our own research!) would certainly be impoverished.

We could not have done this without the invaluable assistance of Kathi Kirigin with computer matters (on Carol's end) and the cheerful help of Alicia Palao and Laura Potter with library matters (on Tracy's end). Additionally, we have both been exceedingly lucky to have had the support of our department colleagues (Carol's at the University of Kansas and Tracy's at the University of Houston), without which a project such as this might never have come to fruition. Tracy adds a note of gratitude to Joe Kotarba, who offered open access to his considerable personal library of qualitative texts, and to Jenifer Bratter and Marilyn Espitia, her fellow methodological muses, for insightful and ongoing discussions.

Considerable time has passed since Tracy first sat in Carol's Field Methods class at the University of Kansas back in the fall of 1989. This was an intellectual turning point for Tracy, the beginnings of a collaborative friendship, and an introduction to the methods that continue to inform her research to this day. Carol began her qualitative journey in Jack Douglas' PhD seminars at the University of California in 1970, following her general methodological training at San Diego State University. Thus, we both come out of the "California School," though once removed on Tracy's part, and we are especially thankful to the teachers and colleagues we have had the pleasure to know and learn from over the years. This thanks includes our students, from whom we have had the opportunity to learn our methods anew each semester. Coming from an interactionist perspective, we are acutely aware of the importance of others in our intellectual development, and in sharing the enchantment of the qualitative approach to understanding social life. And so, it is to all those colleagues and scholars who have gone before us and all the social scientists to come that we dedicate this work. A labor of love and delight, we pass on the challenge to you our readers, to "get into the field" and use these methods to come to see and know your social world.

Go forth and do good (qualitative) work.  ❖

Carol A. B. Warren
Coronado, CA

Tracy X. Karner
The Woodlands, TX

**Chapter One**

# Introduction to Qualitative Methods

Qualitative methods in sociology, like any other methods in the social sciences, involve not only a set of procedures but also an underlying logic sometimes referred to as *epistemology*. It is important to understand this foundation before you go on to learn, and put into practice, the specific methods of qualitative research. Qualitative methods also have a history, which is important both in itself and to the extent that it shapes the present. And qualitative methods have a purpose, or rather a variety of purposes, that range from the wish to change some aspect of society to the desire to capture it on film. This chapter is a discussion of the logic, history, variety of approaches, and purposes of qualitative inquiry, including field research, interviewing, and the analysis of documents and images.

Although field research and interviewing are described in detail in Chapters 3 through 7, a brief definition of these methods is in order here. Both methods involve, ideally, face-to-face interaction with respondents, although some qualitative researchers use the telephone or Internet for interviewing when issues of cost or distance make this advisable. Both methods, since they involve people interacting, are heavily dependent on the social characteristics of the people involved in them—both researchers and respondents—and thus are "experience near" processes (Geertz 1976).

Field research or *ethnography* (sometimes also called participant observation) involves present-time face-to-face interaction in a setting, which can be anything from a bus stop to a casino to a small town. The field researcher enters and spends a certain amount of time interacting and observing in the setting—more time in larger and more complex settings such as the small town, less time in smaller and less complex settings such as the bus stop (the casino is in the middle; one might go there at least once a week for a few months). The fieldworker takes extensive fieldnotes (see Chapter 5) as soon as possible after she leaves the field; these fieldnotes, then, become the basis for ethnographic analysis.

Qualitative interviewing involves present-time face-to-face (or sometimes telephone or e-mail) interaction, but the topic of the interview may be related to the past or future as well as the present. The general format of the interview is a dyad (one interviewer and one respondent), but there may be triadic interviews (one researcher and two respondents, for example, a married couple) or focus group interviews (one or two researchers and a group of respondents). Prior to the actual interviews, the researcher has gone from general research questions to 10 to 15 actual interview questions, which are intended to address the topic of specific interest, whether this topic is the experience of HIV/AIDS, working-class graduate students, or motherhood. These questions form the basis for eliciting narrative stories from respondents, which are recorded and then transcribed to serve as the data for analysis.

Although field research and interviewing are the major qualitative methods, visual and documentary materials can also be studied from a social constructionist perspective. With these methods, instead of "hanging around" a setting or asking questions, the researcher may be limited (as with historical data) to what can be found or (as with internet data) may be unable to verify claims (such as age and gender) through observation. Gold mines of material in visual and textual form still await qualitative researchers, as we shall see in later chapters.

Qualitative and quantitative social research display similarities and differences. Both kinds of research involve a commitment to understanding others, and some dedication to learning or being trained in the specific methods. But quantitative methods are more programmatic (see Box 1.1), beginning with existing social theory and proceeding to the generation of hypotheses from that theory. Data collection consists of devising instruments and measures to transmute social interactions, behaviors, or attitudes into numbers. Analysis is accomplished by means of statistics, with the researcher designing and interpreting the statistical findings to either disprove or support the hypotheses. Contrast the approach of qualitative research in Box 1.2 with the quantitative procedure in Box 1.1. In qualitative research, you alone (or with others in the case of team field research) are responsible for all stages of the research enterprise. Additionally, qualitative research is "experience near" (Geertz 1976)—close to other people and social settings—while quantitative research generates "experience distant" numerical summaries of social life.

The value of qualitative research in sociology has been discussed and debated for decades. While quantitative research can capture important statistical relationships—such as the relationship between gender and income—it is not well adapted to interpretive or social constructionist understandings. Statistics may record relationships between income and gender, but the meaning of being a single mother with a low income, raising six children with little help from an ex-husband, relatives, or the state, can be captured sociologically only by using qualitative methods. Both the statistical and the qualitative are significant components of understanding gender, class, and income in the United States. However, many aspects of social life can only be illuminated using qualitative approaches.

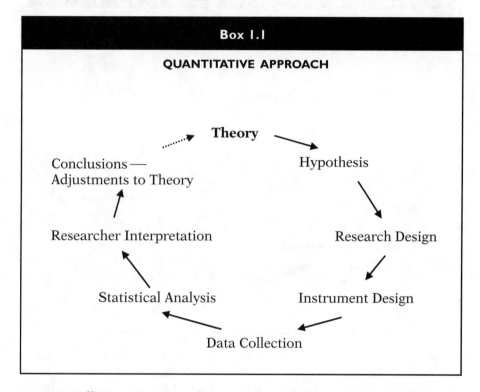

**Box 1.1**

**QUANTITATIVE APPROACH**

Theory

Hypothesis

Conclusions — Adjustments to Theory

Research Design

Researcher Interpretation

Instrument Design

Statistical Analysis

Data Collection

As an illustrative example, consider the meaning of sleep. We all know, individually, what sleep is—we get a good night's sleep, we toss and turn, we count sheep, we have insomnia. But in Jaber Gubrium's wonderful ethnography *Living and Dying at Murray Manor* (1975), the social meanings of sleep are illuminated. In this study of a nursing home, Gubrium explored what he called the different "social worlds" of elderly residents, lower-level staff, and upper-level staff. The residents "passed time" in various ways at Murray Manor, one of which was sleeping. Some of the shared social meanings of sleep are described by Gubrium (1975, 179–180):

> Where one sleeps to pass time makes a difference in how the sleeping is evaluated by others. Sleeping in bed most of the day is judged negatively, but spending nearly as much time sleeping in the Manor's lobby or lounges is considered just a matter of dozing off. The former is believed to be a deliberate plan to *just* sleep,

whereas the latter is treated as one of those things that "happens" when it gets warm and quiet. Dozing off is defined as an event that "happens," even though for some patients and residents it happens fairly systematically.

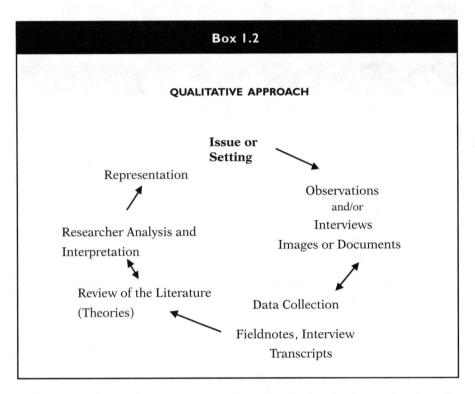

Judgments about sleeping are made not only by the lower-level staff, but by the residents themselves, feeding into the patients' hierarchical status system. Patients may "boast that they 'don't sleep around all day like some others in this place do'" (1975, 179), thus laying claim to a more "normal adult" status than other more "deteriorated" residents.

## The Logic of Qualitative Inquiry

The logic of qualitative inquiry is referred to in a number of ways by qualitative methodologists; our chosen term among these alternatives is *social constructionism* (another common term is naturalism). Social constructionism takes the position that sociologists' knowledge about social life (or any other knowledge about anything, for that matter) involves both understanding the meaning that interaction has for the participants and realizing that any analysis of society is made from some standpoint or perspective that informs the analysis. Let us look at these assumptions in turn.

*In her recent work,* Alive With Alzheimer's, *Cathy Stein Greenblat (2004) visually documents many of the social meanings of sleep found in care facilities. Here one resident is "dozing off" in the day room.*

Photo credit: Copyright © 2004 by Cathy Greenblat. Excerpted from *Alive With Alzheimer's*. All rights reserved. Used with permission.

As you probably know from introductory and other sociology courses, sociology seeks to explore both the macro level of social structure and the micro level of social interaction. From the first assumption of social constructionism, it is clear that constructionist analysis is directed toward the micro level. Social constructionists use qualitative methods to try to understand the meanings that people bring to the social worlds they inhabit and construct—their relationships, groups, organizations, communities, or subcultures. And they use the methods to analyze documents and images generated from documents and texts ranging from thirteenth-century self-help books to the Internet.

To understand the second assumption of social constructionism, it is necessary to make some contrasts between constructionism and positivism as epistemologies. *Positivism* involves a "camera" theory of knowledge, in which it is assumed that if you have a good camera (research design) and film (methods) you can achieve an objective "photo" of whatever aspect of society you are studying. Any cameraperson trained to use the research design and methods (camera and film) correctly would "take the same picture" as any other cameraperson.

This "objective" conception of knowing is often compared with "subjective" knowing based on individual feeling or intuition, and social constructionism is often wrongly described as subjective. Social constructionism proposes that sociological knowledge of the social world is neither objective nor subjective, but *intersubjective—based on the shared meanings and understandings of the people being studied, and the shared meanings and understandings of the disciplinary community (qualitative sociologists) doing the studying.*

While social constructionism and qualitative methods do not always go together, they often do, since field research and interviewing are ideally suited for exploring members' meanings and understandings. Similarly, although positivism and quantitative methods do not always go together, they, too, are ideally suited to one another. Quantitative methods seek to render social life in numerical patterns, whether by surveys related to the macro level of society or numerical scales related to the micro level.

## Generalizability, Validity, and Reliability

Those of you familiar with any of sociology's general methods texts are aware that there are fundamental concerns in social science related to methods; among these are generalizability, validity, and reliability. The purpose of positivist, often quantitative research is to *generalize* from the sample you are studying to the population from which the sample is drawn; for example, from your survey data of a random sample of 500 people to the population of Wichita, Kansas. This generalizability is made possible by various random sampling procedures, just as random assignment to experimental and control groups ensures generalizability in experimental research. Qualitative epistemology is based on the premise that social actors create emergent social worlds specific to time and place. Thus, the notion of generalizability for qualitative inquiry is concerned with social processes (such as power structures, insiders–outsiders, or gender relations) that might be relevant in more than a single setting or interaction. So, when a qualitative researcher uses the term "generalizability" (and they seldom do), the reference is not to the statistical relation of the sample to the greater population, but to common patterns in social interaction and social life.

Qualitative researchers generate thickly descriptive analysis to persuade the reader that the interpretation is plausible, and might or might not be found in other places and at other times. An example comes from ethnographies of bars, which have been done off and on during the past twenty years in various parts of the United States. Obviously, many types of bars exist in many kinds of areas—rural bars with a farm clientele, urban "leather" gay bars, hotel bars serving wealthy travelers, and so on. These are clear differences. But there are also similarities among these bars, such as distinctions between regulars and strangers; the fact that social behavior is loosened by alcohol; a workplace culture with typifications of customers; and often gendered and perhaps sexualized behavior seen among patrons. Although these are not statistical generalizations, anyone familiar with bars in the United States during the past 20 years can recognize these standard elements. In Simmel's (1950) terms, the content of social life (as in a bar) is quite varied, but its form is often discernibly similar.

In positivist, quantitative sociology, several types of *validity* and *reliability* are proposed in the context of scientific objectivity. A few qualitative sociologists are concerned with validity and reliability in a similar way (e.g., see Kirk and Miller 1986). Most qualitative sociologists, however, do not claim scientific objectivity, or seek to test hypotheses. We (for we include ourselves among this group) seek not proof or some sort of statistical correlation, but thick description: is the interpretation provided by the researcher convincing to the reader—does it ring true? The field researcher "wants to provide an account that communicates with the reader the truth about the setting and situation, as the ethnographer has come to know it" (Altheide and Johnson 1994, 496). Qualitative researchers rarely discuss reliability, a concept you may have encountered when studying quantitative methods (Kirk and Miller 1986), though a qualitative sociologist's implied definition of validity is, often, his or her loyalty and commitment to representing the people and settings being studied as fully as possible.

The irony of qualitative validity is that sometimes an ethnographic depiction does ring true to outsiders or strangers to a given social world, while it may not ring true to those who have been written about (see Ellis 1995a). Ethnographers have come to believe that this is because social life is composed not only of interactions but also of intentions; many of our interactions in life fall short of our intentions, and we may not have put our best foot forward. Ethnographers capture the observed experience, rather than the social fictions, of our everyday lives.

An example of the difference between observed interactions and social fictions about those interactions comes from Tamara Sniezek's (2002) research on wedding planning. Although in interviews with prospective brides and grooms, Sniezek found that both participants claimed that they were equally involved in the wedding planning, her field observations told her otherwise. While grooms often made suggestions and comments, agreeing or vetoing, it was the brides and their female relatives who did the legwork, actually finding the stationers, caterers, church, florists, photographers, and clothiers who eventually came to constitute the wedding event. This example also underlines the differences between qualitative interviewing and ethnography as methods. Although both are social constructionist, interviewing is more amenable to the presentation and preservation of social fictions than is ethnography.

In the camera theory of knowledge, validity may also be seen as compromised by bias—holding the camera in such a way that the picture is skewed toward the researcher's own values or beliefs. In social constructionist research, the term "bias" is used in a commonsense way to refer to strong beliefs or feelings that people might have about certain aspects of the social world. For example, a student who sets out to study an abortion clinic and is pro-life has a different bias than a student who is pro-choice. It is quite possible that either, both, or neither of these students would be able to conduct an effective ethnography of this clinic; personal biases alone do not guarantee either well- or badly done qualitative research. However, the awareness that all human activity, including research, is accomplished from a specific standpoint that requires qualitative researchers to state the perspectives from which they write their accounts. Thus, in providing a thick description, qualitative researchers include themselves and how they came to acquire their knowledge as key elements in their representation of people or settings.

## Methods, Theory, and Representation

The relationship of theory to method is different in qualitative than quantitative research. Most quantitative sociological research is *deductive* in the sense that researchers begin with theory (functionalist, conflict, Marxist, or feminist, for example), derive one or more hypotheses from this theory, and test these hypotheses (see Box 1.1). Most qualitative research is *inductive*, with concepts derived from the data gathered. Some qualitative research is then linked to theories of the kind mentioned above, for example, the ethnographic work of Michael Buroway and his students:

> We begin by trying to lay out as coherently as possible what we expect to find in our site before entry. When our expectations are violated—when we discover what we did not anticipate—we then turn to existing bodies of academic theory that might cast light on our anomaly. (quoted in Emerson 2001c, 283)

Much qualitative sociology is conceptual—at a middle level of abstraction—rather than grandly theorizing. Qualitative analyses, as we discuss at greater length in Chapters 9 and 10, are framed within sets of concepts developed during the early part of the century by members of what sociologists call the Chicago School (see below). Symbolic interactionism, which theorizes the relationship between self and society (Cooley 1922; Mead 1934; Blumer 1969), is an important component of qualitative sociology today, as is the work of Erving Goffman from the 1950s through the 1980s on everyday life (Goffman 1959, 1961, 1963a,

1963b). Today, many qualitative methodologists in sociology use symbolic interactionist approaches (and indeed have their own society, *http:/ /sun.soci.niu.edu/~sssi*, and journal, *www.ucpress.edu/journals/si*).

European influences entered the stream of qualitative analysis during the latter part of the twentieth century, when translations of German, French, and other works became more commonplace. The work of Georg Simmel on everyday life (1950) was especially influential in Erving Goffman's work and is still used by sociologists today. In Warren's work on *Identity and Community in the Gay World* (1972), for example, she analyzed a male homosexual community using Simmel's concept of secrecy and Goffman's concept of stigma. Today, qualitative sociologists who study homosexual communities are unlikely to use either of these concepts (Warren 2003). Both methods and theory change over time.

One significant change in the epistemology of methods and theory has been the consideration, in interdisciplinary work from the 1970s onward, of the issue of *representation.* This term refers to the ways in which the interactions and talk of a given social group or individual are represented in fieldnotes, interview transcripts, visual images, and published reports. Representational concerns are wide-ranging; they include a consideration of the rhetoric and metaphors of research (Gusfield 1976), the relative power of researcher and researched (Clifford and Marcus 1986), and the ways in which the researcher shapes the "voices" of respondents (Holstein and Gubrium 1995). Postmodern and feminist theorists in particular have grappled with issues of representation. The significance of these various aspects of representation when doing your own qualitative research is likely to vary according to your instructor's focus. But the general issue of representation has been established in qualitative methods as central to any discussion of the methods.

What is central is this: the qualitative researcher produces an oral report and/or written representation of the social world she is studying, which is itself based on prior representations of the field in the form of fieldnotes or interview transcripts. The researcher then develops the analytic focus of the presentation and the parts of the fieldnotes or transcripts that will be used to illustrate the analytic points made. Clearly, the representation of *reality* that ensues will have elements of "the field" or others' lived experience as part of it, and reflections of the analytic concerns and writing choices made by the qualitative researcher. As such, ethnographies and other studies based on qualitative data are intersubjective representations rather than objective portrayals of the social world, involving the researcher's interpretations and choices as well as the lived world of the respondents.

This intersubjectivity is not seen by qualitative sociologists as a flaw, as positivists see bias; representation is an inevitable part of the process of qualitative research. This does not mean that validity is abandoned, because the researcher strives to examine the world "out there" as closely and systematically as possible. It does mean that research findings are always from some standpoint, perspective, or point of view; they are not unmediated "snapshots" of an objective reality. When you become a qualitative researcher, you strive to become a good writer, but you also strive to become an attentive researcher. The foundation of qualitative research is still in research: that close-up immersion in and examination of lived worlds, first recommended in American sociology by the qualitative researchers of the Chicago School.

## The Chicago School and the Development of Qualitative Methods in Sociology

Like any other social phenomenon, the current status of qualitative methods has been shaped by its history. Although qualitative methodologists may trace the history of qualitative methods as far back as Herodotus (called by some the father of the discipline of sociology as well as history), or to the travelers of the Middle Ages or the missionaries of the nineteenth century, it is generally agreed that the Chicago School was the twentieth-century American cradle (Bulmer 1984; Fine 1995). The Chicago School was responsible for several key features of contemporary qualitative methods, including the use of documents (see Chapter 8), fieldwork (Chapters 3–5), and interviewing (Chapters 6 and 7). And as we discuss below, the conceptual and theoretical frameworks used by many contemporary qualitative sociologists are informed by the symbolic interactionist theories developed by scholars of the Chicago School.

The Chicago School of Sociology, with its interdisciplinary links to philosophy, social welfare, and other schools, flourished in the early part of the twentieth century. The methods used by Chicago researchers revolved around the "case study," a compilation of qualitative and quantitative approaches that highlighted the nature of a given social "case." The collection of documents was a central aspect of many Chicago School case studies, including the assemblage of Polish immigrants' letters analyzed in Thomas and Znaniecki's five-volume *The Polish Peasant in Europe and America (1918–1920)*.

Researchers of the Chicago school regarded the city as an urban laboratory, an ecological system amenable to a sociological analysis based on class and race. These researchers were often activist or reformist, using the case study to understand and solve social problems, locate "social pathology," and point out where reforms were needed. The social problems and "pathologies" studied by professors and students of the Chicago school included inner-city poverty and decay, racism, delinquency, gangs, riding the rails (hobos), and "deviant" sexualities such as homosexuality and prostitution. The tone of some of this research is captured in an unpublished "Glossary of Homosexual Terms" compiled by students at the University of Chicago during the 1930s:

> Older homosexual men were referred to as "Auntie" or "Ella" . . . those who "practice[d] fellatio on men" were designated "goop gobblers," "fruiters," and "flute-players" . . . the terms "trade" and "hustler" were used to designate an otherwise "normal" man who was willing to "permit [a] homosexual to have sex relations with him, usually for money." (Heap 2003, 474)

Many of these "pathology and deviance" topics were the subject of ethnographies by the sociologists of the second Chicago School (Fine 1995) and a subsequent California School. The second Chicago School consisted of scholars who had been trained at the University of Chicago but were not necessarily teaching there. This cohort of qualitative sociologists included David Matza and Howard Becker (see *http://home.earthlink.net/~hsbecker/*), who were influential in the 1960s and 1970s "appreciative" (rather than reformist) studies of "deviant subcultures," a term that came to encompass a wide variety of topics ranging from marijuana smoking among jazz musicians to mental hospitals and juvenile delinquents. The "California School," with centers in Berkeley, Los Angeles, and San Diego, continued the study of deviance throughout the 1970s and 1980s, again with a wide range of "deviance" topics, from nude beaches and homosexuality to drug dealers and topless bars. Some of the studies produced by sociologists from these "schools," including Warren's (1972) study of a Southern California male gay community, used interview as well as ethnographic methods.

Qualitative interviewing, like fieldwork, can be traced to the early twentieth-century case study approach. Chicago researchers interviewed immigrants, delinquents, and others to get their life stories in their "own" words. Among these early studies was Clifford Shaw's *The Jack-Roller* (1966), first published in 1930. This was the story of a delinquent boy, Stanley, born in 1909, whose petty crimes had landed him in correctional facilities in Chicago—the perfect place at the time to find oneself in a case study. In 1975 Stanley wrote to Jon Snodgrass, then at California State University, and offered to tell a second life story; this story became *The Jack-Roller at Seventy: A Fifty-Year Follow-up* (The Jack-Roller and Snodgrass 1982).

While the life history was used to illuminate individual experiences in local context, the Chicago School social scientists also used interviews as a way of trying to understand different social groups, from hobos to gang members. Although some early Chicago school interviews were in the form of questionnaires or were closed-ended, others were open-ended, and more like contemporary qualitative interviews. In a 1939 methods textbook, Pauline Young, who was trained at the

University of Chicago, described the essence of qualitative interviewing as the elicitation of stories:

> When people are least interrupted, when they can tell their stories in their own way . . . they can react naturally and freely and express themselves fully. . . . [Interruptions and leading questions are likely to have the effect that] . . . the adventure into the unknown, into uncharted and hitherto undisclosed spheres, has been destroyed. (quoted in Platt 2002, 37)

While contemporary qualitative sociologists are indebted to the Chicago School, much has changed (of course!) in the 70 some years since. Young's description of the interview as a site for narrative is similar to our understanding of it in the 2000s. In other ways, however, early discussions of the interview differ from today's recommendations and technologies. Tape recorders were not in use for interviewing prior to the early 1960s, and Young stated that it was best for the interviewer not to even take notes. The issue of the interviewer summarizing the interview material versus trying to record it verbatim was debated among Chicago School researchers (Platt 2002, 37); today it is generally assumed that the respondent's words should be captured as completely and accurately as possible.

The purposes of qualitative research have also changed and diversified since the 1930s. For most of the Chicagoans in the early decades of the century, including Pauline Young, the purpose of understanding the social world was to change it—to reform, to end deviance, to restore social order, both to urban Chicago and to the nation. The Chicago research reports were often written from this standpoint. Erving Goffman, in *The Presentation of Self in Everyday Life* (1959), separated himself from the reformist purposes of qualitative methods, seeking to study everyday life as socially constructed. Both traditions have continued in qualitative research: the study of social life as social construction, and its analysis for reformist purposes.

Qualitative research based on the work of Erving Goffman (1959, 1961) and the symbolic interactionism of the Chicago, neo-Chicago, and California schools is our main focus in this text. Many qualitative, scholarly monographs are published by the University of Chicago and University of California presses. Some excellent ethnographies are published as articles rather than books (e.g, Emerson and Pollner 1976; Holstein 1987), but the full-length book format is ideal for the depth of analysis and thickness of description typical of fieldwork representations. Since many classic Chicago school ethnographies are the foundation of our discussion in Chapters 4 and 5, here we discuss, briefly, other non-reformist approaches to ethnography: autoethnography and visual ethnography. But first we will trace the development of reformist qualitative sociology since the Chicago School.

## Ethnography and Social Change

Some contemporary practitioners of reformist sociology (both quantitative and qualitative) refer to their work as applied sociology. Their research is devoted to changing individual behavior, organizational functioning, or both. Applied sociology is often funded by government or private foundations and is directed toward issues currently defined as social problems in need of address. In the 1970s, for example, a major focus of applied research was delinquency and criminality; in the 1980s many efforts addressed homelessness, mental illness, and program evaluation; in the 1990s gerontology and education were important areas of research and social policy debate (see also the Epilogue).

Other qualitative sociologists are more interested in examining the politics of social settings than in implementing or testing social policy. During the 1960s—a time of political change of all kinds—qualitative sociologists began to explore a different vision of the relationship between sociology and social change. They developed a variety of approaches, including action research, which are more politically critical of the status quo than applied research. Some qualitative sociologists continue, in the 2000s, to use qualitative methods not only to understand political or social systems (local, national, or global) but also to try to change them. Among these politicized approaches to social change research are action research and institutional ethnography.

Qualitative *action research* (Whyte 1984) seeks not only to develop understandings of social settings but also to intervene in those settings in ways likely to be helpful to the people being studied. Depending on the emphasis, this kind of research has a number of names, including collaborative action research and participatory action research (Kemmis and McTaggart 2000). Action research is premised on the notion that those conducting the research and the respondents are collaborative equals—the researchers bring sociological expertise to the team, whereas the respondents bring their local knowledge. Both parties are seen as contributors cooperating to accomplish mutually beneficial goals. Since doing the research will benefit the researchers (in terms of publication or career opportunities), it should also benefit the respondents. The researchers participate in the activities of the group being studied, and the respondents participate in research decisions at all stages of the process.

Action research is done by anthropologists and education specialists as well as sociologists, and is often associated with solving local, national, or global social problems. A good deal of action research has been done in school classrooms, with an emphasis on students' and teachers' perspectives, and on the practical help researchers can offer these participants (Kemmis and McTaggart 2000). Other researchers, such as Whyte (1984), have done research among and on behalf of disadvantaged groups such as factory workers, miners, and migrant farm workers in the United States. Anthropologists have conducted action research studies both in this country and in Third World settings. Kemmis and McTaggart (2000, 595) describe the reflexive "spiral" or process of action research as stages of planning a change, implementing the change, observing the process and consequences of the implementation and change, reflecting on these processes, and rethinking and replanning further implementations (see Box 1.3). The respondents and researchers continue to collaborate and reflect on the processes of change. Action research is not a linear process, but a multiphase progression of reflection, discussion, research, and action (implementation of change).

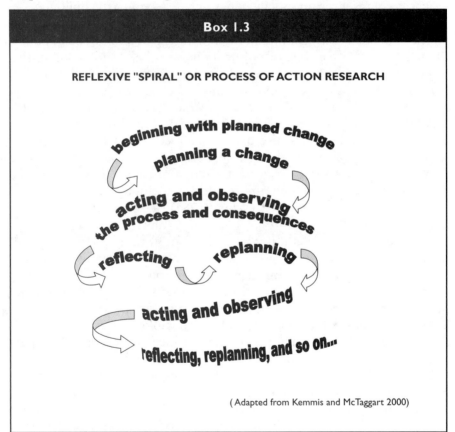

**Box 1.3**

**REFLEXIVE "SPIRAL" OR PROCESS OF ACTION RESEARCH**

beginning with planned change

planning a change

acting and observing the process and consequences

reflecting    replanning

acting and observing

reflecting, replanning, and so on...

(Adapted from Kemmis and McTaggart 2000)

*Institutional ethnography* starts not with an idea of change but with a model of relations of domination and subordination in contemporary global capitalist society. Institutional ethnographers such as Dorothy Smith (1987) study organizations and bureaucracies (institutions) such as nursing homes and mental hospitals, because it is there that these relations are played out among clients, lower-level staff, and upper-level staff, in the context of globalization. DeVault and McCoy summarize the purpose of institutional ethnography as a mode of inquiry:

In contemporary global capitalist society the "everyday world" (the material context of each embodied subject) is organized in powerful ways by translocal social relations that pass through local settings and shape them according to a dynamic of transformation that begins and gathers speed somewhere else (e.g. if the local hospital closes the explanation will not be wholly local). . . . [T]hese translocal relations that carry and accomplish organization and control . . . [are] "relations of ruling." (2002, 752)

Both action research and institutional ethnography seek social change, but in different ways. Action research has as its purpose the meeting of immediate and local needs, while institutional ethnography attempts to dislocate relationships of domination and subordination. Applied research, like that of the Chicago School, uses qualitative methods to understand and, it is hoped, change individual "deviance" or social "pathology." In contrast to all these approaches, authoethnography is concerned more with the self than with benefiting or changing others.

## Autoethnography

Autoethnography puts the self at the center of sociological observation and analysis. The autoethnographer uses his or her engagement in the interaction, or reflections about the interaction, as the data. Two general approaches to autoethnography are emotional (Ellis 1995b) and analytic (Vail 2002; Kivett and Warren 2000). Emotional autoethnography focuses on the researcher's own involvement in, and feelings about, the setting; analytic autoethnography focuses on involvement, but more on cognition within a particular context than on emotion.

The work of Carolyn Ellis (1995a) epitomizes emotional autoethnography, although her dissertation research was ethnographic rather than autoethnographic. For her dissertation, Ellis did a study of "Fishneck," a fishing village in the Blue Ridge Mountains; during the research, she was taken in as a guest by one of the large extended families in the village and became quite close to some of them. After her book on the village was published, the people she wrote about recognized the setting, and some of them did not like what she had said about them, while others felt betrayed. During a return visit many years later, one Fishnecker, Minnie, told Ellis:

M: "That was a lot of nonsense you wrote. I know you was a writin' 'bout me". . . .

E: "How do you know this is about you?. . . I didn't use your names . . . how will they know it's you I'm writing about?"

M: "They'll know," she said confidently. . . . "I thought we was friends, you and me, just talkin'. I didn't know you would put it in no book." (Ellis 1995a, 78–79)

After her return to Fishneck, Ellis turned to autoethnography as a way of avoiding or resolving the ethical and political dilemmas and consequences of research among strangers. In this quote, Ellis is describing the process of autoethnography to a potential graduate student:

I start with my personal life. I pay attention to my physical feelings, thoughts, and emotions. I use what I call systematic sociological introspection and emotional recall to try to understand and experience what I've lived through. Then I write my experience as a story. By exploring a particular life, I hope to understand a way of life. (Ellis and Bochner 2000, 737)

The work of D. Angus Vail (2002) exemplifies analytic autoethnography. Vail studies "tattoo collectors," persons who collect tattoos all over their bodies, in a sort of body suit pattern from neck to wrists and ankles, and then display them to interested audiences. Vail himself is a tattoo collector, with tattoo portraits of Jimi Hendrix, Carlos Santana, and John Coltrane on his legs; he plans to have depictions of the Wagnerian "Ring Cycle" operas covering his back. His work is, like Carolyn Ellis', autoethnographic in that it involves himself—and in this case his own embodied experience of acquiring and "showing" tattoos—in the research enterprise. But it is unlike Ellis' focus in that his interest is in sociological analysis rather than what he refers to as emotional "navel-gazing." Vail's purpose in studying tattoo

*Filip Leu tattooing D. Angus Vail. Custom tattoos are measured by the degree to which artist and collector collaborate on a design.*

Photo credit: Copyright © 2004 by D. Angus Vail. All rights reserved. Used with permission.

collectors is to analyze and convey the perspective of members of this West Coast subculture, not only as he experiences it, but also to represent the social world of other tattoo collectors and artists.

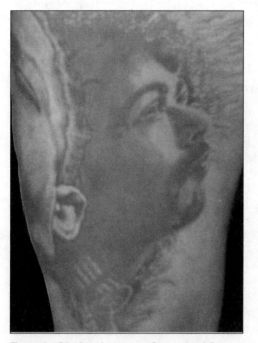

Tattoo by Filip Leu, Lausanne, Switzerland. Portrait of Carlos Santana. Collection of D. Angus Vail.

Analytic autoethnographic approaches may also be used when there are no other means of gaining access to social interaction or experience. Douglas Kivett (Kivett and Warren 2002) did an autoethnographic study of social control in "Sweetwater," a group home for delinquent boys where he worked as an assistant. Kivett and Warren were interested in understanding the circumstances under which social control was not exerted in situations that in some sense called for it. Since in this setting there was generally only one staff assistant present, and the decision to exert or not exert social control was based on that individual's interpretation, the only source of data on such decision making was the assistant's own thoughts and actions.

Kivett and Warren (2002) follow the steps toward the escalation or de-escalation of trouble and social control within the institution:

> A youth's questionable behavior causes an uneasy feeling in the staff person witnessing the behavior, followed by rumination about what has taken place. . . . The vague sense of something wrong is defined in local staff culture as a "gut response," coming "naturally" as the staff member "learns the ropes." (11)

Kivett found that what was crucial to interpreting the boys' behavior as trouble, and thus escalating social control, was staff members' assessment of the intentions and motives behind the boy's behavior. For example, in an instance in which a boy threw a bookbag on the floor, they questioned:

> Was the throwing . . . just that, or was it a meaningful, intentionally negative response to being given an instruction? Was it obedi-

ence of the body only, or the totalizing obedience of the truly docile body? Was it, perhaps, in the local culture, "playing games," or perhaps "limit testing"? (Kivett and Warren 2002, 12)

From such moments and instances social control (and emergent meaning making) in our society is shored up or defused.

## Visual Ethnography

Qualitative research has a strong and growing tradition of visual sociology, using or making still or moving photographs, or analyzing existing visual images (see Chapter 8). Douglas Harper (2002) is a prominent visual sociologist who uses still photography in his work. He notes that "there are at least two alternatives for visual sociologists" (2002, 729). One is to use the camera for observing just as fieldworkers use fieldnotes; these visual observations then become the basis for developing concepts. In his visual sociology of agriculture, Harper displays a photograph of a barn, a silo, and apple trees—one of which is being climbed by a man—and notes that

> Howard Becker suggested several years ago that sociologists learn to analyze photographs by first concentrating on the act of looking itself. Rather than glancing and moving on, give yourself five minutes. Look beyond the quirky, almost humorous construction of the image. See that behind him are a small barn and a silo big enough for the corn of a ten-acre field. Who filled the silo and what animals will it feed? Behind the farmer are two more apple trees. These suggest the family's self-sufficiency. . . . The farmer works alone on a winter day. . . . This reading is only the surface, a scratch at the meaning of the image, but even at this level the photo suggests the contours of a biography. (9)

*Douglas Harper's photograph of a farmer in front of a barn suggests the contours of a lived biography.*

Another approach of visual sociologists is to use photographic elicitation to "confirm and develop existing theory" (Harper 2002, 729). This method involves taking photographs and showing them to cultural informants to see what the images elicit. For example, Harper showed Italian informants his photographs of bicycles and other traffic taken while he was riding a bicycle in Italy. He asked them to comment on what the photos showed them about the role of the bicycle in Italian society. One informant commented:

> The bicycle stands for: rapidity, convenience, physical exercise, danger, risk, challenge, reduction of stress, increase of stress, cancer in the lungs, cold in the winter, hot in the summer . . . flexibility of the [traffic] rules, aggressiveness, attention, negotiation, social conscience, no pollution, autonomy. (2002, 725)

*"Bicycling in Bologna" by Douglas Harper.*

In ethnographic video the visual imagery is the vehicle by which the analysis is communicated. Several of Warren's students have, over the years, combined ethnographic writing with film or video. Laura Scheerer and Jim Whitney, two students of Warren's in Los Angeles, collaborated during the 1980s to do fieldwork on what they at first called "homelessness." As their setting the students chose a public parking lot next to the beach in Venice where many "homeless" people lived in vehicles ranging from wrecked, immobile Volkswagens to large, movable RVs. They found that the people who lived in this setting did not regard themselves as homeless because, after all, they made their homes in their vehicles. Their ethnography focused on the hierarchy of vehicle dwellers that arose from the conjunction of vehicles ranging from the wrecked to the middle-class, and on the "privatization of public space" that occurs whenever the homeless, or vehicle dwellers, settle in any number in public spaces. Scheerer and Whitney called their film "Addressless" (*http://www.sagemtnfilms.com/filmmaking.html*).

Eric Margolis (*http://courses.ed.asu.edu/margolis*), an innovative sociologist and documentary filmmaker, sees film, audiotape, and videotape as ways to more fully represent the spoken traditions of local communities. In his documentary work with coal miners in Colorado, Margolis found:

> The use of non-print media offers opportunities for the investigator to record social processes directly, to explicitly enter into the process, and to record the effect of that interaction. At the same time that I "studied" coal miners, I intended to explore the developing relations between what I was doing and the miners. Not only do cameras and tape recorders open up new possibilities to record social interaction and for sociologists to present their findings, they also have the potential to reduce the dualism experimenter/experimental subject. Reflexive research designs utilizing non-print media have the potential to provide checks on the work by encouraging "subjects" to participate actively in the research and take a critical role in the presentation of research findings. (Margolis 1994, 130)

*Margolis (1994) conceptualizes the editing process as the place where biography and history intersect. For "Coal Mining as a Way of Life," a slide show of tentative findings was given in the town and residents were asked to provide feedback to guide the editing process in this public editing meeting in 1975.*

*Visual sociologist Mima Cataldo's images of women in New York City's Chinatown suggests the contours of biographies within neighborhoods and communities.*

The use of either still or visual images in qualitative sociology poses special problems in human subjects protections. As you will see in Chapter 2, researchers are required, in most cases, to promise confidentiality to their respondents; where photographs or videos are used, this promise can be neither made nor kept. Sociologists who use visual images such as Harper (2001), Duneier (1999), and Greenblat (2004) have chosen to define themselves more as journalists than as sociological researchers, thus invoking the protections of the first amendment rather than coming under the strictures of Institutional Review Boards (IRBs; see Chapter 2).

## Qualitative Interviewing: The Collective and the Individual Story

As Gubrium and Holstein (2002) note, we live in an interview society. All kinds of interviews are featured on TV; we could probably be watching an interview at any time of the day or night. We may be interviewed for admission to colleges or for jobs. Although face-to-face qualitative interviews are less common in our everyday lives—most likely—than survey questionnaires, we are familiar with the basic question-and-answer format of the interview. From a social constructionist and symbolic interactionist perspective, interviews are the primary method by which researchers facilitate *narrative*, or the telling of stories.

In interview narratives, selves and individual histories are "continually reinvented in the service of contemporary psychological and political aims" (Rosenwald and Ochberg 1992, 4). Thus, interview narratives are more than a simple mirror of life events; they are embedded in temporal, geographical, political, cultural, and social fields—all of which lend shape and form to the story. In addition, these stories reflect and define both the interviewee and the social context. "Narratives allow us to create who we are and to construct definitions of our situations in everyday interactions" (Riessman 1992, 232). All interviews, then, tell both a collective and an individual story, but the analysis of interviews may focus more on one or the other. When social scientists, historians, or folklorists use narrative to explore the collective story, they refer to interviews as oral histories, folklore collections, or ethnographic interviews. When they want to examine the individual story within the collective narrative, they refer to life history narratives or biographies.

Oral history interviews provide "firsthand testimony that may assist [scholars] in describing historical events or the experience of social process" (Smith 2002, 711). Scholars who use oral histories are well aware that "in common with other types of evidence, interviews contain a mix of true and false, reliable and unreliable, verifiable and unverifiable information" (Smith 2002, 712). Thompson, therefore, suggests that oral history interviews should be used in historical research with the same cautions that apply to all historical research: (a) assess each interview for internal consistency; (b) cross-check information found in interviews with as many other published, oral, and archival sources as possible; and (c) read the interview with as wide a historical and theoretical understanding of relevant subjects as possible (1988, 240–241).

Similarly, folklorists are interested in the collective story. In many cultures, stories are like gifts, "lovingly imparted" and "associated with prior tellers, keeping their wisdom and influence alive" (Narayan and George 2002, 824). In American culture, collective stories include not only our own American history, but also fairy tales such as Cinderella and Jack and the Beanstalk. Folklorists' interviews can illuminate both the cultural and individual meaning of tales. In a 1980s interview study of women's and men's memories and meanings of fairy tales, the researcher found that women remembered these tales more than men did. In addition:

> Girls and women sometimes chafed at the messages in fairy tales, and some also reworded the stories to carry alternate endings. So, for example, a 9-year-old girl who preferred the character of Jack in "Jack in the Beanstalk" to Cinderella suggested that perhaps

Cinderella could recover her slipper from the prince, and then "maybe she doesn't marry him but she gets a lot of money anyway and she gets a job." (quoted in Naryan and George 2002, 824)

Ethnographers use informant accounts to gain understanding of a particular culture and way of being. Anthropologists conduct ethnographic interviews as part of their fieldwork; the "ethnographic interview is a bid on the part of a researcher to get an interviewee to converse openly about a set of issues of concern to the researcher" (Narayan and George 2002, 820). Spradley notes that the "ethnographer's main tool for discovering another person's cultural knowledge is the ethnographic interview" (1979, 60). He identifies thirty or more types of ethnographic questions that can be asked in an interview, the most important of which are *descriptive, structural,* and *contrast* questions.

*Descriptive questions* are designed to elicit examples of the informant's language, which is the basis of cultural meaning. These are, according to Spradley, the easiest to ask (1979, 60); his example is the question "Could you tell me what you do at the office?" *Structural questions* reveal what Spradley refers to as "*domains,* the basic units in an informant's cultural knowledge"; an example is, "What are all the stages in getting transferred in your company?" (1979, 60). *Contrast questions* elicit cultural meaning directly, by asking for the "dimensions of meaning which informants employ to distinguish the objects and events in their world." A typical contrast question would be, "What's the difference between a *bass* and a *Northern pike*?" (Spradley 1979, 60).

Since all individual stories are embedded in culture and in history, in some sense—as we have already noted—there is no distinction between the collective and the individual story. However, some interviews seek to highlight individual biographies, either for therapeutic or research purposes, or some combination. Karner (1994) explored the individual narratives of inpatient Vietnam veterans to understand their individual stories: their understanding of United States culture and the impact the Vietnam War had on their lives. However, because individuals are dependent on the cultural resources at their disposal to tell their story, qualitative interviews allowed Karner to focus analytically on both the individual story and its reflection of the collective story. For example, without cultural resources (such as language, common understandings, shared experiences), certain experiences can remain outside the bounds of telling. For example, some of the veterans' traumatic combat situations were considered "unimaginable" and "unspeakable"—that is, they defied narration. A qualitative interview can facilitate both telling the personally unspeakable events and reintegrating the individual experience into the social context:

The word *context* literally means to weave together, to twine, to connect. This interrelatedness creates the web of meaning within which humans act. The individual is joined to the world through social groups, structural relations, and identities. However, these are not inflexible categories to which individuals can be reduced. . . . The general constructs of race, class, and gender are essential, [but] they are not rigidly determinant. Context is not a script. Rather, it is a dynamic process through which the individual simultaneously shapes and is shaped by her environment. (Personal Narratives Group 1989, emphasis in original)

By telling stories to and about each other and ourselves in interviews, we "fashion ourselves and our worlds" (Shoemaker 1991, 356). Indeed, interview narratives constitute the "ideological terrain" of self-representation and formation (Ganguly 1992, 29). As representations, stories are not just the recounting of past experiences or memories; they are a cultural device for the expression of self and experience. The narrator reconfigures him- or herself with each story and with each telling.

Life history interviewing is another term for the interpretation and representation of individual (within the collective) experience. As Atkinson notes, an "individual life and the role it plays in the larger community are best understood through story."

A life story is the story a person chooses to tell about the life he or she has lived, told as completely and honestly as possible, what the person remembers of it and what he or she wants others to know of it. . . . The . . . life story is the narrative essence of what has happened to the person. It can cover the time from birth to the present or before and beyond. It includes the important events, experiences and feelings of a lifetime. (2002, 125)

In studies of self-help groups (see Irving 1999; Denzin 1989a) and of people-changing institutions over the past 10 years, qualitative sociologists have noted the linkages between individual stories told in these settings and the ideologies promulgated by them (e.g., Miller and Holstein 1996; Loseke 1992). In a study of a battered women's shelter, Loseke (1992) explores the process by which a woman is defined in the setting as "a battered woman" and eligible for "intervention." Using an ethnographic approach, Loseke traces how the broader collective stories about battering and abuse are used by the staff members to interpret and typify help-seeking women's narratives—that is, how a woman comes to be defined as an eligible victim in need of assistance as opposed to a woman who is just having a spousal disagreement.

In his work on interpretive biography, Denzin (1989a), links the personal story to the collective story—and ethnography to storytelling—with examples from research on and membership in Alcoholics Anonymous. He points out that the stories told by AA members are individual, with their own events and turning points, but they are also collective. Denzin transcribes a story told at an open AA meeting by Bill, a self-defined alcoholic, and explores its dynamics:

> As Bill speaks, he throws his story out to the audience who hears it. This audience becomes part of the story that is told. A third structure emerges. Not only is Bill talking about his alcoholic self, he is telling his stories to other alcoholic selves. A group self is formed; a self lodged and located in the performative occasion of that "open meeting." (1989a, 72)

And, one might add, a fourth structure emerges as Denzin writes his book, that of the academic meanings of individual and group stories and selves. The four structures that emerge in Denzin's analysis provide a striking example of the complexity of qualitative inquiry. As we noted at the beginning of this chapter, the richness of meanings to be found in social settings and in individual and collective stories is the reward of the sociologist who uses qualitative methods. But what are the individual and social purposes of seeking this reward?

## The Purposes of Qualitative Research

The reasons for pursuing qualitative sociological research vary historically and locally with the individual, the sponsoring organization, and the contextual political economy. An individual sociologist may wish to pursue promotion and tenure in her department, or (once tenured) make money directly (royalties) and indirectly (increases in salary) by writing a well-received ethnography. Her sponsoring institution, a university or college, may or may not reward writing based on qualitative research over that based on quantitative, and may value some research topics over others. The research may be funded or not, the funding level may be large or small, and the funding can come from a variety of local, national, international, private, or governmental sources. Certain topics may be "hot," and others cold and dead, often in the context of current media attention to them.

But whatever the reasons, and whatever the sponsoring institution or social context, it is important to remember that the motives for pursuing research are connected inextricably with the consequences of that research—that is, all social science research has political implications. Contemporary critiques of interviewing processes (Briggs 2002; Gubrium and Holstein 2002; Richardson 1990) illuminate the political consequences of social science methods, a theme we return to in the Epilogue. From choosing a topic to selecting respondents to interviewing and analysis, researchers' activities are part of the social order at the micro level, through the interview encounter, and at the macro level, as part of the nexus of knowledge and power. Qualitative methods allow the researcher to both acknowledge power differentials and to resist them. As feminist, action, and institutional sociologists have pointed out, the effect of research on the settings and respondents of qualitative research are also important. Feminist sociologists have illuminated and at times attempted to change the hierarchy of gender dominance in our society. Action researchers have made the local and immediate welfare of settings and respondents part of their agenda, while institutional ethnographers have an eye on more long-term social change in society's relations of domination and oppression. Applied sociologists seek to change individual behaviors (such as criminality or drug addiction), but they may also hope to reform the organizations that deal with these individuals (such as prisons, schools, or nursing homes).

For some qualitative researchers, the purpose of qualitative research is obligatory—something that has to be done because of a class assignment or a job. For most, however, it is a kind of personal passion: the satisfaction of a boundless curiosity about the social construction of our social worlds. What Reinharz and Chase have to say about feminist interviewers also applies to other qualitative researchers, who "choose research topics that are deeply personal." This type of choice "tends to make the interview [or ethnographic] process emotionally intense for both interviewer and participant" (2002, 227). Even when research topics are chosen because of considerations such as funding, the process of doing qualitative research can engender intensity and a kind of cognitive passion. Warren began to study the mental health and legal system because of grant funding, and wrote an ethnography of decision making in a mental health court (Warren 1982). This initial research led to several other research projects, including an interview-based study of 1950s housewives diagnosed with schizophrenia (Warren 1987), and a history of electroshock in America (Kneeland and Warren 2002) using documents and visual images.

Your use of this textbook may be limited to finding out about qualitative research, or perhaps doing one or two exercises such as observing and writing fieldnotes, doing an interview, or analyzing a set of magazine advertisements. If, however, you are assigned to do something less limited—even, perhaps, a paper based on fieldwork, interviewing, or textual analysis—you may find that you too are drawn to the method. We certainly hope so! But whatever the level of your involvement in qualitative research, it is important to understand that it is framed within the set of ethical, legal, and political issues we discuss in Chapter 2.

## Suggestions for Further Reading

Becker, Howard. 1998. *Tricks of the Trade: How to Think About Your Research While You're Doing It*. Chicago: University of Chicago Press.

Bulmer, Martin. 1984. *The Chicago School of Sociology: Institutionalization, Diversity, and the Rise of Sociological Research*. Chicago: University of Chicago Press.

Denzin, Norman K., and Yvonna S. Lincoln, eds. 2000. *The Handbook of Qualitative Research.* Thousand Oaks, CA: Sage Publications.

Emerson, Robert M. 2001. *Contemporary Field Research,* 2nd ed. Prospect Heights, IL: Waveland Press.

Fine, Gary A., ed. 1995. *A Second Chicago School? The Development of a Postwar American Sociology.* Chicago: University of Chicago Press. ❖

## Chapter Two

# The Law, Politics, and Ethics of Qualitative Research

**S**ocial research does not occur in a vacuum; it takes place under specific sociohistorical conditions. And in the twenty-first century, those sociohistorical conditions include a set of important legal, political, and ethical issues surrounding both the subjects of social research and the researchers themselves. These human subjects issues, in addition to various laws pertaining to social research, affect all funded and unfunded student and professional social science research.

The politics and legalities of doing research with human subjects vary considerably depending on the discipline with which the researcher is associated. If you are a journalism instructor or student interacting with or talking to "human subjects" for the media, you may ask any questions you wish, and use the names of the subjects in your published research; your work is protected by the First Amendment and your notes are protected by law from subpoena. Your only obligation to your subjects is to identify yourself as a journalist. If you are a sociology student or instructor, however, you may not interact with or talk to respondents unless you have received permission from your college or university's Institutional Review Board (IRB). You are not protected by the First Amendment, and your notes are not protected by law from subpoena.

Both sociologists and journalists have professional associations with ethical guidelines for the treatment of human subjects; sociology's is the American Sociological Association (ASA). The entire text of the ASA code of ethics can be found on the Internet at *www.asanet.org/ members/ecoderev.html*. The basic principles elaborated by this code of ethics are given in Box 2.1.

---

**Box 2.1**

**Basic Principles of the
American Sociological Association
Code of Ethics**

- Research should not harm respondents.
- Participation in research must be voluntary, and therefore respondents must give their informed consent to participate.
- Researchers must disclose their identity and affiliations.
- Anonymity or confidentiality must be maintained for respondents unless explicitly and voluntarily waived.
- The benefits of a research project should outweigh any foreseeable risks.

(Adapted from *http://www.asanet.org/members/ecoderev.html*)

---

Despite the existence of professional codes of ethics and of IRBs, debates continue over several issues in field research, including overt versus covert participant observation and the general issue of deception in social research. Various discussions of whistle-blowing have also occurred in ethnographic research under circumstances where the fieldworker becomes privy to illegal or unethical behavior by people in the setting. These and other issues in qualitative research are not easily resolvable by guidelines and codes, because everyday life is not governed by guidelines and codes, but rather by the unfolding of situations. However—and also like the rest of everyday life—anything a qualitative researcher says, does, or writes during the course of his research can render him liable to legal action by respondents.

## The Law and Qualitative Sociological Research

The law has become relevant to the conduct of ethnographic research in this country in two contexts: complaints or legal action against ethnographers by people related to the setting, and the subpoenaing of fieldnotes by legal representatives. One well-known ethnographer, William Foote Whyte, was the subject of a complaint to the American Sociological Association by the adult offspring of one of his key informants for the book *Street Corner Society* (1943). Like many such complaints, the central issue was one of seeming betrayal by the ethnographer, in this case Whyte's key informant, "Doc." After Doc's death, his two sons were interviewed about his reaction to the book:

> The oldest son answered, "Mr. Whyte would not be pleased to hear what my father had to say. My father considered the book untrue from the very beginning to the end, a total fantasy." I was ex-

tremely puzzled and remarked that on various occasions Whyte had mentioned that his father had gone line by line through the drafts and had approved of them. . . . They answered that their father did not even know that Whyte had written a book on their [*sic*] research. (Boelen 1992, 29)

Naming "Doc" as Ernest Pecci, Whyte claims that they did go over the manuscript of the book together (Whyte 1992, 59–60). However, "As I expected, when the book came out, he undertook to distance himself from it," mainly because of the possibility of other street corner society members identifying him and themselves in the text and not being pleased with the portrayals (Whyte 1992, 60). Whyte adds: "Doc's sons state that I had exploited their father. While I grant that I got more from the relationship than he did, that was not my intention" (Whyte 1992, 61). Although this and several other cases did not eventuate in full-fledged litigation, they serve as a reminder that not only disgruntled respondents, but even the offspring of disgruntled respondents may use the law to express their sense of betrayal.

## The Brajuha, Scarce, and Leo Cases

A number of attempts to subpoena the fieldnotes of qualitative sociologists in the twentieth century have resulted in court trials, and others were settled out of court. If your instructor wants you to undertake, as well as read about field research or interviewing, you should be aware of three published graduate student cases in order to make a realistic assessment of possible difficulties that can occur. These are the Brajuha (Brajuha and Hallowell 1986), Scarce (1994), and Leo (2001) cases.

In the first published case, Mario Brajuha, a graduate student at the State University of New York, was conducting field research in the 1980s while working as a waiter in various New York restaurants. One of these restaurants was destroyed by fire while he worked there, and arson was suspected by investigators. Brajuha's fieldnotes were subpoenaed by federal and county district attorneys. He refused to turn them over, but did agree to provide copies edited for confidentiality; eventually the subpoena demands were dropped (Brajuha and Hallowell 1986).

In the second case, in 1992, Rik Scarce was doing dissertation research in the sociology department at Washington State University on the radical environmental movement. Upon receipt of a fieldnotes subpoena for a grand jury investigation, he invoked (a legally nonexistent) "academic privilege" under the First Amendment. The judge rejected his argument and held him in contempt of court; his appeal against this conviction was unsuccessful, and Scarce spent 159 days in jail (Scarce 1994).

Richard Leo, the third student case, had done dissertation field research in police interrogation rooms in 1992–1993 in a "large urban police department" in California (Leo 2001, 262). Six months after he had finished his research, a public defender learned of his observation of the interrogation of his client and subpoenaed Leo to appear at a preliminary hearing. Leo did appear at the hearing, and did "betray . . . my promise of confidentiality" to the detective involved in the case by turning over his fieldnotes and testifying (2001, 276).

These three graduate student cases, with their different contexts and outcomes (although all involved fieldnotes dealing with some kind of illegal behavior), underline the significance of writing fieldnotes that protect, as far as possible, the confidentiality of the persons being observed. It has long been seen as important to protect confidentiality in published qualitative research, but it is now necessary to begin the confidentiality process earlier, at the point of fieldnotes. Actual names and clearly identifying details should be removed or changed in all written materials pertaining to qualitative research.

In addition, these cases point to the necessity for sociologists to have the umbrella of First Amendment protections given to journalists. Although journalists are not completely protected by the First Amendment, they are on much firmer legal ground than sociologists when it comes to the inviolability of their notes and sources. The protection of human subjects is extremely important—as we will see below—but so is the protection of researchers as well as journalists by some kind of "academic privilege" equivalent to "journalistic privilege."

## The Protection of Human Subjects

The federal government sets standards for the protection of human subjects in social as well as biomedical research; colleges and universities must institute procedures implementing these standards. College and university IRBs are charged with overseeing research with human subjects to ensure their protection. In order to conduct funded or unfunded research on campus, even observation of public places, the sociologist—professor or student—must write up a proposal for the IRB detailing the research design and procedures. Qualitative researchers, whose research always involves observing, interacting with, or talking to respondents, are particularly affected by human subjects regulations.

Although some IRBs are not particularly concerned with field research in public places, others restrict even this seemingly harmless form of research. Field research in quasi-public places (such as restaurants or bars), workplaces of other kinds, and private places (such as clubs or families) often requires the permission of those in the setting being studied as well as the sponsoring institution. Some settings, such as health service organizations, mental hospitals, and prisons, have their own IRBs to which potential researchers must submit their proposals. Thus, for a single research project, the researcher may have to gain the approval of a number of IRBs. In a study of managed care organizations that Karner (Montgomery, Kosloski, and Karner 1996) participated in, nine separate IRBs had to give their approval before data collection could begin (four managed care IRBs—even though three were part of the same larger organization—four state agency IRBs, and one university IRB). IRB committees require specific documentation of various components of the research process, a requirement more closely suited to quantitative than to qualitative field research. See Box 2.2 for a list of the components required in most IRB proposals.

---

**Box 2.2**

## Components of an Institutional Review Board Proposal

I.   Research design and specific aims

II.  Methods and data collection procedures
   A.   Data collection instruments and questionnaires
   B.   Interview questions

III. Informed consent procedures
   A.   Proposed consent forms
   B.   Proposed consent "scripts" used in informing potential subjects
   C.   Written information to be given to subjects agreeing to participate which includes
      1. Subjects' rights
      2. Clear idea of procedures and aim of research
      3. Any benefits the subject will receive
      4. Any potential harm to subjects

IV.  Any potential harms to subjects
   A.   Argument for necessity of data collection plan
   B.   Plan to minimize any anticipated harm

V.   Debriefing procedures or services offered to subjects that might be needed due to participation

---

If researchers wish to interview as well as (or instead of) interact with respondents, the proposal to the IRB must include a list of the questions that will be asked, and anticipated behaviors to be observed. Many times field researchers are unaware of the questions that they will want to ask or all the types of behaviors they will encounter in a

setting prior to entering the field, which makes this sort of prior documentation speculative at best.

Federal guidelines also specify certain populations as "special"
ones to whom special protections are extended in human subjects
guidelines. To do research with individuals at either end of the age
spectrum—children and adolescents under 18, and some elderly populations—the researcher will generally need to obtain the approval of
guardians, who may be parents or adult children caregivers. These
populations are seen not to be fully capable of consenting to participation. Research with prisoners is often not permitted, since their social
situation implies that they are not free to voluntarily consent to act as
the subjects of research. Furthermore, research into "sensitive" topics
such as sexual behavior or drug use, or combat activities will generally
receive closer scrutiny by IRBs than research that seems less sensitive,
such as preferences for ketchup brands.

## Protection From Harm

What are the human subjects being protected from? One protection is from stigma—the possibility of being "found out" by published
or unpublished research as a criminal, drug user, child molester, or
such. Elaborate procedures have been devised to avoid the identification of subjects in published, and even unpublished, research. In order
to send out a survey (and resend it if there is no response by a given
date), a quantitative researcher has to know the name of the recipient,
but once the survey document is received, the respondent may be further identified only by a number. Thus, by the time survey research is
published, there is little reference to anything other than numbers.
Survey researchers can promise their respondents both confidentiality
and anonymity with little difficulty.

But the issue is different for qualitative researchers. They observe,
interact with, and talk to people, and in many cases know their identities and names and sometimes even their families and where they live.
The data of qualitative researchers are people's words and appearance.
So, qualitative researchers cannot promise respondents anonymity
(we know who they are!), but they can provide, and reassure respondents of, confidentiality. Confidentiality involves not only obvious
things like not using respondents' names and addresses, but also less
obvious things like not describing them in enough detail so that they
could be identified by others—while not changing details so much that
the meanings associated with persons are lost.

Federal guidelines also seek to protect human subjects from the
possibility of distress: being asked questions that provoke emotional
reactions such as shame, guilt, or sorrow. In biomedical research, of
course, human subjects protections also refer to bodily harm—indeed,
it was with issues of bodily harm and biomedical research that our

society first concerned itself with the protection of human subjects from researchers.

Human subjects protections as we know them today began, as so many things begin, with media publicity concerning abuse. The Nuremberg trials brought photographs and accounts of the treatment of concentration camp prisoners that made Hitler's genocidal schemes public, and horrifying, to the world. In his camps, physicians had experimented biomedically on adults and children, destroying their bodies and minds in the process. The horrors of Hitler's agenda in Europe, together with ethically problematic research in this country, made twentieth-century politicians and lay people aware of the need to have strict controls in place for any biomedical experimentation on human beings.

In the United States, the Tuskegee Syphilis Study serves as one of the most egregious examples of ethically problematic research. (See Jones [1993] for a detailed account of the study.) Partly because it was federally funded, and thus at the time, sanctioned by the government as well as the medical profession, the Tuskegee study focused concern on issues of informed consent and its importance for voluntary participation. Without full information and disclosure, research subjects' participation cannot truly be considered voluntary.

In the early part of the century, biomedical researchers in Tuskegee, Alabama, received funding from the U.S. Public Health Service to study the impact of untreated syphilis on the human body. For 40 years (1932–1972), over 400 African American men ill with syphilis participated in this federally funded study. Since the objective of the study was untreated syphilis, even after an effective treatment was developed these men were overtly denied the medications. The researchers went so far as to contact the physicians of their participants to persuade them not to treat the research subjects. The study also offered free health care to the participants so that they would not seek care elsewhere. Furthermore, to ensure that autopsies could be done after death, the researchers offered free burial services, thereby gaining access to the bodies without having to gain family consent.

Unfortunately, the Tuskegee study is not an isolated example. In 1963, two physicians at a Brooklyn, New York, hospital conducted a cancer study where 22 elderly patients were injected with live cancer cells without their knowledge (Katz 1972). In the Willowbrook Hepatitis Experiment, 1956 to 1972, uninfected mentally ill children were given viral hepatitis in order to study the course of the disease (Barber 1976). The journalists who discovered these studies provoked enough public outrage that laws were passed to protect human subjects from such misuses of biomedical experimentation. In 1966, the first federal Public Health Service policy for the protection of human research subjects was issued. It was, however, limited to medical and clinical experimentation (see Warren and Karner 1990).

From the 1970s onward, the federal government extended protections for human research subjects to include the social sciences as well. The 1966 policy for biomedical and clinical research served as the model for the federal government's approach to social science research (Reiss 1979). This was a step that many social scientists found—and find—distressing. Social science research can indeed cause social and emotional difficulties for people: for example, if respondents are engaged in unlawful or stigmatized behavior (such as illegal drug use, excessive violence in combat, or extramarital sexual liaisons) and are identifiable, they could presumably be held accountable by the law, or stigmatized within their own social circles. If they are asked in interviews about distressing subjects—their troubled relationship with their parents, perhaps, or how it is to be biracial—they may become emotionally upset. However, these kinds of problems are arguably not comparable to Tuskegee and Hitler and are part of everyday life as well as research into everyday life.

Nevertheless, social science researchers, and the codes of ethics that have been established in the last few decades, recognize the importance of protecting their respondents from harm (see Box 2.1). Qualitative researchers are required to be—and want to be—careful about ensuring that their respondents' identities remain confidential. They are also generally trained to ask questions in ways that are helpful rather than distressing, and to provide resource information about counseling resources should interviewing (for example) become distressing. However, we agree with many of our fellow social science researchers in the twenty-first century who also feel that the restrictions on social science research have gone too far in this country. On many campuses, even ethnographic research in public places such as bus stops, a few years ago deemed "harmless" by federal and IRB guidelines, is being scrutinized. We also are rather unhappy at being lumped together in the same ethical realm with the Tuskegee research team and Adolf Hitler.

It is also difficult to easily use dichotomies such as "harm" or "benefit" in the interactional, situated world of ethnographic research in particular. In *Street Corner Society* (Whyte 1943), it might have seemed beneficial rather than harmful for Whyte's key informant, Doc, to become interested in getting out of his lower-class, street-corner circumstances. But Doc did not succeed in his ambitions, and became frustrated, according to his sons, harmed rather than helped by his association with Whyte. But, surely, the harm (if that) was of a type that affects us all in our interactions with others, every day. Doc was not injected with hepatitis or cancer cells, nor was he left with untreated syphilis or forced to undergo physical experiments without anesthesia; rather, he did not get a job for which he was not deemed qualified:

When . . . Frank Havey . . . was starting the store-front recreation program, [I] persuaded him to hire Pecci as director of one of the centers. He did an outstanding job, but unfortunately, funding for the program ran out after 6 months. . . . [Later] I learned that Havey had an opening on his regular staff for a boys' worker. I phoned to urge him to appoint Pecci. . . . Apparently the board was not prepared to appoint a high school dropout, no matter what abilities he had already demonstrated working with boys. (Whyte 1992, 61)

## Informed Consent

IRBs and federal regulations are concerned not only with protection from harm but with *informed consent*—voluntary participation in the research combined with an awareness of its purposes and procedures. IRBs generally require researchers to write an informed consent statement that respondents then sign; situations may occur in which informed consent can be delivered orally and for which the IRB will require a "script." In qualitative research, informed consent forms can be used easily with interview research, but the issue is much different in field research. If you are sitting at a bus stop observing the behaviors and interactions of those around you, it is not possible to request and obtain consent from bystanders and passersby.

The issue of informed consent in field research is one still being grappled with by IRBs and researchers today, and is resolved in different ways at different institutions. Your instructor may define such field research as "student training" rather than as IRB-covered research. Or the instructor may obtain an IRB approval for your class as a whole rather than for each individual project. If you are doing interviews, however, individual proposals will, according to federal regulations, probably have to pass your institution's IRB before the research can proceed. Informed consent may be oral, but it is generally written; an example of a letter of informed consent to be given to respondents is given in Box 2.3.

Informed consent can be, and has been, itself a topic for qualitative research. At a university psychiatric hospital, Charles Lidz and his colleagues (1984) observed the interactions surrounding informed consent to electroshock therapy (ECT) between staff and patients. They learned that the degree and kind of explanations offered by staff varied by many factors, including the patient's psychiatric symptomology and the presence of relatives in the room. They also learned that patients had a variety of interpretations of what they had been told:

Patients' understanding was . . . typically incomplete and occasionally misdirected. . . . it seemed often to be idiosyncratic and experientially based. . . . disclosure by the staff, even when fairly substantial, seemed to play a relatively small part in the patients'

**Box 2.3**

## Sample Letter for Informed Consent

Dear Ms. X,

The Department of Sociology at the University of X supports the practice of protection for human subjects participating in research. The following information is provided for you to decide whether you wish to participate in the present study. You may refuse to sign this form and not participate in this study. You should be aware that even if you agree to participate, you are free to withdraw at any time. If you do withdraw from this study, it will not affect your relationship with this unit, the services it may provide to you, or the University.

**The purpose of this study** is to learn more about how individuals with diabetes understand their illness and treatment protocols. **Procedures** for this study include two one-hour interviews with a sociologist in which you will be asked questions about your experience of living with diabetes. The interviews will be tape-recorded for accuracy and later transcription. We do not anticipate any potential **risks** to participants in this study, nor do we anticipate any direct **benefits** to those who participate.

If you agree to participate, your information will be kept **confidential**. Your name will not be associated in any way with the information collected about you or with the research findings from this study. The researcher(s) will use a study number, initials, or a pseudonym instead of your name. Furthermore, you may withdraw your consent to participate in this study at any time. You also have the right to cancel your permission to use and disclose information collected about you, in writing, at any time, by sending your written request to: Dr. X at the Sociology Department of the University of X. If you cancel permission to use your information, the researchers will stop collecting additional information about you. However, the research team may use and disclose information that was gathered before they received your cancellation, as described above.

### Participant Certification:

I have read this Consent and Authorization form. I have had the opportunity to ask, and I have received answers to, any questions I had regarding the study and the use and disclosure of information about me for the study. I understand that if I have any additional questions about my rights as a research participant, I may call (XXX) XXX-XXXX or write the University Institutional Review Board, University Road, University Town, [State, zip code].

I agree to take part in this study as a research participant. I further agree to the uses and disclosures of my information as described above. By my signature I affirm that I am at least 18 years old and that I have received a copy of this Consent and Authorization form.

_____                    _____

Type/Print Participant's Name                               Date

_____

Participant's Signature

Jane Smith, Principal Investigator,
Department of Sociology, University of XXX, University Road, University Town, XX
phone: XXX-XXXX

understanding. . . . patients tended to cite their own and other patients' experiences much more frequently than they cited information they had received from the staff in justifying their decisions [to have or not to have ECT]. (Lidz et al. 1984, 317)

This is only one of many examples you will encounter when doing qualitative research (or for that matter living everyday life) on the issue of interpretation by participants of what was said or done in an earlier situation. In comparing research we had previously been engaged in (Karner and Warren 1995), we found that the clinical setting of a Veterans Administration hospital and the psychiatric context of the *Madwives* study (Warren 1987) often led interview subjects to conflate research with clinical treatment despite the fact that they had been informed that they were participating in a research study and different (nonclinical) individuals were conducting the interviews. As this illustrates, you cannot assume that the participants' understandings match your own.

Some ethnographic settings are such that it might be possible to obtain informed consent from everyone present; we have seen this done, for example, in small, closed self-help group settings such as Gamblers Anonymous that met once a week. There have also been attempts to make informed consent a continuous part of ethnographic research. For example, in Mitch Duneier's *Sidewalk* (1999), the use of turned-on tape recorders functioned as a continual reminder that the street booksellers' lives and words were being observed and recorded.

Some qualitative researchers, such as Mitch Duneier and Douglas Harper, use still photographs in their research, while others, such as Joseph Kotarba and Eric Margolis, use videotape or film. Using the identifiable images of other people in sociological work requires informed consent, although some visual sociologists object to this on First Amendment grounds. It seems odd, they say, that journalists can talk to anyone, and publish anyone's name or image, without requiring informed consent (in most cases), just because they identify themselves as journalists. Yet, somehow, as we noted above, the same First Amendment provisions do not protect social science researchers.

## Confidentiality, Publicity, and Anonymity

When journalists write, they inevitably make public the lives and statements of their respondents without confidentiality. Sociologists, however, are expected to keep their respondents' identities a secret while publishing general information about their lives and statements. These IRB guidelines, as we have seen, are premised on the idea that publicity might harm social science respondents by stigmatizing them in some way, if their identities are put into print. This issue of confidentiality and stigma has been a concern of IRBs, professional associations, and individual researchers for several decades.

Although there has been some concern about publicizing subjects' lives in the latter part of the twentieth century in the context of ethnographers becoming "spokespersons for deviant subcultures" (e.g., see Warren 1972), a more recent ethical debate concerning similar issues arose during the early 2000s. Some ethnographers who identified their subjects were criticized for sanitizing and glamorizing the lives of their subjects (Wacquant 2002). If respondents are identifiable by names and even photographs (as in Duneier 1999) in published work, then the sociologist writing about them might be tempted to skew his findings or analysis in ways protective of those respondents. Sociologists who do identify their respondents deny that this strategy leads them to "naively fall in with my subjects, romanticizing their lives and depicting them as saints" Duneier (2002, 1552).

As a novice researcher, your instructor will inform you about any IRB reviews your work might entail; whether your instructor is able to define what you will be doing as training rather than research at your institution, or if a blanket IRB approval will be obtained for the entire class. But whatever the formal procedures, it is incumbent on you to protect the confidentiality of your informants and try to refrain from distressing them in any way outside the bounds of everyday social interaction. The first issue—confidentiality—is easier in large urban areas than in small towns, where even naming a particular kind of self-help group such as Gamblers Anonymous can narrow the possibilities down to one.

## Ethical Issues in Qualitative Research

Over the years, fieldworkers in particular have written extensively about ethics in qualitative research as they encounter issues and dilemmas they see as "ethical" ones. Some of these are mentioned in codes such as the ASA guidelines (for example, the issue of sex with respondents, discussed in Chapter 4), while others may not be discussed in any written form but may arise nonetheless. All social science fields face two key ethical dilemmas: the issue of deceptive research, and the Cartesian imperative to treat others (in this case, research subjects) not as means to an end but as ends in themselves. These two key dilemmas take particular forms in qualitative sociological research: the issue of covert versus overt roles in fieldwork, and the clash of citizen versus research roles if abuse is observed in your setting. Both these issues are debated in the context of changing views of what constitutes justifiability in the search for knowledge about society.

## Deception in the Field

There has been an extensive and ongoing debate for several decades over the issue of deception in social science research. Experimental psychologists, in particular, have long relied on experimental procedures in which subjects are not aware of what is really going on—for example, the famous Milgram (1963) experiments in the post–World War II United States. In these experiments, recruits were informed that they were giving electric shocks to research subjects concealed from them, whereas in fact no humans were being shocked in the experiment. Some of these subjects were captured on camera in extreme emotional distress over obeying the experimenter and giving increasingly more severe shocks to the concealed (and screaming!) "victim"—but nevertheless continuing to obey.

Although Milgram and other such experiments over the next 60 years have been subject to considerable ethical dispute, deceptive research continues to flourish on college campuses in Psych 101 courses, where undergraduates are subject to all kinds of experiments, including many involving deception. Like the Milgram subjects, these psychology students are "debriefed" *after* their participation, but the possibility of emotional harm from being deceived has not convinced most campus IRBs to discontinue Psych 101 experiments. The same IRBs, however, would be unlikely to permit covert field research, which has been condemned by the American Sociological Association as well.

The Cartesian insistence that humans should treat one another as ends in themselves and never as means to other ends would, in its most literal interpretation, prohibit all social science research, or perhaps all research not directly beneficial to the respondents involved in it. In doing qualitative research with other human beings, researchers may treat subjects as ends in themselves—be polite, careful, sincere, and interested—but they are inevitably also treating them as a means to the end of understanding and interpreting settings (and, for some researchers, publishing books or articles, teaching, and perhaps amassing some share of fame and fortune). Obviously, since we are sociologists who have done research and we are writing this book, we do not accept a literal interpretation of the Cartesian strictures.

## Covert Versus Overt Field Research

Covert research is passively deceptive in the sense that qualitative researchers either do not reveal their research intentions or are actively deceptive, where they are pretending to be something they are not. For example, Leslie Irving, (1999) in studying a Codependents Anonymous group, was not a codependent herself, but attended the meetings anyway and said nothing about her research intentions. On the other hand, Irving could have (though she did not) pretended to be a codependent and participated in telling codependent narratives. Passive deception is more acceptable to many sociologists than active, as this mirrors an approach often found in everyday interactions.

Active deception—someone pretending to be something he or she is not—is doubly problematic. First, it is often impractical, since pretending to be something you are not may entail a good deal of knowledge (which you may not have) and some acting ability (which you also may not have). Second, most qualitative sociologists today would also deem such research unethical, although the matter has been contested for at least the past 30 years. The most debated study with regard to active deception may be that of Laud Humphreys (1970), who dressed in leather and served as a watch queen (lookout) for men engaging in homosexual encounters in park restrooms. He observed the license plates of the participants, had a friend obtain their home addresses from the Department of Motor Vehicles, and then, after disguising himself, approached the men for a "neighborhood survey." Thus he was able to collect broader background data on the participants than he would have been able to obtain otherwise.

The issue of not revealing one's research intentions is regarded by some qualitative sociologists as ethically problematic, and by others as not. Researchers might join a support group or field setting that they feel they are legitimate members of, but conceal the fact that they have joined specifically for the purpose of research. Some researchers who define themselves as having problems for which there are self-help groups join such groups with mixed agendas, seeking both personal involvement and research opportunities; several of Warren's students, for example, studied Overeaters Anonymous for both research and self-defined weight problems. Additionally, some researchers find the opportunity for a study arising from their own lived experience, and retrospectively their participation in their own lives could be viewed as unintentionally deceptive as they begin to revisit their former interactions as a source of data.

Public-place field research is almost by definition covert, since one cannot stand at a bus stop or walk down a street informing everyone present or passing by of one's research intentions and status. It is justified, however, both by the public, available-to-all nature of the setting and by the fact that people observe others all the time in public settings. Sociologist Erving Goffman (1959, 1961) has documented in numerous studies of everyday life how people self-consciously present themselves to others, interact with acquaintances and strangers, use public space, and obey or deviate from everyday norms. This body of work is outstanding, and it is unimaginable that human subjects regulations or overly controlling "ethical" regulations might have prevented Goffman from doing this work, or disallow future Goffmans.

Doing overt field research, which is not generally perceived as ethically problematic, means that at least one or some of the members of the group under study know that you are a researcher and have given you permission to "hang around" in the setting. However, this does not mean that everyone at all times knows that you are a researcher. Everyone in a closed, small self-help group might be aware that one in their midst was an overt field researcher, but this would not be the case in a setting where people come and go. Richard Johnson (2002), for example, studied a rural Kansas "sale barn" where local folks auction cattle and various other animal and material goods. Although he was given permission by the owners of the sale barn to hang around on Saturdays when the auctions were in session, not all the sellers, buyers, or members of the sale barn community knew, every Saturday, that Johnson was doing research. Over time, however, many regulars did come to address him as "professor" and ask him how his studies were going.

The opposite happened to Warren (1982) when she was doing field research at Metropolitan Court. Although she was given permission to study the court by her key informant, the judge, and he sometimes introduced her as a sociological researcher, he more often introduced her as a law or nursing student, and she was most often regarded by others in the setting as a student (being fairly young at the time and even more young-looking). At a private psychiatric hospital where Warren later researched overtly, she soon came to be pulled into the duties of the hard-pressed psychiatric technicians; forgetting her non-tech, research status, the head nurse of the unit tried on several occasions to get her to accept work shifts. Warren did not do so, partly because the hospital was more than a hundred-mile round trip from her house, and partly because she was afraid that as an unlicensed, untrained person she might bring some unintended harm to the adolescents on the ward.

Karner's (1995) field experience on a post traumatic stress disorder unit at a Veterans Administration hospital presented yet another dilemma of identity. Because the unit routinely had clinical students "rotating" through for training, some of the unit staff assumed that she was just another clinical student. The veterans Karner interviewed and observed were for the most part unaware of what a sociologist is and had almost no familiarity with social research. Thus, though the guidelines and procedures for informed consent as sanctioned by both her university and the VA were followed closely, the subjects' lack of knowledge of sociology limited the possibility for fully informed consent.

Punch (1994) goes so far as to propose that all fieldwork has an element of mutual deceit; that both subjects and researchers are practicing impression management. Some subjects may wish to present the most positive aspects of themselves, while others may overstate their involvement in the researcher's stated interest. Meanwhile, researchers set out to ingratiate themselves within a community or setting and must develop a sense of rapport and trust with potential subjects that can take both diplomacy and concealment.

## Ethical Dilemmas in the Field: Researcher Versus Citizen

Although federal human subjects regulations may be overly concerned about the possible harms done to respondents by qualitative sociologists, it is certainly possible to fear doing harm (as Warren did when she had to deal with disturbed adolescents for the first time) or to observe harmful activities on the part of others. These possibilities are particularly salient in institutions populated by relatively helpless clients, including prisons, mental hospitals, nursing homes and other facilities for the aged, institutions and homes for the developmentally disabled, and general hospitals. Some researchers who have researched or done work in such settings have documented occasions in which their wish to continue researching in the setting has clashed with their wish to see something done about particular conditions or activities that they have been privy to—researcher vs. concerned citizen.

"Blowing the whistle" as a concerned citizen is not something that facilitates continued research access, and several field researchers who have encountered problematic situations in the field have declined to do so, including Stephen Taylor (1987) in his study of a ward for the mentally retarded, and several ethnographers who studied the police. Taylor says that "the ward was a terrible place" (290) in which abuse by the attendants ranged from yelling, threats, and teasing to physical assaults: "it was not uncommon for attendants to hit or slap residents," and

> when attendants were bored or in a jovial mood they compelled one resident to swallow lit cigarettes or instructed another to perform fellatio on one of his peers. (291)

Taylor notes that there were four choices of action facing him when he observed abuse: intervention, leaving, whistle-blowing, and continuing to do the study without any kind of citizen response. He decided on the latter and continued the study. His argument for prioritizing researcher over citizen is that more was to be gained in the long run by accumulating knowledge about issues, problems, and stresses in the field setting than by whistle-blowing in the short run. He notes:

> Drawing on what I had learned about institutions, I have written descriptive reports for use in several court cases and for media exposes. Based on related research, I presented U.S. Senate testimony on conditions in the institutions and the federal government's role in perpetrating abuse. . . . Had I not continued my research . . . I would never have had the commitment or knowledge for these activities. (1987, 300)

Studies of illegal police violence by John Van Maanen (1988) and others also highlight the tension between research access and the presumed obligations of citizenship—and, for that matter, between the law and the actual practice of police work. Emerson (2001a, 34–35) describes two ethnographic studies of the police use of illegal force: Van Maanen's fieldnotes on the violent arrest of a drunken bar patron, and Jennifer Hunt's interview with a patrol officer who repeatedly hit a driver who had embarrassed her by driving away while she was trying to ticket him. Emerson comments:

> These descriptions convey a sense of police work as patrol officers might themselves understand and talk about it. . . . The use of force in circumstances not prescribed by law is not only viewed matter-of-factly, as part of the job, but is assumed to be justified or "normal" in particular contexts and under certain circumstances. . . . but not in any and all. (2001a, 35)

Sociologists are for the most part a bit uneasy about prioritizing the researcher role over citizen, especially in cases where the violations documented are extremely serious. Ken Levi did a series of intensive interviews with a hit man without revealing his identity or crimes to the authorities, and commented on the ethical issues:

> A question might arise about the ethics of researching self-confessed "hit men" and granting them anonymity. Legally, since Pete never mentioned specific names or specific dates for possible future crimes, there does not seem to be a problem. Morally, if confidentiality is a necessary condition to obtaining information about serious offenders, then we have to ask: Is it worth it? Pete insisted that the hit man had retired from the profession. Therefore, there seems to be no "clear and imminent danger" that would justify the violation of confidentiality, in the terms set forth by the American Psychological Association. (1981, 48)

A number of Levi's colleagues did not agree, and his article was greeted with considerable controversy.

These cases illustrate the kinds of ethical dilemmas intrinsic to ethnography. If ethnography's purpose is to understand social worlds as the members themselves understand them, then observing abuse of patients or police violence, or interviewing hit men, is likely to be a part of the process of developing such understandings. Furthermore, if sociology's purpose is to develop knowledge about society, then, as Taylor implies, the value of the knowledge gained by continuing to do research is greater than the value of the outcome of blowing the whistle—the termination of research involvement.

There are also the matters of gratitude and trust in field research. Ethnographers who are permitted, as outsiders, to be part of a setting's activities are often quite grateful to the people who opened their lives to the researcher, and thus are not inclined to "blow the whistle" on them. Such whistle-blowing violates the trust that members have placed in the ethnographer, as Van Maanen (1983) noted in his discussions of the reasons for not blowing the whistle in his police research.

It is no accident that the ethical dilemmas we focus on here are from research done primarily in the 1970s and 1980s. It is much more difficult to obtain access to settings where policy violations or illegal activities might be observed in the 2000s than it was 20 years ago, including police ride-alongs, prisons (where Levi located and interviewed his hit man), and institutions for the mentally ill or retarded. Although Taylor (1987) was given permission by the institution's administration to research his setting, it is also possible to engage in covert (or only partially overt) research while working for pay or as a volunteer. This is what Timothy Diamond did in his 1990s study of institutions for the elderly, *Making Grey Gold* (1992). Diamond trained and worked as an aide, one of the few men and one of the few nonminority aides in the various settings in which he worked and did research.

So, is it ethical to gain entrée to institutional settings not via IRB approvals but via paid or volunteer work? This brings us back to the issue of covert research. The easy answer is no, since such tactics violate the principles of informed consent and involve deception as to one's intentions. It is reasonable for you to engage in field research in settings in which you already work or that you frequent, such as a bar or restaurant, and you would probably be given IRB approval to do so. But, while you are a student researcher in training, do not try to get into a prison, mental hospital, or other such institution as a paid or unpaid worker (or client!) by volunteering or working there. In our view such research should not be undertaken by students. Your instructor is responsible for the conduct of your research, so you should not do anything to get her, as well as yourself, in trouble; the same goes for team research and its hierarchy of members. However, entering an institution by "the back door" as a paid or volunteer worker is sometimes justifiable, in our view, by skilled individual researchers.

Why do we see such research as justifiable by individual researchers? One of the major premises of sociology is that we need to understand relationships of power and domination in our society. Sociologists have found over the decades that studying elites is rather difficult, because there is far less access to elites than to nonelites—but some ethnographers have won acceptance among aristocratic, professional, or business circles. Studying the vulnerable and oppressed in society was once much easier, but is now made more difficult by IRB regulations preventing access to settings such as mental hospitals and prisons. It is arguable that research in such institutions is impossible or difficult not because the inmates or clients need to be protected from researchers, but because the owners and managers of such institutions prefer not to be under the scrutiny of an outside researcher.

One argument for doing the research anyway, covertly by becoming a worker, is that public institutions should be accountable to the public, and anyone should have access to them. And although many of our contemporary care-and-control institutions are private and corporate, including the nursing homes studied by Timothy Diamond (1992), they take public money in many forms. Thus it is also justifiable, in our view, to study private institutions that have been licensed by the state and take state funds such as Medicaid. In short, if you become a professional sociologist and ethnographic researcher, you might want to do as Timothy Diamond did, but not now as a student and researcher-in-training.

The law, politics, and ethics of qualitative research are as complex as the settings, interactions, and individuals toward which such research is directed. Although the First Amendment protects journalists—indeed, permits them to interview, identify, and name people—it does not protect sociologists, leaving us open to the possibility of lawsuits connected with our qualitative studies. The extension of human subjects protections from biomedical to social research has meant the presence of the long arm of politics (national, local, university, and perhaps international) as well as the long arm of the law in the conduct of qualitative research. Informed consent, confidentiality, and the absence of risk or danger to respondents are all extremely important issues, but in their actual implementation by IRBs, they may be at the point of hampering or short-circuiting important qualitative sociological research.

During the past decade, professional associations, including the ASA, have developed ethical guidelines of their own in response to and in the context of federal regulations. Although ethical guidelines and federal regulations are often quite specific about what is or is not permissible in social research, various ambiguities also derive from the ambiguities inherent in everyday life itself. Ethical debates may exist over overt versus covert social research and the general issue of deception, but the field researcher's identity and stated purpose are not simply absorbed and reflected by the people in the setting. And the ethical issues surrounding dilemmas of research and citizenship in qualitative research are not resolvable by general principles, but must be negotiated in the field by individual researcher/citizens.

As you, having decided on your setting and received permission to do your research (by your instructor, IRB, or both), prepare to enter the setting, think about four issues: (1) Be aware that the law is *not* on your side; (2) Even if you cannot obtain informed consent from everyone all the time, keep the spirit of informed consent alive by occasional reminders or symbols (such as jotting notes) of what you are up to; (3) Protect the confidentiality of your informants by not using their real names, and by not giving descriptions of them that are accurate enough to identify them; (4) Use all the courtesies and kindnesses of everyday life in your interactions in the field—although these courtesies and kindnesses may not always keep others from harm, they are the best we can do in fieldwork, as in everyday life.

## Suggestions for Further Reading

Duneier, Mitchell. 1999. *Sidewalk*. New York: Farrar, Straus, and Giroux.

Humphreys, Laud. 1970. *Tea Room Trade: Impersonal Sex in Public Places*. Chicago: Aldine.

Katz, Jack. 1972. *Experimentation With Human Beings*. New York: Russell Sage.

Lee-Treweek, Geraldine, and Stephanie Linkogle. 2000. *Danger in the Field: Ethics and Risk in Social Research*. Routledge.

Punch, M. 1994. "Politics and Ethics in Qualitative Research." In *The Handbook of Qualitative Research*, ed. Norman K. Denzin and Yvonna S. Lincoln, 83–97. Thousand Oaks, CA: Sage Publications.

Romm, Norma R. A. 2001. *Accountability in Social Research: Issues and Debates*. New York: Plenum Press. ❖

# Chapter Three

# Field Research

*Setting and Entrée*

Field research, also known as ethnographic research, is based on interacting and talking with people in a setting. In this chapter, the first stages of field research are discussed: selecting a setting, access to it (referred to by sociologists as *entrée*), and ways of gaining access. Chapter 4 describes the incorporation of the researcher into the setting, the establishment of roles and relationships, research bargains, and leaving the field and its aftermaths. Chapter 5 tells you about what is perhaps the most significant task associated with field research: writing fieldnotes.

"Interacting and talking with people in a setting" sounds simple, but it is not. What is a setting and how should I find one? How should I interact? What should I say and what should I refrain from saying? Will I be the only researcher doing the study or will I be part of a group? Will they let me study them? How will I leave? What should I write down in my fieldnotes? How do I balance field research and fieldnote writing against my other social and academic obligations? All these questions and others are characteristic of the ethnographic enterprise.

To make matters even more complex, as we noted in Chapter 1, there are also a number of different approaches to, or ways of doing, field research. The approach that forms the basis for this book, and the one that we have practiced in our own ethnographic studies, is what John Van Maanen (1988) calls "realist ethnography." Realist ethnography takes a middle position in the debate over reality versus representation (see Chapters 1 and 10). We realist ethnographers know that a published study is an interpretive representation of a setting, not an exact replica or mirror. But we also think—because we have tried our best to observe and write fieldnotes diligently, carefully, and for an adequate length of time—that our account represents a reality in which even members of the setting might recognize themselves and their world (see also Emerson, Fretz, and Shaw 1995).

Before considering the first step in ethnographic research of selecting a setting, we want to say a few words about circumstances in which researchers do not choose their settings but rather settings are chosen for them. Sometimes graduate students and possibly undergraduates are hired as part of a team research project of which field research is a part or the whole. Concerns in earlier decades that "hired hands" might skip details or even falsify data (Staggenborg 1988; Noblit and Burcart 1975; Roth 1966) have prompted team researchers to put safeguards in place. In the mid-1990s, Karner managed a multisite interview project in which she trained several local interviewers in a number of different geographic regions of the United States (Kosloski, Montgomery, and Karner 1999). Local interviewers were selected for their language skills and familiarity with various immigrant groups to be interviewed. Quality control measures such as comparison with other service and family data that were being collected, regular contact with the interviewers in the field, and a local supervisor were crucial in alleviating "hired hand" concerns.

Students may be assigned their research topics by the instructor, either individually or as part of a group research assignment. Research-methods instructors often assign students to take fieldnotes in open campus settings such as libraries or cafeterias just to have the experience of writing notes and trying to analyze them. But whether for hired hands or supervised field research, the team research supervisor or instructor selects settings that the student can gain access to. Gaining access and selecting a setting are the first two problems of doing field research.

## Choosing a Setting

Some students come to classes in qualitative methods fully prepared with topics or settings that they want to study. In cases where topics such as motherhood or danger have no settings, methods other than field research may be more suitable. What, then, *is* a setting?

Consider, for example, the mental health court Warren studied in Los Angeles, which for the sake of confidentiality she calls Metropolitan Court (Warren 1982). The court is a building on a street; in that sense, the setting is architectural, with floors and walls and roofs. But that is not the "interacting and talking with people" setting. What provides access? This building has one courtroom that provides easy and immediate access to the casual visitor. In the hallways, patient/petitioners wander around and talk with their court-appointed attorneys.

Offices abound: the district attorney's office, the public defender's office, the judge's chambers, and offices for bailiffs, court reporters, and mental health personnel Warren had never before heard of when she first visited Metropolitan Court. There are also the bathrooms, cafeteria, and other assorted spaces. So, what is the setting?

For the student ethnographer, the most suitable answer is: the courtroom, or a courtroom if the courthouse has more than one. A study of the public rituals of the courtroom would be your best bet for doing a semester or quarter ethnography of Metropolitan Court, or any other court for that matter. Even traffic court can be a fascinating study ethnographically. Warren's fieldnotes from a Kansas courtroom in the early 2000s (see Box 3.1) can give you some idea of what you might find in this kind of public setting. Wider definitions of the setting will take more time; Warren's (1982) study eventually encompassed the judge's chambers, the attorneys' offices, and the hallways. It took her seven years to write about this setting.

What is also interesting about the Metropolitan Court example is that it may also be seen as several settings rather than one. Each of the subsettings in the court building—the courtroom, the hallways, the judge's chambers, the district attorney's office— sustained their own patterns of social interaction and talk. In a way, each interactional subsetting was its own social world, a point also made by Jaber Gubrium in his study of *Living and Dying at Murray Manor* (1975). In this ethnography, Gubrium described the different social worlds of Murray Manor, a nursing home: the worlds of upper-level staff, of lower-level staff, and of patients.

> Each world provides its participants with a way of looking at and understanding daily life at the Manor. And each has its own logic: its own ideals, sense of justice and fair treatment, method of expedience, prescribed duties, rhetorical style, and proper mode of making decisions. (1975, 37)

If you have the opportunity to choose a setting, one not assigned by an instructor or team leader, be flexible (see Box 3.2 for aspects of choosing a setting). Realize that unless the setting is extremely small and clearly bounded in time and space (such as an 8–10 member Smokers Anonymous group that meets once a week on Tuesdays at 6 p.m.), you will probably not be able to study it in its entirety. It is acceptable to study one classroom in a school, or one courtroom in a courthouse, especially in a study that will last only a few weeks or months. Although a few ethnographic works are comparative (Sudnow 1967; Lyman 1993), these are generally book-length; shorter studies are usually confined to one setting. So the first principle of choosing a setting for a semester-long project is to be modest in your aims. As indicated in Box 3.2, other considerations are relevant if the setting is pub-

## Box 3.1

### Traffic Court as a Fieldwork Setting

I enter the courtroom from the hallway, and find myself in the usual type of courtroom setting: the judge's chair and desk elevated on a platform, with (in this case) her name engraved in large gold letters on a wooden sign, facing the audience. Instead of a witness box a podium is placed in front and just to the right of the judge's desk. A middle-aged, white male sheriff, in uniform and with a gun in his holster, hovers around the judge's desk eyeing the crowd and the people coming in.

[symbols of authority and power; the elevated platform, the sheriff, his uniform and his gun to keep order, the judge's name in front of the anonymous crowd. I feel guilty of something although I haven't done anything, my presence in the courtroom is simply to observe.]

And it is quite a crowd. As I walk in I am facing the judge's platform with the podium facing me, and rows of folding chairs lined up on either side of the room. It looks like every chair is full—there are perhaps fifty people in the room of all ages, although only one who might be under 18. I spot one vacant seat in the middle of a row of chairs to the right, and take it. People are still streaming in, looking around for vacant seats. A man in the back by the entry door tells them to sit or lean against the walls, which they do, starting at the back but soon spilling against the sides. The sheriff warns a young woman off a part of the wall that is beyond the rows of chairs and toward the judge's platform.

Most of the people seem to be here by themselves, or at least they are not interacting with anyone; they either stare at the judge's platform in a waiting stance or occupy themselves with shuffling and looking at papers they have brought with them. A few people are talking with one another in a muffled, whispery tone.

A woman sweeps into the room from a door behind the platform, wearing black robes, her eyeglasses on top of her head. She is white, perhaps in her early 40s, with long dark hair and a severe expression on her face. As she begins to sit, the sheriff shouts, "All rise and order in the court!" Everyone shuffles to their feet, and there is pretty instant silence.

[these rituals of authority work; we the audience have to stand before our judge, and we have to be silent unless and until we are invited to speak]

The judge bangs a gavel on the desk in front of her. A man, not in uniform but in khaki pants and a white long-sleeved shirt, comes down the aisle between the rows of chairs and says, "All here in the matter of . . . [I couldn't hear what he says] please rise, we are going to another courtroom." He opens a door to the right of the room and gestures toward it. About 15 of the people in the room stand up and make their way with various degrees of difficulty through the door. No one else in the room seems to be moving or talking, although a few brave souls who have been standing move quietly to take a couple of vacated chairs. . . .

[Later] the judge said, "Now what I am going to do is I am going to enter a plea of not guilty for you and then when I call your name you will come forward—" she gestures to the podium. . . . [I am intensely surprised by this, as I thought that people in court, even traffic court, would make their own plea, and, indeed, somewhat later still]. . . . the judge calls out a name and a middle-aged white woman comes to the podium. The judge says, "I have entered a plea of not guilty for you." Almost interrupting, the woman says, "Can't I just plead guilty and just get it over with?" [although I could not follow the next brief interchange, I gathered that pleading guilty and getting it over with was not possible]

(Excerpted from Warren's fieldnotes)

lic (easy access) or private (may be more difficult) and if the research requires Institutional Review Board (IRB) approval.

---

**Box 3.2**

**Evaluating Setting Appropriateness**

I.   Access
   A.   Public or private space
   B.   Internal IRB required

II.   Geographic Issues
   A.   Proximity
   B.   Transportation availability
   C.   Weather

III.   Interest
   A.   Of the potential subjects
   B.   Of the researcher

IV.   Cost
   A.   Time
   B.   Money
   C.   Emotional (dis)comfort
   D.   Other involvements (schoolwork, employment)
   E.   Other social relationships (friends, dates, parents)

---

## Accessibility, Interest, and Cost

A setting may be feasible (public space with no IRB required), but as Box 3.2 also indicates, you still need to think about its accessibility, interest to you, and cost. Public settings are often feasible and accessible, private ones generally less so. You should be able to do an ethnography of a bus stop or a public courtroom, but you are not likely to be able to do an ethnography of the West Wing of the White House. This is of course an extreme example—the White House is not only a private space, but a highly secured one as well—but it does illustrate the first principle of accessibility: the public-private continuum of settings.

This example also illustrates the second aspect of accessibility: geographic proximity. Unless you happen to live in Washington, D.C., the White House is an inaccessible setting for reasons of geography, as well as privacy and security. A bus stop on campus would probably be a better choice for your field research than a bus stop far from either campus or your residence.

You also might not be interested in either the bus stop or the White House. People's interests come from many places: reading, the media, political participation, leisure, work, and religious affiliation—all different aspects of your personal biography. Sometimes, students are interested in researching something they find fascinating but know little about directly, such as prisons or mental hospitals. Other students are interested in features of their own biographies; for example, a student whose parent is a member of Alcoholics Anonymous may want to study self-help groups.

However, the mental hospitals, prisons, workplaces, and other bureaucracies often of interest to student and faculty researchers are essentially (especially in a one-quarter or one-semester course) off-limits to student field research. Not only does the researcher's proposal have to pass the University's IRB (see Chapter 2), but institutions also often have their own IRBs that further scrutinize researcher proposals. Even if this process is successful—which it well might not be—it might take upwards of a year to get permission for research. By this time your class would be long over!

The student who wanted to study an Alcoholics Anonymous group would face an ethical dilemma. Some meetings of AA and other self-help groups are open to the public, and thus are quasi-public rather than private settings. However, the essential characteristic for entry into the meetings is possession of the identity of which the self-help group is all about: alcoholic, gambler, narcotics user, smoker, or codependent, among others. A researcher who considered herself to be one of these might have legitimate entrée into the setting; a researcher prepared to pretend such identity would be in violation of ethical standards in place for at least the past two decades (e.g., see Humphreys 1970 and Chapter 2). Even the researcher whose entrée was legitimate might be considered ethically compromised if he did not identify to the group as a researcher as well. (See Irving 1999 for a discussion of this issue.)

Some settings are accessible in principle, but are difficult to enter if the researcher does not share certain beliefs or values with the members. Nancy Tatom Ammerman (1987) wanted to observe a Protestant fundamentalist congregation she called Southside. She foresaw problems because fundamentalists were likely to count her, as a sociologist, among the "'secular humanists' who have corrupted traditional ways of thinking" (Ammerman 1987, 10). However, because she was a "committed Christian" able to say "'yes'" to the question "'Are you born again?'" Southside's pastor gave her permission to do the research (Ammerman 1987, 10–11). Patricia and Peter Adlers' youthfulness, somewhat hippie appearance, and tolerant outlook on the use of soft drugs made the drug culture they studied accessible to them (Adler 1985, 13).

Public settings such as bus stops or parks are clearly the most accessible settings since anyone (at least in theory) can be there, but students often resist studying everyday life settings because "nothing interesting ever happens there." We would like to encourage you to think about studying everyday life in public settings, not just because it is easier with respect to IRBs but also because it is infinitely captivating, as the work of Goffman (1959, 1961) has shown us. Everyday life pulses with interaction rituals, spatial norms, presentations of self, deviance, sanctioning, and social control all around us in settings such as the bus stop and the grocery store.

Quasi-public settings such as bars and restaurants also present interesting locations for research. They are public in that anyone can enter (although restrictions such as age or dress codes may restrict access), but they are owned by and operated in the private sector (or, in the case of an armed forces commissary, by the state). If you are going to do field research as a quasi-customer (rather than a worker) in such a setting, you will need to be aware of the responses or potential responses of management or owners, often referred to by ethnographers as "gatekeepers," to your presence in the setting, as Gary Alan Fine (1996) did when he observed restaurant kitchens (see below).

Another aspect of choosing a setting is cost not only in terms of money and time, but also in less tangible factors such as self-esteem. Some research settings will obviously and from the beginning involve fixed dollar costs (e.g., observing audience behavior in your local movie theater unless you have free access). Other settings may not have fixed and obvious costs but can come to involve financial elements, as Elliott Liebow (1993) found when he studied a shelter for homeless women who asked him for rides and loans. You should also calculate the financial cost involved in transportation to or from the setting, and the temporal cost to you of selecting that setting.

Some settings are clearly more costly in terms of time than others. Sociologists and anthropologists who study whole villages have to invest a great deal of time in learning the culture; thus so that entire community studies are not suitable settings for an individual student researcher engaged in one-quarter or one-semester courses. In terms of time, settings where you are already a member may be ideal, although what you learn from them may not be as challenging as would be the case if you become a "stranger in a strange land." Settings that are available all or most of the time and where the interaction is fairly routinized or ritualized are ideal for beginning field research: bars, bus stops, restaurants, grocery stores, and other such places.

Other costs to consider in some field research settings are physical and emotional. A bus stop, inviting in the late summer at the beginning of the semester, might be less so in the incipient winter at its end. A setting that takes you away from family members used to having you around may take its toll on your personal relationships. And a setting you feel uncomfortable in or ambivalent about might also be one you should consider avoiding. One student Warren had was very uncomfortable with gambling, and was disconcerted by what she regarded as her boyfriend's compulsive gambling. She chose to study a local casino in order to try to understand more about gambling, but was never able to even take good fieldnotes because of her disgust at the activity she was trying to observe.

## 'Starting Where You Are'

Thus far, we have discussed settings of which you, the researcher, are not already a member. There is a long tradition of field research, however, that relies on varying kinds and degrees of membership or potential membership in the setting to provide entrée, something that Lofland and Lofland (1995, 11) have called "starting where you are." As we pointed out in Chapter 1, a researcher who also wishes to lose weight might join Overeaters Anonymous for both research and personal purposes if she thinks she fits OA's definition of overeater. A student working his way through school by waiting tables at a local restaurant might decide to do field research in that restaurant because he already has access to the setting and is in a good position to understand its patterns of interaction (although he might want to think about this carefully in the light of possible legal issues, as discussed in Chapter 2).

"Where you are" in a setting has a profound impact on the access you will have to the various worlds of interaction and talk within a setting. A worker in a bar or restaurant may do field research on workplace culture, as Spradley and Mann did with *The Cocktail Waitress* (1975), while a customer is likely to be limited to studying customer-customer and customer-worker interaction (for example, see Cavan 1966). A stranger walking into a bar for the first time will probably have to become a customer—sit at the bar, buy drinks, interact and talk—to understand the patterns of interaction in that setting. In some settings it is really not possible to be or remain an outsider and do field research.

Several of Warren's students over 21 have done ethnographies of bars and restaurants where they have been either workers or customers. One bartender-student was in a good position to do a somewhat autoethnographic analysis that focused on the significance of the bartender in bar interaction—as the person dispensing the drinks (or not!), as typifier of customers as *regulars, strangers, funny drunks,* or *on the wagon,* as a focus of talk and interaction at the bar, and in collaboration with the cocktail waitresses. An ethnography of a bar from the vantage point of the bartender will be different than one from the vantage point of the customer.

Many qualitative studies have been done by researchers who are already members of a setting, from Howard Becker's analysis of the world of jazz musicians in the 1960s to Rick Fantasia's (1988) study of a wildcat strike that occurred in an iron foundry to Kristin Esterberg's (1997) study of lesbian and bisexual identities in the late 1990s. Other studies are accomplished by the researcher becoming a member of the setting, such as Timothy Diamond's *Making Grey Gold* (1992), a study of nursing homes. Diamond trained as a nursing assistant and worked in several of these homes, usually as the only white male among a staff of African-American women workers. His analysis of how nursing home corporations "make grey gold" out of the pensions and social security of residents, and the minimum wage labor of nursing home aides is an example of institutional ethnography (see Chapter 1).

Sometimes "starting where you are" is a matter of geographical proximity or even serendipity. When they moved to Southern California to attend graduate school, Peter and Patti Adler (Adler 1985) rented a condominium next to a young man they called "Dave." After hanging out with Dave for a few weeks and noting his drug use and apparent lack of employment, they came to the conclusion that he might be a middle-class drug dealer. They report: "We watched Dave and continued to develop our friendship with him" until interactions with some of Dave's friends made it clear that he was a "member of a smuggling crew that was importing marijuana weekly and 40 kilos of cocaine every few months" (Adler 1985, 14). Thus began Patti Adler's study of drug dealing (1985).

Your commitment to the setting marks the time to enter or reenter it. If you are a member of a group—a bartender, an Alanon member, a lesbian activist, a tattoo collector—your commitment to researching, as well as being part of, that group is in itself a kind of entrée (see Thorne 1980). But if you are not a member, you will have to present yourself to the group as a field researcher: a person in everyday life who looks to be of a particular gender, age, social status, race, or ethnicity.

## The Embodied Researcher: The Presentation of Self in Fieldwork Entrée

As a method involving everyday interaction and talk, field research is not unlike everyday life. One of the things we have all heard is that first impressions are very important—and this is no different for field research than for any other kind of interaction. The kind of person you look like, the way you dress, your demeanor, voice, accent—everything about you affects first impressions in field research (or interviewing) as in other arenas of everyday life. In large-scale interview research, interviewers are trained in how to dress and how to approach different types of respondents, but presentation of self is often not part of the direct training of sociological fieldworkers (although anthropological fieldworkers studying non-Western societies are generally more aware of the issue; see Warren and Hackney 2000).

As we will see in subsequent chapters, entrée is not a one-time event but rather has a number of different meanings. In this chapter we will consider two of these meanings: agreement by the people in the setting that the researcher will be permitted to do field research (an unnecessary step if you are doing fieldwork in a public setting such as a bus stop or in a setting of which you are already a member), and the moment at which the researcher enters the flow of everyday life in the setting to join in the interaction and talk. Both aspects of entrée depend on the researcher's embodied presentation of self. This facet of fieldwork is not always as obvious as in the case of a tattoo collector, who literally shows off his body, but it is always a salient background feature of social interaction in fieldwork as in everyday life. (See Chapter 4 for more on this.)

Your presentation of self, or front, in Goffman's (1959) terms, is made up of things you cannot change and things you can, things you do change, and things you do not. Some of the things you cannot change (at least not easily) include your gender, height, age, and skin color. Anthropologists studying societies in other than the First World have found that gender, age, skin color, and nationality are particularly significant embodiments when seeking entrée to societies structured by these ascribed characteristics (see Warren and Hackney 2000). Race, ethnicity, and gender are also significant ascriptions in contemporary American culture, and can function to shape or defeat entrée.

In thinking about doing ethnographic research on homeless African American book vendors in New York's Greenwich Village, Mitch Duneier felt that he would have to "bridge many gaps between myself and the people I hoped to understand" (2001, 168). These gaps included race, social class, religion (he is Jewish), and occupation. He concluded that "none of these differences seemed to be as significant as that of race. Actually the interaction between race and class made me uneasy, although I was unaware of that at the time" (168). One of the book vendors, Hakim Hasan, wrote a note to Duneier that said he was suspicious of him:

> My suspicion is couched in the collective memory of a people who have been academically slandered for generations. . . . African Americans are at a point where we have to be suspicious of people who want to tell stories about us. (Duneier 2001, 169)

After a couple of months of informal meetings in which Hakim and Mitch discussed issues of race and research, Hakim said that Mitch could start his ethnographic observations at his book vending table.

Embodiment as a race-d, class-ed, gender-ed and age-d person is the first entrée consideration for fieldwork seeking acceptance among strangers; the second is demeanor. Our general advice is to conform, politely, to the standards of appearance and behavior expected within the setting. If you are to study a law firm, you might consider dressing as "professionally" as the people who work in the firm. If, on the other hand, your setting is a construction site, a hardhat and tools might help you to fit in, but also might look odd if you are not working at but only researching the site. In that case, jeans and a T-shirt would probably be adequate.

Sometimes field researchers have to decide how much they are willing to give up, or compromise, to achieve an appropriate presentation of self for a given setting. Warren once had a female student with a shaved head whose chosen setting was a beauty parlor. Although she preferred her shaved head to a head of hair, she was willing to grow her hair back in order to be able to fit in with the workers and customers at the beauty parlor. It was the view of the class members, including Warren, that her entrée without hair would have been much more problematic than with hair.

In Richard Leo's research into police interrogations, he knew he was getting into a setting that is "tightly knit and intrinsically conservative. . . . Any outside observer or researcher of interrogation practices may thus be viewed as a potential whistle-blower" (2001, 262). Leo tried in several ways to gain the trust of the officers he wanted to observe, including what he called a "chameleon strategy" (Leo 2001, 266) of attempting to fit in. He not only cut his hair short and shaved closely, he also pretended to share their "personal, administrative, and political biases" (267). Leo's chameleon strategy involved adapting not only his clothing, but also his talk to the setting:

> I feigned conservative politics; I openly shared their bias against abortion and in favor of the death penalty; I affirmed their antipathy toward homosexuality; and I described my intimate relations with women in the same crude manner and sexist language that is common in police culture. In short, I fabricated a nonthreatening research persona in order to establish rapport with the detectives, acquire their trust, and gain observational access. (2001, 267)

Not every setting requires chameleon-like adaptation, but most profit from courtesy. Politeness is part of the smooth functioning of everyday life, and this is no less the case for ethnographic settings (exceptions might include, for example, biker bars). As an individual or a representative of your college or university, you want to approach others with courtesy, not like the student who introduced himself at an AA meeting by saying, "I'm here to study boozers."

Over decades of ethnographic work, field researchers have found that they can as often as not achieve entrée into their chosen settings as long as they are polite and try to fit in. Sometimes, however, entrée does not go as planned. Warren had one student who wanted to study a health care facility that served low-income Hispanics. She spoke Spanish fluently and dressed and presented herself appropriately; however, she never achieved entrée to the setting as she had conceptualized it. What she wanted to study was interactions between health care providers and patients—interactions that took place in private rooms in the clinic. Although she never did gain access to these rooms, she became a fixture in the waiting room of the facility, and was able to write an ethnographic paper on waiting room interactions. Once again, this student's experience illustrated the principle that "a setting" may consist of several different social worlds.

In our American culture, gender, age, ethnicity, race or nationality, and apparent social class are very significant aspects of interaction in everyday life; it is not surprising, then, that they are equally significant to the conduct of field research, from first impressions onward. Federal law forbids discrimination in employment, housing, and other areas on the basis of gender, race, and in some cases sexual orientation, but this does not mean that the settings you might be interested in researching operate without any such discrimination. Ethnographers have written about various aspects of embodiment in the conduct of field research in places other than the Western world; anthropologists have stressed ethnicity and nationality, age, and gender, while sociologists have stressed gender. This does not mean that age, race, and other ascribed statuses—and first impressions—are not important in sociology. But especially since the 1970s, with an increasing cognizance of gender in sociology, women and men doing fieldwork (often young women and men doing undergraduate or graduate-level research) have been a focus of ethnographic discussion.

## Gender and Fieldwork Entrée

Your gender may facilitate or prevent your doing research in particular settings. If you are a woman, for example, you are unlikely to gain entrée into male homosexual bathhouses, although you could probably hang around some male gay bars. In other settings, either a man or a woman could gain access, but they might be treated very differently according to gender; this has been the experience, for example, of field researchers who study police. Gender expectations related to the dress, demeanor, and behavior of women and men are also relevant to entrée into various settings, and the conduct of research once inside (see Chapter 4). Ethnographic methods writing has also examined issues of danger for researchers, particularly violence against male researchers, and sexual violence or sexual harassment directed against female researchers (see Chapter 4).

One area of research that has flourished during the past 10 years is research into lesbian and gay settings (Robinson 2003). This is an obvious area in which the gender of the researcher is of paramount significance in gaining entrée. Some settings in this area may be completely or almost completely closed to one gender: women's music festivals, for example, are open to lesbians and to other women, but may be closed to men and to transgendered males-to-females and females-to-males. One of Warren's students, in a study of a women's music festival in Minnesota, found that the only men permitted in the grounds were those associated with cleaning crews; when they came into the grounds to clean, the women were warned away from them. This setting, clearly, would not be one for a male to attempt to enter.

We return to Warren's 1980s research in Metropolitan Court as an example of different access accorded to male and female researchers in the setting. Warren, as a (then) young female, was warmly welcomed by her gatekeeper and key informant, the judge. He made a "mascot" out of Warren (something that has been noticed by women fieldworkers from at least the mid- into the late twentieth century), and she was able to accompany him around the court and onto the bench. A young man who wanted to do research in Metropolitan Court a couple of years later was permitted to do so by the judge, but was pretty much ignored by the judge as he went about his business. This young man, instead, made friends with the male head of the public defender's office, and made him his key informant (see below). And this difference in entrée and access affected the subsequent conduct and focus of the two studies: he saw more of the public defender's side of the court's business, while Warren saw more of the judge's and district attorney's activities.

In preparation for her entrée into Metropolitan Court, Warren visited it briefly to see the kinds of clothing worn by the professional workers in the setting. After making this observation, she dressed like them: this was the early 1980s, so Warren wore a blouse, skirt, and jacket, styled her hair long, and wore makeup. Whatever the setting for your research, it is generally advisable to dress and conduct yourself in a manner befitting the general and gendered expectations of the setting. To do otherwise invites a rejection of your interest in entrée. Before you approach a setting to which you are a stranger, be sure that you have some idea of expected dress, demeanor, and appearance.

## Approaching the Setting

Chapter 2 detailed the formal steps necessary before beginning some, if not all, ethnographic research. These preparatory stages of field research involve attempting to gain entrance into the setting during the same time period in which you are negotiating with your institution's IRB: there is no point in gaining IRB permission to do an ethnography of a setting that will not let you in!

Gaining admission to a setting in which you do not already have a role and where people do not know you begins with the first contact. This first contact may best be made by your instructor or supervisor or by you, depending on the setting and what your instructor thinks. Among the possibilities for seeking admission are telephone calls, letters, e-mail, or a personal visit. Which one is used depends in part on the comfort level of the researcher with a given approach, and in part on the nature of the setting, including its formality or informality, IRB requirements, local customs, and the historical time period during which the research takes place. More than 20 years ago, Warren initiated research contact with a psychiatric hospital serving adolescent patients (a formal organization) by visiting the hospital in person and asking to see the hospital administrator. It is possible that such a direct and informal approach would not work today.

During the late 1980s and early 1990s, Karner developed a formal, businesslike approach to contacting individuals in larger organizations that she still uses. She often calls or e-mails (and this works best if you have identified a third-party introduction) to request an informational meeting with key persons in potential settings. As students, you can often contact a potential subject and tell them you are interested in learning more about their work or organization. Most people are quite receptive to interested students. A student of Karner's sought a meeting with the CEO of a large energy corporation; she called repeatedly, leaving messages with his secretary. Her tenacity eventually won out, and the CEO returned her call and facilitated her entrée. Though it took the student over a month to achieve her goal, it is unlikely that she could have invested that kind of time showing up at his office (if she could get past the security guard each day).

For more formal settings, such as large businesses, more formal approaches may be more customary and, perhaps, better received. Yet, much field research takes place in settings not as formally organized as a psychiatric hospital or energy corporation. People in settings such as coffee shops or gyms may be more receptive to students who show up and ask to talk with them rather than to e-mails, phone calls, or letters. It is much easier to put someone off with these more "distanced" approaches. Whichever approach you use, however, it is important to discuss beforehand with your instructor, what you will do, say, or write since you, as fieldworker, are also a representative of your college or university.

In approaching a setting, you should take into account not only your own presentation of self, but also anything about the setting that might be relevant to either allowing or denying you access—if you have this information. Some settings, such as police departments or mental hospitals, are liable to fairly frequent controversies, political battles, and other difficulties, which can make them inhospitable to ethnographic research. In September 1969, W. Boyd Littrell (1979) proposed a study of the administration of criminal law in Fairfield County, New Jersey. His project was approved by Fairfield assistant prosecutors, but

> in November 1969 William T. Cahill, a Republican, defeated the Democrat Robert Meyner in the gubernatorial election. A new prosecutor from a different political party would soon be appointed and the entire project would have to be cleared again. I re-

alized then that my project and I were part of the patronage granted by New Jersey democrats. (1979, 237)

This change in gatekeepers required that Littrell renegotiate, and even redesign, his research.

## Gatekeepers

*Gatekeepers* are those individuals or groups who can grant or deny initial access to a setting—usually a formal organization—and, luckily, they do not always change while entrée is being negotiated. In Warren's (1982) research with a mental health court in Los Angeles, the contact person was the judge—as is the case with any study of courtrooms. In Karner's (1995) research in a Veterans Administration hospital, the contact person and gatekeeper was a professional staff member on the unit she wished to study. In other kinds of organizations, you might have to find out whom to contact—the manager-owner of a restaurant, say, or the top administrator of a nursing home. If these gatekeepers accept your presence as a researcher, other people in the setting will have little choice other than to extend at least a courtesy acceptance to you (more on this in Chapter 4).

Gary Alan Fine (1996) describes the steps to his research entrée into four restaurant kitchens in a large urban area using the restaurants' gatekeepers. He contacted people he knew at each restaurant from a prior stint at a culinary institute (three head chefs and a manager) and sought introductions to head managers or owners. To this second level of gatekeeper, Fine clarified that he had the chef's approval and that he would not evaluate the restaurant (i.e., he was not a food critic in professorial disguise). He told these gatekeepers that he just wanted to stand and watch, and that if they felt his presence interfered with the business he would terminate the research. All agreed, although one requested a formal letter. Fine spent a month observing in each restaurant for six days a week, and reported no problems with the gatekeepers.

In his study of police interrogations, Richard Leo (2001) did not have such an easy time with gatekeepers. Like Littrell (1979) some 20 years earlier, he was initially blocked from doing research because the chief and the captain "feared my study could generate negative publicity for the organization" (Leo 2001, 264). However, when his Ph.D. adviser was asked to do an evaluation study of the police department, this "created a strong incentive for the police chief to be in the good graces" of this adviser. Leo was then permitted to undertake his research, but still had difficulty persuading individual detectives to allow him to observe their interrogations (2001, 264).

Once having been accepted by the "powers that be" as a researcher, you may have a date and time of entrée set for you, or you may have some choice in the matter. Once his gatekeepers—owners, managers, and chefs—had agreed to Fine's kitchen observations, he chose a day to begin his research, one based on prior knowledge of the contingencies of the setting. He began his research at a time that he knew the kitchen staff would not be busy, so he could explain to all of them individually what he was doing. No one refused to allow him access to their work lives, and everyone he asked for an interview said yes: "Like the head chefs, they were flattered that someone of 'importance' was interested in their lives" (Fine 1996, 244).

If you are given a time and place to enter the setting, be punctual. You can also expect that your gatekeeper will give you a tour of the set-ting, then perhaps leave you in the hands of an assistant or someone else who will feel a sense of responsibility for "entertaining" you. Over time, in general, that sense of responsibility and entertainment on the part of setting-members will fade, and they will go about their busi-ness, getting used to your presence in the meantime.

Warren's research subsequent to *The Court of Last Resort* (1982) illustrated several of these issues in acceptance and entry. A few years after the ethnography of this court was published, she became inter-ested in studying court hearings in which potential electroshock patients sought to avoid being given that particular treatment. Instead of approaching the new judge (whom she did not know), Warren approached (in person) the head district attorney in the court whom she had known from earlier research. He said he would check with the judge, and then called her to say her research had been approved, and she should show up the following Monday at 8.30 a.m. when an ECT hearing was scheduled.

The following Monday at 8.30 a.m., Warren showed up promptly to learn that this hearing had been canceled, and that few electroshock hearings were even scheduled. Thus, while hoping that an ECT case might occur within her lifetime, she decided that it might be useful to spend time looking at the court records of past cases. Her interest in entrée was not only into the courtroom to observe interaction, but also into the files to gain some understanding of the background to these cases. IRB permission to do this was not an issue at this time (the mid-1980s). The district attorney gradually allowed Warren access to these records. At first, he pulled them by case number and read them to her. Then, he pulled them by case number and let her look at them. Some months later, he gave her free access to the files, allowing Warren to pull and return them as and when she saw fit.

This anecdote illustrates the stage-like quality of entrée: it may not be a one-time event, accomplished once and for all for the remainder of the research. The researcher is first accepted as an observer, then appears somewhere in the setting. But once in the setting, access to dif-ferent parts of the setting may require further entrée activities; in the court Warren had access to the district attorney's office and the courtroom but not, this time around, to the judge's chambers. In addition, the point of entrée is to enter into not only physical settings but also the social meanings, which requires more than simply the co-presence of researcher and setting members. If Warren had access to the district attorney's office, but whenever she was there the attorney felt compelled to go elsewhere to discuss their cases (which is what happened at one point in the first phase of her Metropolitan Court research), then her entrée would mean little. These continued entrée processes are part of the long-term conduct of field research, which is discussed in Chapter 4.

It is clear from the discussion of field research so far that issues such as entrée and access are common to all settings, but also that a variety of issues occur in different settings. While it is not possible for us to cover all the possibilities that might arise or emerge in your field research, some aspects of the research process are common to various types of settings. In many settings, but especially in bureaucracies and other organizations, key informants play a role in introducing and sponsoring the fieldworker. And in other settings, but especially in community studies, the go-along with key informants provides insight into the meanings a setting has for individuals within it. In still other settings, including but not limited to ones in other countries, the researcher may initially be seen as a spy.

## Key Informants

In organizational field research, key informants may smooth your way into different situations and connections. Some of these key informants are the gatekeepers who initially permitted entrée into the setting, and indeed, gatekeepers may remain key informants as the research progresses. Other key informants may emerge during the process of research, providing access to new settings or other parts of a setting. During Warren's Metropolitan Court research she became interested in visiting the mental hospitals from which the court drew its petitioners. She got to know one of the visiting mental health counselors responsible for connecting patients who asked for *habeas corpus* writ hearings with court personnel to schedule the hearings. After some socializing and discussion of her research interests, this mental health counselor invited her to ride along as she went back to the hospital and continued her work with the patients. Warren was very grateful, and took her up on her offer. The opportunity to see the interactions between counselors and patients before they came to court was a valuable step in the further understanding of the organizational network within which the court was one part.

Though it is not unusual to identify helpful individuals in settings, sometimes their desire to assist the researcher can outweigh their allegiance to their own organizational protocols. While still a young and somewhat naïve graduate student, Karner approached a staff member at a local AIDS foundation about the possibility of meeting and interviewing individuals with HIV. The staff member enthusiastically offered to have Karner accompany her on home visits to clients of the foundation. When the director of the organization discovered the staff member's activities, she nearly lost her job, which put an end to Karner's access. Thus, it is wise to be wary of eager offers to help for many reasons.

Generations of field researchers have, in fact, warned novice fieldworkers that key informants may be problematic in some ways. It is a truism of anthropology and everyday life that members of a setting who are immediately warm and welcoming may be outsiders in their own circles looking for acceptance among newcomers. The twelfth grader who immediately looks for friends among incoming tenth and eleventh graders is one example among many. It is no use cultivating a key informant who is somewhat of a pariah among her or his own people. The rule of thumb in settings where key informants present themselves is to wait and see, at least a little bit. Of course this is not what Warren did with the mental health counselor, but this was because this particular mental health counselor was not a part of the court, the main focus of her study, but of an associated organization.

Key informants are not always pariahs in their own worlds; they may be friendly people who are welcoming to any stranger who comes along, including ethnographers. And in some settings, such as bars, friendliness to strangers is encouraged and facilitated by the loosening effect of alcohol. Friendliness and sociability do not always mean truth telling, however, as Box 3.3 indicates. Key informants are perfectly capable of inventing stories and giving the researcher various kinds of runarounds.

Ethnographers have sometimes found key informants in a setting who understand or are connected in some way with the research enterprise. This kind of understanding can greatly facilitate entrée. Esther Newton, an anthropologist interested in studying male drag performers in Chicago in the mid-1960s, sat in on drag shows—then quite "taboo" (Newton 1972, 133)—and also wanted to interview performers. She approached one impersonator who "replied that he had majored in anthropology in college and . . . would willingly talk to me" (Newton 1972, 134). This man became, over time, "at least as dedicated to the study as I was" (Newton 1972, 133). Recently, a student of Warren's who is studying, and a member of, the Society for Creative Anachronism, found a key informant in a fellow SCA member who is also an anthropologist.

---

**Box 3.3**

### Key Informants at Play

Another problem sometimes occurs when community members know that a sociologist is doing research—they put you on. This is not a problem confined to prostitute respondents who are paid for giving data and feel they have to give the poor john a really good story. Especially in a community where sociability is the main activity, and putting people on is one of the happenings, this can happen very often, and certainly happened to me from time to time: Here is one example from my study of *Identity and Community in the Gay World* (Warren 1972, 170–171).

> Gene said to me in conversation at the bar this evening "There was this guy from Local College doing research as he called it, and he was really gorgeous, really groovy, and straight. Well, we all really gave him a bad time, told him all of these things, like we used bananas up our ass, and he wrote it all down—for weeks. It was fun." I asked Gene why it was fun, and he indicated that it provided a change from the same old routine at the bar.

> Alex told me with a straight face this evening that he and Jake get their kicks sitting on their roof with raincoats and boots on. I saw a certain gleam in his eye when he said it, and he added, "Tell that when you write your book."

---

## The Go-Along

The go-along is a method that combines field research with interviewing, but the interviewing is done in an ethnographic context. Go-alongs have been used in ethnographic research in Hollywood and other communities in the Los Angeles area during the late twentieth and early twenty-first centuries (Kusenbach 2003). They involve walking along with, driving with, or basically shadowing key informants as they go about their daily routines, seeing what various aspects of their environment mean to them.

In the Hollywood research, Maggy Kusenbach found that going along with people who lived in the community illuminated the biographical meanings of community membership to residents, something not ordinarily highlighted either by ethnography or by off-site interviewing. For example, Maggy walked through the neighborhood with a realtor, who spoke of the property values and resale histories of the houses they passed; to him, the meaning of the neighborhood was intertwined with his occupation as realtor. As she walked with a retiree, Ross, who had worked in the city's department of street lighting, he noticed the lighting:

> Ross points out something to me that I have never noticed before; the fact that the street lights in Gilmore Junction are installed on only one side of the street and that there are only three of them in

> the entire block. He tells me what this particular type of lamp is called, "Cobra," and he also says that these lamps are much too high. . . . Ross also says: "I always take notice of the lights!" He tells me that when he traveled in Venice (Italy), the hometown of his wife, he realized that the streetlights were very yellow, unlike in the U.S. (Kusenbach 2003, 473)

Ross also "likened the property on the corner of his block to a 'jungle'" because of its wild, dense foliage. He did not approve of this jungle look, preferring "civilized" and tidy gardens. Another go-along, Jill, a musician in her late forties, used the same term, "jungle," to refer to the garden, but in her case the term was used approvingly; she "just loved" how it looked (Kusenbach 2003, 475).

Studies of urban space can be done from the standpoint of the stranger-observer, as Lyn Lofland has done in her ethnographic work (1998). But the go-along enables the fieldworker to gain access to the individual, as well as the collective, meanings of participating in public interaction. As Maggy Kusenbach summarizes:

> The position of the lonely, outside observer well suits studies of public space because anonymity reigns here and the dominant principles of interaction are based on categoric, not personal knowing. But it takes a more familiar, intimate vantage point to understand the dynamics of interaction in communal (and private) realms—and this is where walk-alongs have a considerable edge over ethnographic methods. (2003, 472)

Thus, when personal approaches to interaction are being studied in a localized community, the go-along form of ethnographic interviewing can be invaluable.

## The Researcher as Spy

A researcher who has gained entrée to a setting through one or a group of key informants may find that she is initially assumed to be a spy by other people in the setting. This presumption is particularly common in non-Western societies with a colonial history. In field research in this country, the spying presumption is most likely in hierarchical organizations, where conflict and antagonisms may occur within and between groups. When Gary Alan Fine did his study of restaurants in *Kitchens* (1996), management had allowed his entrée. He comments:

> One day early in the research one of the kitchen workers whom I had not previously met, seeing me constantly jotting in my notepad, inquired if I was conducting a time study. . . . Paul, the head chef, jokes about me being a spy, adding that "he's watching to make sure we work." (1996, 234)

Management's interest was in ensuring that the kitchen workers worked up to speed, and did not eat—"steal"—the food. However, Fine's fieldnotes often documented these forms of "minor deviance":

> Felicia . . . eats a piece of the roast beef that had been trimmed off and giggles when she sees me watching. She says to me laughing: "Are you going to put this in your book?" . . . Lee, a dishwasher, takes some of the beef and jokes to me: "Which part will we steal today?" I am expected to legitimate their deviance, or, better, to participate in it. (1996, 234)

Over the course of the research, according to Fine, the question of who he represented remained unclear to the workers, although it was clear that he did not report to management (1996, 234). Fine did, however, refer to himself and his fellow ethnographers as "spies . . . like myself" (1996, 233).

Barrie Thorne's (1971) experience studying the draft resistance movement in Boston in the late 1960s provides a political example of the researcher as spy. "The issue of betrayal of trust was thrust upon me in a direct and painful way," Thorne writes, "when I eventually realized that some of the movement members had come to regard me with great suspicion, wondering if I was a 'Fed'" (1983, 227). Within the movement, infiltrators from the F.B.I. were referred to as "Feds." Given her role as a researcher, Thorne reflected on the similarities between her activities as a field researcher and what a "Fed" would do:

> I also was myself doing a kind of spywork not unlike what I imagined a Fed would do, I was systematically observing; I kept my ear out for a range of information and detail . . . I asked the kinds of questions a Fed would also want to know: "When did you turn in your draft card?" "What led up to that decision?" "What organizations had you been in?" And I listened attentively, committing the responses to mind for later recording. (1983, 229)

Good fieldwork does have many of the elements of spywork.

Though Thorne's study was of a radical political group, similar dynamics may also occur in mainstream organizations. Bureaucracies are hierarchies, and as such may be rife with cliques, gossip, backstabbing, and other activities of great interest to "spies." In her ethnography of police work, Jennifer Hunt also found that her informants initially viewed her with suspicion. Hunt notes that any stranger doing research on urban police is liable to be seen as a spy, but a woman even more so. Not only was the police department she studied embroiled in a lawsuit charging gender discrimination against female officers, but she also found that

> the role of spy was consistent with my gender identity. As a civilian and a moral woman I respected the formal order of the law and the inside world of the academy. As both FBI and police internal secu-

rity also represented the formal order, it was logical to assume I was allied with them. In addition, no policeman believed a woman was politically capable of fighting the department to promote honest research. Instead, the dominant elite would use me for their own purposes. (1984, 289)

Unlike Thorne, who began as a member then became a researcher in the radical political group, both Fine and Hunt were given entrée to their settings by gatekeepers, and consequently were initially seen as spies by those lower in the hierarchy who did not, however, have any choice in the matter. This was also true of Warren's Metropolitan Court research; although anyone could attend hearings in one of the two courtrooms, it was only by the permission of the judge that she was able to wander around the "backstage" area of offices. At times, as in Warren's research and Hunt's, some of this initial suspicion remained, and some interactions were hidden from the researcher. At other times, as in Fine's study, suspicions of spying were replaced by a greater trust and acceptance.

Once having selected and been accepted into a setting, you are in a position to begin your field research in earnest. If you are studying an organization, permissions have been granted both formally and informally, gatekeepers have been helpful, and perhaps remain available to you as key informants. Or alternatively, you have been in as a member already, for weeks to years, but now you are in as a researcher, changing the ways in which you observe and interact with people in the setting. You may have decided to do visual ethnography using a still or video camera, or an autoethnography, or a "realist tale." With any of these approaches—as stranger or member, as ethnographer or autoethnographer—you are going to have to pay a different kind of attention to the setting as a qualitative researcher than you do in everyday life. You will find yourself attending to things with intensity and in ways that are unfamiliar—and typically quite tiring. You will find yourself making and unmaking various kinds of relationships with informants, and taking on or being cast into various social roles (Chapter 4). And you will be writing fieldnotes (Chapter 5).

### Suggestions for Further Reading

Agar, Michael. 1996. *The Professional Stranger: An Informal Introduction to Ethnography.* San Diego: Academic Press.

Anderson, Elijah. 1990. *Streetwise: Race, Class, and Change in an Urban Community.* Chicago: University of Chicago Press.

Diamond, Timothy. 1992. *Making Grey Gold: Narratives of Nursing Home Care.* Chicago: University of Chicago Press.

Erikson, Ken, and Donald Stull. 1998. *Doing Team Ethnography: Warnings and Advice.* Thousand Oaks, CA: Sage Publications.

Kusenbach, Margarethe. 2003. "Street-Phenomenology: The Go-Along as Ethnographic Research Tool." *Ethnography* 4 (3): 455–485.

Whyte, William F. 1984. *Learning From the Field: A Guide From Experience.* Newbury Park, CA: Sage Publications.

Additionally, these are the main journals within sociology that publish contemporary ethnographic research as well as methodological discussions:

*Journal of Contemporary Ethnography*
*Qualitative Sociology*
*Journal of the Society of Symbolic Interaction*
*Ethnography* ❖

# Chapter Four

# Roles and Relationships in Field Research

$\mathbf{T}$his chapter is about doing field research once you have achieved initial entrée, or—in the case of preexisting membership—once you have begun to explore the field as researcher as well as member. The key interactional issue for the field researcher as stranger is the development of new roles and relationships; for the member-researcher, it is how existing relationships develop and change. For the stranger-ethnographer, what is problematic in interaction is figuring out who is who and how to fit in; for the member-researcher, it is how to maintain existing roles and relationships while adapting them to research. In this chapter, first we will explore the incorporation of the stranger and second the reincorporation of the member.

In the case of undergraduate students, field research may be limited to a semester or less, while graduate students or professors may conduct field research for a year or more. Warren studied Metropolitan Court for a total of seven years, although she visited the court only a few times a week for a few hours at a time. But however short or long your stay in the field, interacting and talking with its members is likely to have a profound influence on you, and perhaps you will have some influence on them, as well. As in all other arenas of social life, the personal, culturally meaningful characteristics we discussed in the last chapter, such as gender and nationality, shape the roles and relationships occurring in the field.

The term *role* refers to the individual's place within a social setting or network of social relationships. The fieldworker who enters a setting takes on (in her or his mind) the role of fieldworker. Other setting members, however, may assign to her or him the role of mascot, apprentice, or a variety of other roles that researchers have been assigned during their fieldwork, roles associated with gender and other characteristics. The fieldworker may also develop particular kinds of relationships with setting-members, which in published ethnographic research have included everything from enmity (not a good idea in field research!) to sexual liaisons (ditto!!). The ethical standards and guidelines discussed in Chapter 2 should be reviewed as you continue your fieldwork, because the intersections of roles and the development of relationships inevitably bring with them ethical dilemmas in the conduct of fieldwork.

*Incorporation* refers to the ways in which people in a setting define the researcher, and accord him or her a particular role or social place in that setting. This process has to do not only with the personal and social characteristics of the researcher but also with the setting and its members as things go along, and change, over time. Since most of you will probably be doing your research in the surrounding community rather than abroad, we will confine our examples mainly to research conducted in the same country or area rather than (as typically occurs among anthropologists) in Third World or other countries where both language and nationality are issues.

Since the 1960s, the literature on incorporation into roles and relationships in field research has identified a number of key themes. One such theme is the significance of personal characteristics, or *embodiment*, in the process of fieldwork. Gender and race have received the most attention in the methodological literature in sociological field methods, particularly the issues confronted by women studying a variety of settings, and men—black and white—studying race. Certain common themes appear in these discussions, including the setting-members treating young women researchers as mascots and young men as apprentices. Sex in the field has been discussed for 30 years in sociology, longer in anthropology, in themes ranging from consensual sex to sexual harassment and rape. The issue of danger sometimes appears in these sexual narratives, and at other times in narratives of males researching violent subcultures.

## The Embodied Self of the Field Researcher

The ways in which a field researcher is incorporated into the field are dependent on many factors, including the researcher's gender, race, age, appearance, and other characteristics, and the ways in which the researcher's characteristics match or not the characteristics of setting-members. In sociology, the personal characteristics that have been written about the most by ethnographers are gender, race, and class. Women and men sociologists from the 1960s to the present have studied settings both predominantly or all female or male, and mixed. Since the 1940s, both white and black sociologists, most of them male, have studied black lower-class males in urban areas, especially Chicago.

The access fieldworkers have to the people and the interactions in these settings, as well as the incorporation of the fieldworker into the setting, is dependent on embodiment, as indicated in Chapter 3. Only a male researcher will, for example, gain entrée into an all-male gay bathhouse. His incorporation into the setting will depend on the way he seems to fit into the setting—whether, for example, he is young and handsome, or elderly and ungainly, and whether he seems or presents himself as gay, straight, or bisexual. If he is young, handsome, and engaged in covert research, he can expect to be incorporated into the setting as a candidate for sexual as well as sociable activities.

Being the same gender as all or most of the members, or being a different gender, may bring about different conditions of incorporation. Anthropologists who study highly gender-stratified and even gender-separated societies have long noted the importance of same-gender research in fieldwork. In 1885, anthropologist Edward B. Tylor stated that

> to get at the confidence of the tribes, the man of the house, though he can do a great deal, cannot do it all. If his wife sympathizes with his work, and is able to do it, really half the work of investigation seems to fall to her, so much is to be learned through the women of the tribe which the men will not readily disclose. The experience seemed to me a lesson to anthropologists not to . . . ward the ladies off from their proceedings, but rather to avail themselves thankfully for their help. (quoted in Wax 1979, 517)

At that time, the researching "ladies" were often the wives of ethnographers rather than trained ethnographers themselves.

In some settings, opposite-gender researchers may have the advantage. In Elliott Liebow's fieldwork with homeless women, he described how being a male was useful to the conduct of his research, while his age (late middle age) and Jewishness did not seem to be problematic (1993, x). He noted, "Most of the women probably liked having me around. Male companionship was generally in short supply and the women often made a fuss about the few male volunteers" (1993, xi).

Other characteristics of the body have also been the subject of discussion among ethnographers. Liebow said of his body: "I am 6'1" and weigh about 175 pounds. I had a lot of white hair but was otherwise nondescript" (1993, x). Who knows what might have happened had he been young and handsome, or black and weighing 400 pounds? Anthropologist Rosalie Wax, in her analysis of gender and age in fieldwork during the 1940s through the 1970s, noted that in her study of a World War II Japanese internment camp, "perhaps the fact that I was a strapping five feet ten and weighed (then) about 180 pounds helped a bit" in enabling her to evade danger and threat (1979, 521).

Certain themes have emerged over the past 30 years in the methodological literature on ethnography. Young women have experienced being treated by powerful males in various organizational settings as mascots—that is, when, as "dancing daughters," they could avoid the sexualization of interaction that sometimes also occurred. Young men have reported being treated by powerful males in similar settings as apprentices: people eager to learn about the setting in possible preparation for becoming a member. That is not to say that women are never defined and treated as apprentices, or men as mascots or sex objects during the process of field research, just that these have been the most commonly inscribed experiences.

## Researchers as Mascots, Apprentices, and Dancing Daughters

Liebow referred to his gender in the homeless women study as a "resource" (1993, xi). Many women fieldworkers have documented gender-as-resource in a variety of settings, including the fieldworker as mascot, sexual object, or dancing daughter. More than 30 years ago, Arlene Kaplan Daniels, engaged in fieldwork and interviewing with military psychiatrists, noticed that her male respondents treated her like a mascot: someone nice to have around, but not taken very seriously. Daniels recounts how one officer explained her presence: "She's a great girl. She's our mascot. She studies us" (Daniels 1967, 286). Ten years later, Lois Easterday and her colleagues noted that the research "mascot is accepted simply for 'being'" rather than for research competence (1977, 343). More than 20 years later, Laura Adams noted the same patterns in her research on bureaucrats in Uzbekistan. She became a mascot to these middle-aged men, being a "good girl" in dress and demeanor, and "approving of [her hosts'] nation-building projects" (Adams 1999, 340–342).

For men, the functional equivalent of mascoting female researchers seems to be apprenticeship. William Foote Whyte (1992) noted this research role in his retrospective discussion of his own fieldwork among "corner boys" several decades earlier; he was an apprentice to the art and task of "hanging out" on the corner. In his ethnographic, videotaped study of pawnshops, Geoff Harkness (2003) noticed that the pawnshop owners and managers identified him, and identified with him, as a fellow heterosexual white male interested in making a buck. They presumed that his interest in the pawnshop extended not only to videotaping but also to possible work as, or investment in, pawnbroking. Forrest, in discussing his apprenticeship research in "hidden worlds" such as spiritualist groups, comments:

> Apprenticeship is largely a matter of attitude and . . . can be carried out in almost any setting. . . . The apprentice attitude is one of sincere questioning with a willingness to be taught about the meanings behind the actions in a given milieu. (1986, 437)

How one is perceived can also vary by whom one is interacting with even within the same setting. When Karner was researching a unit of a Veterans Administration hospital where clinical interns were common, she was treated as an apprentice. Her key informant, who did not have internship supervisory responsibilities, took great care to place Karner in this role, introducing her to the Veterans Administration procedures as well as explaining and elaborating about treatment philosophies. Other clinical staff members on the unit who routinely supervised *real* interns—and knew Karner was not one—viewed her as a mascot of her key informant. However, the veterans seemed to see her role differently. One veteran dubbed her the "translator." If they could have Karner understand their combat experience and its aftermath, she could then translate it to the rest of society. Thus, the veterans treated her more like an apprentice—but one seeking knowledge or awareness rather than skill. As Karner's experience illustrates, it is not that women could not be treated as apprentices, nor men as mascots in some field settings, it is just that, thus far, women have written mainly about mascoting and men about apprenticeship.

The "dancing daughter" is, like the mascot, associated with women rather than men, but while mascoting represents the response of men in the field to women, the dancing daughter represents a strategy of women researchers in a field of men. The "dancing daughter" attendance upon the powerful male(s) in the setting is busy, cheerful, and just out of reach. Warren used this strategy in the early 1980s with the judge of Metropolitan Court (Warren 1982). More than a decade later, Laura Adams, (1999) who was also treated at times as a mascot during her research in Uzbekistan, reported that the former administrator of a television company told people that she was his "little daughter" (1999, 361). The "dancing daughter dances to attract her 'field father's' eye and keep it paternally (not sexually) on her" (Warren 2001, 217).

## Sex in the Field

The literature of fieldwork has considered sex as well as gender as an aspect of field relationships. This literature refers to several aspects of sexuality: consensual sex, sexual objectification or harassment, and sexual danger. Erich Goode (1999, 2002) notes that although emotions, intimacy, and sexuality are often part of field research as they are of everyday life, social researchers rarely discuss this issue in the articles and books they publish (1999, 302), although there is plenty of gossip among ethnographers about "lurid assignations, couplings, trysts, and other linkages between ethnographers and those they 'observe'" (Fine 1993, 283).

One of the few sociologists who has written about his own sexual behavior in the field is Erich Goode (1999, 2002). Goode describes his sexual experience in three research endeavors, including an ethnographic and interview study of the National Association to Aid Fat Americans (NAAFA; by 2002 renamed the National Association to Advance Fat Acceptance). He says that "sex represented my unconditional entry into NAAFA. . . . only by dating was I seen as a full-fledged member of the organization"; however, dating "recklessly and promiscuously" was also his "undoing" as a NAAFA member (Goode 1999, 314). The point of revealing these sexual activities, according to Goode, is that "sex was a central fact of my investigation of that setting, and any honest account had to take note of it" (1999, 314). A critic of Goode, Clifton Bryant, finds Goode's and others' justifications of their sexual activities in the field "far from persuasive," and states

> there is little real evidence that sex with informants . . . actually enhances the researcher's integration into the community, facilitates the research process, or sharpens or enriches research insight. Instead, the accounts . . . would seem to be essentially self-serving, methodologically spurious, and an effort to normalize hedonistic tendencies. (1999, 327)

Whatever position you take on these debates in the abstract, in your own student research our advice to you is to refrain from sex in the field! The consequences of sex with respondents could range from lawsuits directed at you and your institution to sexual danger to you as an individual. And such liaisons can affect, as many aspects of fieldwork do, your relationship with other people both inside and outside the setting.

Most of the literature on sex and gender in fieldwork has been written by women fieldworkers during the past half century, and is focused on issues of sexualization, sexual objectification, sexual harassment, and even sexual danger in the field. For many women fieldworkers, being treated like a mascot or dancing daughter is preferable—and may head off—being treated as a sexual object. Although the term "sexual harassment" was not in general use 30 years ago, Joy Browne documented the sexualization of interaction that occurred while she did research in a used car lot during the 1970s:

> As I progressed with my project, it became important to note that I was a young woman. Irrelevant as it might have seemed at the outset, the fact that used car lots have little shacks that can cozily accommodate a salesman (nearly all are men, and all those I encountered were men) created a methodological problem. I had to develop a method of convincing a sometimes over-eager informant that I did not want to be that kind of participant. (1976, 78)

By the 1990s, fieldwork accounts of being treated as sexual "fair game" had become less oblique, and were framed as sexual harassment. Terry Williams and his colleagues noted that in their urban street ethnography project and in other settings,

> Several female ethnographers have had their fieldwork severely constrained or have had to terminate it completely . . . due to the sexual expectations and demands of other males in the research setting. The threat of sexual assault or rape is a real concern for most female ethnographers and staff members. (1992, 363)

One of these female ethnographers wrote that when treated as "fair game," she usually would "just move away or shift to a conversation with someone else" (Williams et al. 1992, 355).

Despite his own experiences and revelations, Goode (1999) warns that sex in the field can be dangerous to the researcher in a number of ways, especially for women. One survey he cites reported that 7 percent of female anthropologists reported rape or attempted rape against them in the field. Goode notes,

> For all researchers [sexual liaisons] may make a research enterprise less viable, close off avenues of information, and upset and anger participants. . . . [S]ex on the job traverses much of the same landmined territory. (1999, 314)

As stated before, with regard to potential sexual aggression, a researcher needs to use common sense and social awareness in the field as in everyday life. This is also the case when studying settings where other forms of violence may occur.

## Ethnographers and Violence

It is not only women who can be endangered by sexual—and nonsexual—violence in ethnographic research. Men who research settings in which male violence is commonplace may also face the consequences of such immersion. While studying motorcycle gangs, Hopper and Moore (1990) were threatened with physical violence when events did not unfold as the bikers liked. The bikers did not like questions, uninvited comments, or humor directed against events such as wrestling on TV that they took seriously. For example,

> At times when we were not expecting any problems conditions became hazardous. . . . [O]ne morning in 1985 we walked into an area where bikers had camped out all night. Half asleep and hung over, several of them jumped up and pulled guns on us because they thought we might be members of a rival gang that had killed five of their "brothers" several years earlier. If Grubby, a biker who recognized us from previous encounters, had not interceded on our behalf, we could have been killed or seriously injured. (1990, 368–369)

Although these two male ethnographers escaped actual violence, others have not been so fortunate. Sanchez-Jankowski (1990), who studied gangs in New York, Boston, and Los Angeles, was subjected to physical violence by gang members.

The ethnographer may not only be endangered but may also endanger others. In a British study of bouncers (men, and sometimes women, who are hired to keep order in bars and nightclubs), Simon Winlow and his colleagues focused their analysis on the male working-class parameters of social worlds such as those of bouncers. They comment, "In this field doing research was dealing with violence, and sometimes doing violence" (2001, 537). Bouncers are not paid very much, and

> the real benefits of the occupation are grounded deep within masculine working-class culture and self-identity . . . with its powerful appreciation of bodily power, personal and group respect and violent engagement. . . . Being a bouncer allows a demonstrative cultivation of a hyper-masculine persona: from body language to the cut of their clothes to the way they smoke their cigarettes. (Winlow et al. 2001, 541)

The one member of the research team who got a job as a bouncer was liable to violence by bar customers, and also had to engage in violence when the job conditions made this necessary: "It was impossible to avoid problematic interactions with bar customers, who might well be drunk or under the influence of drugs, and it was impossible just to stand and observe" (Winlow et al. 2001, 543). Incorporation into the social world of the bouncer involved, inevitably, participation in violent encounters.

Danger in field research may involve sex, violence, or violent sex, for women or for men fieldworkers. However, there are also dangers in fieldwork that do not involve violations of the body, most notably the danger of arrest when studying illegal behavior. Although he did not think about this issue at the time, Laud Humphreys (1970) could have been arrested, under sodomy laws of the time, for being an accessory to felonious sex acts. The Adlers were afraid of being arrested during their research into the "wheeling and dealing" of drugs in the context of their own drug use. They comment, "We broke the law ourselves. . . . it would have been impossible for a nonuser to have gained access to this group" (Adler 1985, 24).

The Adlers did not get arrested and completed their research successfully. Their research was, as noted in Chapter 3, facilitated by their shared social class and racial identifications: middle class and white. Other research involves different constellations of class and race, including a long tradition, in ethnography, of African American (mostly male) scholars studying African American lower-class males.

## Race, Ethnicity, and Class

The ethnographic tradition of male ethnographers writing about men and masculinity (Winlow et al. 2001) is fairly recent, as are gender studies. However, a longer tradition exists of Anglo, white male ethnographers (and some African-American male ethnographers) writing about race. Many of these works are set in Chicago, since the university campus is on the edge of a black ghetto area. Early Chicago classics in this genre include William F. Whyte's *Street Corner Society* (1943) and Elliott Liebow's *Tally's Corner* (1967). More recent examples in the Chicago style but that take place elsewhere include Mitchell Duneier's *Slim's Table* (1994) and Elijah Anderson's *Streetwise* (1990) and *Code of the Street* (1999). These works, like those on women in the field, analyze racial differences and similarities of race, class, and sometimes gender as they affect the conduct of field research.

Mitchell Duneier (who is white), for example, recounts an occasion on which he went with an African-American photographer, Ovie, to a bookstore to have a picture taken of some major ethnographic books. Ovie thought that they should ask permission of the bookstore's manager to clear a shelf of its for-sale books and replace them with the ethnographies, but Mitch did not want to bother. This event taught Mitch something about being black, or white, in public space:

> In a very sensitive way [Ovie] pointed out something I knew in theory but had not acted on in the situation: As a white man I go through life believing I can take liberties that black men would never think of taking. One can only imagine what would have happened if a black man had been seen putting books in a bag. . . . I felt stupid. If anyone should have been aware of the situation, it was a sociologist who was writing about black men. (1999, 166)

There were other occasions of ethnic and racial differences between Duneier and his respondents in his New York study of homeless African-American male street book vendors (1999). He used tape recorders, continually running, to capture the interaction that took place at the vendors' tables. At one point during his absence from the scene, a conversation was recorded that questioned his research motives in the context of race, ethnicity, and class. The vendors were wondering why he did not study rich people who have yard sales instead of them:

> He's not questioning them. . . . He's questioning us! He want to know how did the homeless people get to do it. . . . Not really trying to help us. He's trying to figure out how did the homeless people get a lock on something that he consider *lucrative*. . . . You gotta remember, he's a Jew, you know. They used to taking over. (1999, 337)

It is not surprising that Duneier concluded, as he was publishing his study as a book, that at times he thought that "the truce I thought I had developed [with the book vendors] was nothing more than an illusion" (1999, 14). In ethnography, race and ethnicity, like gender, may be deeply and dichotomously divisive in our culture, as in our social institutions.

Being of the same race, ethnicity, or gender does not, however, guarantee an ethnographic experience free of difficulty. Dorrine Kondo, a Japanese-American woman, studied family and workplace in Japan during the 1980s.

> My ambiguous insider/outsider position in the field may have made the issue of identity and selfhood especially acute, but other studies by white female ethnographers and by Japanese American men suggest that my experience was not a unique one. (Kondo 2001, 199)

Although she was Japanese by heritage, she did not speak perfect Japanese, she had not been socialized into Japanese gender norms, and she was an American citizen. Thus it was culture and nationality, not ethnicity or race, that formed the basis of ethnographic difference for Kondo.

## Incorporation: Finding a Place

By now it should be clear that incorporation into the setting is a matter of negotiation between the embodied researcher and the members. The literature on incorporation from the 1970s onward (although the process was not referred to as incorporation in the 1970s in sociology) discussed entrée (see Chapter 3), choosing a research role, and other themes such as the research bargain (more recently referred to as the useful researcher), going native, being proselytized to convert (generally to a religion or cult), emotions in the field, and leaving the field.

In early (1970s and prior) sociological field research, the presumption was that the researcher chose the role he or she would play in the field—a presumption that was behind the discussion of covert versus overt roles. By the 1980s, sociological ethnographers had come to the realization (as their anthropological colleagues had done earlier) that incorporation into the setting involved more than the researcher choosing and acting out a role. The respondents had their own definitions of the situation, ones that might vary greatly with the researcher's self-definitions. Gary Alan Fine, in his ethnography of restaurant kitchens, introduced himself as a sociologist who was writing a book. His respondents kept the book part in focus, but also imagined movies; further, they interpreted him as a psychologist rather than a researcher. One cook said, "The book will be *Portrait of a Cook*. I'll have my name up in lights. The movie will be filmed in an insane asylum." Others saw Fine as a "psychologist" or "psychoanalyst," judging "are they crazy or sane?" (1996, 236). Informed consent (see Chapter 2) may require respondents to hear about the researcher's intentions and identities, but it does not force them to define him according to his revelations. People outside university settings often do not make distinctions between social science disciplines such as psychology and sociology.

Fine describes incorporation as partly situational and partly a series of stages. He notes that in the four kitchens he studied for one month apiece, it was "a continuing stream of joking" that transformed him "from researcher to worker, from observer to full participant" in the eyes of the cooks (1996, 236). At times he was not permitted to observe, including nights when less expensive "specials" were served, and times when workers were being trained by observing the kitchen (when it was too busy and too crowded for the ethnographer). Though further into the research process, Fine writes, "I was present on equally busy nights. . . . later in the research, when another server was being trained, I was allowed to observe"(1996, 235).

Incorporation into the social world of one part of a setting may mean estrangement from other parts, as Warren found in her research in Metropolitan Court. Acceptance by the judge and the district attorney's office meant, almost automatically, nonacceptance by the public defender's office. Even in leisure rather than work settings the researcher can be torn between different cliques, as Warren found in her research, 30 years ago in the gay male community of a Southern California city (see Box 4.1).

---

**Box 4.1**

### Competing Relationships in Field Research

The gay community is made up of multiple cliques whose members shift and change, and do not necessarily get along with one another. . . . I got to know several cliques quite well, but kept some distance from them in order to move into other situations. . . . Sometimes these tactics were successful, and at other times they did not do as well.

> Dick called me up and invited me to go to Beach Town for Sunday brunch with that new set of "wealthy queens" he's always talking about, so of course I accepted. Justin called almost immediately afterward and suggested that "our group" get together for Sunday brunch. . . . I knew that Justin resented Dick's defection from "the crowd" so I indicated unspecifically that I had another engagement, which bugged him. Joe, I hear, has been commenting to some of his friends, "Carol's too good for us now, she's always up at Beach City with those rich bitches up there." When I called and invited him over, he was quite cold, and claimed he had something planned "every weekend for the next three months."

. . . As I got to know more people I was invited to more and more homes, often at the same time, and had to weigh increasingly carefully the question of where to go, making sure that I didn't always go where it would be most fun, where everybody liked me, or where I felt most at home.

Warren, Carol. 1972. *Identity and Community in the Gay World*, 173–174. New York: Wiley-Interscience.

Many other issues of incorporation into settings have been written about by sociological ethnographers in many contexts. There may be research bargains in which the researcher is expected to be useful in the setting in return for continued access. *Going native*, a possibility in research where the setting somehow "fits" the researcher, has been seen as a problematic feature of field research since the Chicago School. In some settings, particularly religious cults or sects, the fieldworker (no matter what he says) is perceived and treated as a potential convert who is expected to go native. Thus, leaving the field can be a relief (as in a setting where there is escalating and unwanted pressure to convert), or it may be continually delayed in the face of what can become almost an addiction to one's setting.

## The Research Bargain

Ethnographers have written extensively over the last 30 years about the research bargain that is part of fieldwork. Incorporation into a setting—being permitted to hang around, interact, and talk with people—is a gift of time and attention. Both fieldworkers and respondents may see this gift as something that needs repayment. People in some settings may seek information or even intervention from researchers perceived as experts. Other settings are so busy and active that anyone around, even the overt fieldworker, is pressed into service of some kind. This aspect of incorporation into a setting—essentially making use of the researcher—is sometimes referred to as the *research bargain*, and the researcher as a "useful" one.

Gary Alan Fine refers to the circumstances of the bargain as "The Plimpton Effect," recalling a "journalist-essayist who briefly participated as a member of professional sports teams" (1996, 236). In his ethnography of restaurant kitchens Fine peeled potatoes, retrieved food from storage, strung beans, and stirred soup when asked. As the research continued, he was jokingly asked to "work the window," mop, cut meat, and "take over" (1996, 237). Agreeing to do these tasks was his "gift" to the workers who were willing to let them into their lives and give him information; their "gifts" to him came in the form of "pleasant little bribes" of food (1996, 237). Fine comments on the place of the research bargain in organizational ethnography:

> The cooks liked me, and I became, in some measure, a member of the group; yet, simultaneously I was and would remain an outsider, potentially affecting their lives and reputations. By bribing me and telling me about their lives they hoped to gain my support. Because they work in scenes that they do not entirely control, and because I have access to those who control them, they were at my mercy. I, in turn, was at their mercy to the degree that I was allowed to operate, briefly and marginally, as one of them. (1996, 238)

Leo (1995) sought access to interrogations of suspects by research bargains with detectives ranging from taking them pastries to listening sympathetically to their "war stories." He also helped out in the office by answering phones or doing other minor bureaucratic tasks, since unoccupied observers just hanging out seem suspicious in police settings. And, as we saw in the last chapter, he used a "chameleon strategy" to fit into this conservative and macho setting.

Dorrine Kondo describes the processes by which she, as a Japanese American who did research in Japan, was incorporated into the work and home lives of her hosts. In return for initial and continued research access, Kondo was "bombarded with requests to teach English, a story familiar to any American who had been in Japan" (2001, 198). However, she was also required, over time, to be more and more incorporated into

> the demands and obligations of Japanese social life. . . . People asked me to take part in many social gatherings. . . . Though at the beginning stages of my field research I welcomed all such invitations, the requests and solicitous care shown to me occasionally elicited feelings of invasion. I felt bound by chains of obligation, to my sponsors, my relatives, my friends, and my co-workers. (2001, 198)

In settings where social life is stratified by gender, gender may shape the demands of the research bargain. Kondo was also asked by her host family to help out with the cooking and serving of food. Although she did not mind doing these domestic chores, she was disturbed by the expected behaviors of the men she served, who would "ask for a second helping of rice by merely holding out their rice bowls to the woman nearest the rice cooker and maybe, just maybe, uttering a grunt of thanks in return for her pains" (2001, 193). Similarly, when Warren was doing field research in a residential drug rehabilitation center in Los Angeles in the early 1970s, she was put to work in the kitchen, washing dishes. Such activity was part of her incorporation as the norms of the setting required that everyone be doing something (even the fieldworker); Warren was put to work in the kitchen because that is where the women in the setting worked.

Other research bargains involve the seeking of goods or money. In his ethnography of *Tally's Corner*, Elliott Liebow (1967) found that the poor street corner men he was studying asked him for small amounts of money, a request that he found difficult to refuse. Thirty years later (and at the same age of 37), Mitch Duneier (1999) confronted the same issue during his ethnographic research with African-American street magazine and book vendors. As time went on, he was asked for money more often and for larger amounts. Two of his key informants told him that "these men asked me for money on a regular basis because they thought that as a college professor and a Jew, I was 'rich' enough to afford the donations" (Duneier 2001, 184). Although Duneier at first handed out small change willingly, he was not "rich" ("I could hardly afford the tapes I was using to record the street life") and eventually had to limit the scope of his "donations."

Duneier's respondents also sought to use what they perceived as his expertise and high position in the social structure to navigate their lives. He was asked what he regarded as "simple" things such as what the law might be in a given area, and more complex ones such as providing a reference, or finding (and paying for) a lawyer. He even intervened in the setting: together with an Australian architect he designed a "new and improved" vendor cart for the book salesmen. A food cart manufacturer they approached refused to make the book carts for the vendors on the grounds that the local business and legal controllers of Greenwich Village "want to get all the [vendors] off the street . . . [but] You want to put them on, Mitch! Why you making so much trouble, Mitch?" (Duneier 2001, 186).

As a novice researcher, you may find yourself in situations where your basic human sympathies are brought into play or where, as Fine notes, you are asked to perform services to "cope with the [members'] frustration of seeing the researcher standing around, watching, 'doing nothing'" (1996, 237). It is fine to do small favors for respondents—giving them a few cents for a phone call, perhaps—but it is probably best to refrain from offering major assistance. Giving rides in cars could result in accidents, or bringing someone into your home could have negative consequences. Again, this probably sounds old-fashioned—and it is. But as our old-fashioned relatives used to say, "better to be *safe* than *sorry.*"

## Going Native

"Going native" refers to being immersed in the field to such an extent that the fieldworker becomes a member. Going native has been regarded as problematic because it may result in the field researcher setting aside the research and becoming a member of the group instead. This may or may not be a good thing, depending on what the group represents and the values of the person doing the judging. Warren once had a student who was doing field research at an air traffic control facility; he subsequently dropped his sociology graduate studies and passed the air traffic control exam, becoming an air traffic controller. He did not regard this instance of "going native" as a problem, and neither did Warren, since he seemed happier as an air traffic controller than he was as a sociology student.

Field researchers often do regard it as problematic, however, when their students "go native" into religious cults or other deviant or stigmatized groups. Another student of Warren's, for example, was tempted by the religious cult among whom she was doing overt research (but who, naturally, regarded her as a potential convert). She had just moved away from her family to Los Angeles and was lonely and without close ties. As it became clear that going native was a real danger, she switched to another setting.

In addition to being personally problematic, going native—also referred to as overinvolvement or overrapport—may be "dangerous" to analytic integrity. As Adler and Adler summarize,

> Becoming too closely aligned with one group in the setting may prevent the researcher from gaining access to the perspectives of other groups in the scene . . . [and] bias researchers' own perspectives, leading them to accept uncritically the views of the members . . . as their own. (1987, 17)

Over the decades since the Chicago School, ethnographers have urged their students not to get overinvolved, even lost, in the setting, noting that a balance of immersion and distance is possibly the best place from which to represent others' worlds (Emerson 2001a).

The concept of going native implies that the field researcher has willingly become a member of the group, as did the student who became an air traffic controller. But some settings, especially religious cults and groups, actively seek to convert the researcher, trying to persuade her to become a member. Sometimes conversion efforts are successful, as in Bennetta Jules-Rosette's (1975) conversion to an African cargo cult that she was studying. More often, field researchers expend an enormous amount of energy and strategizing avoiding the conversion attempts of the religious or political groups they study. In a 1980s study of the Jesus People, David Gordon (1987) comments:

> Field research with proselytizing groups presents difficult problems for field researchers. Such groups usually expect commitments from those who are knowledgeable about their point of view. Should the field researcher fail to make this commitment there is the possibility that further access to the group will be ended . . . [or] continuous proselytizing directed at the researcher can create emotional responses that adversely affect field relationships. (1987, 267)

Several other researchers have commented on the discomfort (Rochford 1985), tension (Robbins, Anthony, and Curtis 1973), or annoyance (Peshkin 1984) they felt in the face of continued conversion attempts. One way to deal with these attempts is to go native (discussed above); another way is to pretend to go native by acting like a member, a strategy attempted by Peshkin (1984). From the point of view of the leadership of a cult or sect, the refusal of the researcher to convert, especially over time, may also become annoying. In John Lofland's (1966) research with the Moonies, or Divine Precept cult, once the leader of the group he was studying decided that Lofland was not going to convert, she wanted control over his research. He eventually left the group.

Gordon (1987) notes four possible responses to continued pressure to convert: (1) feigning conversion and switching to covert research; (2) going native or studying a group whose beliefs one already holds; (3) remaining a nonbeliever and refusing to discuss one's own beliefs with the group; or (4) remaining a nonbeliever and discussing one's beliefs with the group. In discussing his use of the fourth strategy, Gordon notes the problems associated with it:

> Six months into my study, the leader of the group asked me if I "knew the Lord yet." When I replied, "no," he said, "Well, why not? You've had plenty of time. You know it says in the Bible that Jesus is like a stone and either you will trip over it someday or it will crush you . . . you've been coming here and hearing all about Him, and one of these days you're going to have to face up to Him". . . . These are the kinds of pressures that lead field researchers to experience fear of expulsion, anxiety, and guilt. (1987, 272)

As Gordon (1987) notes, gaining entrée into and developing initial relationships with members of proselytizing groups is easy precisely because they want converts. Maintaining relationships over time, however, depends on the members' notions of a proper time frame for conversion, which the informant quoted above saw Gordon as beginning to violate. Gordon responded to pressure by joining more group activities such as prayer meetings or singing, but the members also stepped up the pressure by involving him in more and more detailed discussions about his beliefs in contrast to theirs (1987, 275–276). Finally one member said to him: "Why don't you just throw all this stuff [his tape recorder and notes] away and get saved? I think we're going to bring you downstairs and just hold you down until you get saved" (1987, 276).

The older methodological literature framed the research role as a matter of the ethnographer's choice, for example between, covert and overt research (Humphreys 1970). But during the past decade or so, ethnographers have become more attuned to the ways in which respondents incorporate them into the setting, according them a role or social place. Although you can control your appearance, demeanor, and presentation of self, you cannot control the ways in which others interpret your presence, or how they see you. Although Warren always introduced herself in the mental health court as a sociology professor from the University of Southern California doing field research, she was almost inevitably interpreted and introduced to others as either a law student or a nursing student. Most young females who came around the court were law students or nursing students, so in the worldviews of respondents, she was as well.

## Emotions in the Field

In this chapter we have touched on some of the emotional aspects of doing fieldwork: the intensity of the experience, the closeness of the relationships that can develop, the play on human sympathies that can occur, and the tension of resisting conversion while maintaining a role in the setting. Previously, in Chapter 2, we also discussed some of the emotional stress brought about by covert research and the emotional energy needed to maintain social "fronts," as well as the conflictual ethnical dilemmas that researchers have wrestled with when observing cruel and hurtful behaviors in the field. Yet, students are often surprised to find they have emotional responses to their experiences in the field. Sanders advises that we should not shy away from emotional messiness:

> If our ultimate goal is to truly comprehend the rich variety of perspectives and experiences that shape interaction processes, however, we must not avoid involving ourselves in, and empathetically sharing, the sorrow and joy, pain and conflict, that are integral features of social life. (1998, 192)

In doing fieldwork, the goal is to understand the setting from the inside—to gain an understanding that is as close as possible to that of those being studied. It is a process of achieving closeness, both in physical proximity and emotional insight. The balance of experience-near fieldwork—"how ethnographers 'do closeness' on the one hand and 'do distance' on the other" (Emerson and Pollner 2001, 240)—alternating periods of immersion in the setting with periods of reflective withdrawal (such as to write fieldnotes), is the dance of the fieldworker, and it can be an emotionally challenging one. Because you, as the researcher, take on a social role in the setting and initiate and negotiate interactions, it is never a neutral or passive process; it is one fraught with all the social and emotional aspects of everyday life—only intensified. In Box 4.2, Karner's fieldnotes document her emotional response to a particularly disturbing interaction that she witnessed. As a researcher, you are looking to gain entrée, wanting to be accepted as an insider and confidant, exploring new worldviews and belief systems. Your ethnographic agenda, however, does not protect you from responding as a person. You are still you, with all your own sensitivities, insecurities, needs, and desires. And any personal interactions have the potential to be problematic (Johnson 1975).

Some researchers will be drawn to the unknown, to settings that seem exotic to their own lives. This sense of exoticism, Rosalie Wax warns, can leave the researcher "so fascinated by the new, exciting, and significant things he is learning, that he may spend months passionately and persistently thinking of nothing else" (1983, 192). This is the emotional and compelling nature of fieldwork. Other ethnographers will be drawn to settings that allow them to somewhat safely learn about their own lives. One of Karner's students sought out a support group for adult survivors of childhood sexual abuse for her fieldwork site as a means of understanding her own experience by studying others with similar backgrounds. Karner believes that her initial interest in studying violent veterans was an attempt to understand the male violence she had witnessed in her own life.

---

**Box 4.2**

### Emotions in Fieldwork

. . . later as I was leaving, I saw the veteran who had just been discharged in an unpleasant and intense staff meeting, he had gone to his room and was now dragging his guitar behind him. As soon as he saw me, he started "those goddamned mother-fucking fools" etc. I pretended not to notice and went down the back stairs.

(at lunch yesterday, a unit nurse said that this veteran reminded her of a little boy with his dad's shoes and hat on . . . trying to be a man . . . a little cowboy trying to be a big cowboy . . . the way he tucks his pants into his boots and he drags this guitar around.)

At the bottom of the stairs I found the tall, thin vet with long, curly, dark hair. . . . "is it always this intense?" I asked, shaking my head, overwhelmed (the discharge meeting had been very emotional for me—I heard this little boy pleading for what he saw as his last or only chance at having himself back).

The tall vet patted me on the back, "This is the easy stuff, wait 'til you get into trauma [therapy] group—there are just so many triggers, everything seems to pull someone's trigger." . . .

I said, "I'm just so overwhelmed . . . I just . . ."

Another vet answered, "Yeah, just wait until you get to trauma [therapy group], you think this is intense—that gets into some real heavy stuff that you've thought about for years and you've wanted to talk about but couldn't." . . .

Asking another veteran who was nearby how to make sense of all of this—he said, "You just keep listening hoping something will fall through the cracks and will click for you . . . just keep listening." [He must be a qualitative researcher at heart!]

(Excerpted from Karner's fieldnotes)

---

Still other scholars write about their fieldwork experience as personally transformative. In *Missing Pieces: A Chronicle of Living With Disability* (1982), Irving Zola documents his fieldwork in a town in the Netherlands where everyone was physically disabled and no one was stigmatized due to physical limitations. Zola credits this experience with his subsequent acceptance of his own disability. However, other researchers report less positive emotional responses. Johnson makes two major points about the conduct of fieldwork:

> First, in any complex social setting the personal relations between an observer and the individuals he studies will emerge gradually and will be problematic. . . . Second, the complicated personal relations involved in field-research project[s] will necessarily create patterns in the field observations. (1983, 205)

As people with feelings and responses, fieldworkers are never passive observers no matter how unobtrusive they attempt to be.

Emotional responses to respondents and to oneself are reflexive in complex ways. In looking back over her experience doing fieldwork at a holistic health center, Kleinman acknowledged feeling both angry and frustrated with the participants, as they did not live up to her political expectations. The consequence of her emotional response, Kleinman believed, caused her to delay the start of planned individual interviews.

> in close relations with participants, we only expect [to feel] good will. When we break the feeling rule by failing to have those good feelings, we may accuse ourselves of empathetic incompetence. (Kleinman and Copp 1993, 28)

Having negative responses in the field led Kleinman to doubt her abilities as a fieldworker, but through reflection she later came to consider her feelings as a tool that added depth and complexity to her analysis.

Fieldwork occurs in a social setting—within the "mini-dialectic of personal relations" (Johnson 1983, 205)—and has all the opportunities for emotional response that are present in everyday life. Wearing your researcher hat does not protect you from reacting to your experience in an emotional—that is, a very human—way. We can only remind you, as a beginning researcher, that fieldwork can be an emotionally compelling experience. Ideally, you will not be surprised to find yourself entranced by the wonder of learning about your social others, though for many of us, this is exactly the draw of the experience—near work that we do. This draw is one reason why ethnographers may at times be unwilling to leave the setting they are studying.

## Leaving the Field

Eventually all things good or bad come to an end. The rule of thumb for leaving the field is this: your observations are no longer yielding new and interesting data. Warren left Metropolitan Court the first time, for example, when she realized that during her observations of *habeas corpus* writ hearings—having observed more than a hundred by this point—her attention was wandering. Because of Warren's mascot status with respect to the judge, she was not going to gain entrée to the meaning-world of the public defenders' office. Thus, figuring that she had spent enough time in the district attorney's and judge's offices, Warren left the field.

Leaving the field sometimes has emotional as well as sociological elements. Field researchers often become very attached to "their" settings and the people in them, partly because of the intensity of the observational experience in comparison with everyday forms of social attention (which are often mixed with large doses of inattention). One of Warren's graduate students, Richard Johnson, studied sale barn auctions in the rural Midwest and found it difficult to stop going to the Saturday auctions he had attended for a year, even though it was time to focus on writing the ethnography. He had become a quasi-member of the setting, socializing with the members and even being pressed into service as an auctioneer (a "useful researcher" kind of research bargain we discussed earlier in this chapter).

At other times the emotions generated by leaving are related to people rather than the setting itself. As Emerson notes

> Many ethnographers have noted the difficulties of extrication and disengagement from the field due to the . . . intense interpersonal ties between fieldworker and informants: . . . Leaving the field will typically transform these relationships, in some instances ending them entirely, in others diminishing contact to the point that informants feel abandoned. (2001, 140–141)

Negative as well as positive emotions may surround the process of leaving the field. Taylor (1991), who was disgusted by the way in which staff treated the mentally retarded at the state institution he was studying (see Chapter 2), says that he

> began to feel terribly inauthentic. I found it difficult to keep up the facade, yet could not confront the attendants without blowing my cover and letting them know I had misled them about my true feelings. So, without even calling an end to the study in my own mind, I simply stopped visiting. (1991, 244–245)

Although in fieldwork the "stages" of research, fieldnote writing, and writing of the ethnography overlap, they don't overlap so much as to permit you to remain in the field beyond the period of useful observation. This point in time varies depending on the complexity of the field project, but it does come. As indicated above, some field researchers do go native—perhaps usefully in the case of getting a job, perhaps dangerously in the case of joining an extremist group. But in most cases, and certainly for undergraduates studying sociology, it is necessary to leave the field either when you have become very familiar with it, or when your instructor suggests you should leave.

Even after leaving the field, the ethnographer may not sever ties with all its members, but continue to maintain contact with one or more of them for some time afterward. The Adlers point out that fieldworkers sometimes

> continue to form friendships, especially with key informants, that are lasting. Through these people they can manage contact with the group for several purposes, including follow-up research and future re-entry. (1987, 79)

But leaving the field, like doing the research, is not just about the researcher. Riemer notes that leaving the field thoughtlessly can have consequences for future research and researchers. To "get out quickly" and "with little thought for the persons they used for the study" can cast discredit not only on the researcher but also on the profession or discipline as well (Riemer 1979, 177).

When Karner began preparing to leave the Veterans Administration hospital, she timed her departure to coincide with the final staff meeting to evaluate the last veteran she had been interviewing. This meeting typically occurred on the day before the veteran would leave the unit as well. This scheduling provided a natural closure for both the unit staff and the remaining veterans, and also gave Karner the opportunity to publicly express her gratitude before leaving the field.

## Reincorporating the Nonstranger

The fieldworker who is doing fieldwork in a setting she is already a part of faces somewhat different challenges of incorporation than the stranger-researcher. The Adlers' (1987) discussion of membership roles in field research highlights the possibilities available to the nonstranger. But whatever the researcher's role in the field (bartender or customer in a bar, say), the ethnographer must decide to either keep the research agenda private (a kind of covert research role) or reveal it to all or some of the setting's members (an overt research role).

In her ethnographic study of a lesbian community in a midwestern college town, Christine Robinson (2003) initially decided that she would not share her research agenda with her respondents, a position acceded to by the university's IRB. She had moved to the college town to work on her Ph.D. in sociology, and had affiliated with the lesbian community in town before deciding to do her ethnographic dissertation on the community. Later in the study, however, she decided to end the covertness of her participant observation and let people know that she was doing the study.

Field researchers who also want to interview members of their group must, of course, reveal their research agenda. The decision to do interviews as well as field research was one of the factors that convinced Robinson to let her respondents know what she was doing. Similarly, Kristin Esterberg, who refers to herself as an "open lesbian"

(1997, 5), did interviews and a survey as well as field research among lesbians in the "small eastern community" she studied. She reports no consequences or difficulties either for the research process, the data, or her own social circles in her switch from member-only to member-researcher.

The way in which the field is understood and interpreted may also be affected by being a member in it. At first glance it would seem useful for the researcher to be a member of the field of research, with its purpose of understanding members' world of meaning. And, indeed, various problems of entrée and accessibility are solved by membership. But the member may take so much for granted in his settings that his fieldnotes end up as thin descriptions. A graduate student of Warren's who was a nun was also doing field research on her own order for a Ph.D. dissertation. In her first set of fieldnotes she wrote, "we prayed." This meant something very specific to her, and something so familiar that she did not write it down as a nonmember would. So Warren had to ask her: What do you mean by "we prayed"? Did you kneel down? bow your head? recite aloud? contemplate silently? Eventually a thickly descriptive account of praying was derived from the question-and-answer session.

## Membership Roles in Field Research

Peter and Patti Adler have written about a range of membership roles in field research, from the complete participant to the detached observer, with various possibilities along the continuum between these extremes. They note that complete membership roles in field research are of several types: (1) the "master status" of the fieldworker is the same as those in her setting; (2) subcultural, recreational, political, or occupational statuses are shared; and (3) the researcher has gone native or converted (1987, 69). In contemporary fieldwork, it is often option 1 or 2 that constitutes the context of student research.

Students interested in gender, social class, ethnicity, body type, or sexual preference, and who share "master statuses" of these types, may choose to study settings in which they are "natural" members. There is a tradition, for example, of lesbian or gay researchers studying lesbian or gay settings (Krieger 1983; Esterberg 1997; Robinson 2003). Helen Rose Ebaugh (1977), a former nun, did research on religious orders. Jennifer Hackney (1996) and others who have struggled with issues of body and weight have done research in settings such as Weight Watchers or Overeaters Anonymous.

While "master status" settings are one aspect of "starting where you are," settings such as workplaces are another. Ethnographic research on bars has illuminated social relations both from the point of view of workers (work members) and customers (leisure members). In their study of *The Cocktail Waitress* (1975), James Spradley and Brenda

Mann studied a bar in which Mann was already a member, employed as a cocktail waitress. They found that cocktail waitressing was a good example of "women's work in a man's world," in which the waitresses were subordinate to both the bartender and the clientele.

In the member role of customer, Sherri Cavan (1966) visited a number of "taverns" in San Francisco, investigating both types of bars and social interaction within bars. Her typology of bars included "marketplace" or pickup bars (both homosexual and heterosexual) and "home territory" bars of the sort immortalized in the 1980s television series "Cheers." Within different kinds of taverns, various types of customers ranged from "the stranger" to "the regular," and different social interactions flowed from those statuses. Both Spradley and Mann (1975) and Cavan (1966) highlighted the significance of gender in bars as workplaces or leisure places, and the role of alcohol in loosening up social behavior. What do you think you might find in a similar study of bars in the 2000s?

Fieldwork roles are negotiated between the ethnographer and the members of the setting, and may change over time. No matter how the ethnographer wants to present himself—overtly or covertly, savior or spy—incorporation occurs at the pace and in the ways of the setting. Fieldwork relationships begin with first impressions, and continue in a variety of directions, some wanted and some unwanted. The substance of fieldwork interaction, and thus the data of fieldnotes, emerges from this nexus of roles and relationships in the field, and ends only when—and if—the researcher leaves the field and has not remained as native or convert. During the process of fieldwork, the researcher may decide to interview some of the respondents as well, as Kreiger (1983) did in her study of a lesbian community. As we shall see in Chapters 6 and 7, interviewing, the second major qualitative method, has its own roles and relationships as well. But first, we turn to a discussion of the documentation of fieldwork, the writing of fieldnotes.

## Suggestions for Further Reading

Adler, Patricia A., and Peter Adler. 1987. *Membership Roles in Field Research*. Thousand Oaks, CA: Sage Publications.

Anderson, Elijah. 1999. *Code of the Street*. New York: W. W. Norton.

Kleinman, Sherryl, and Martha A. Copp. 1993. *Emotions and Fieldwork*. Thousand Oaks, CA: Sage Publications.

Mitchell, Richard G., Jr. 2002. *Dancing at Armageddon: Survivalism and Chaos in Modern Times*. Chicago: University of Chicago Press.

Warren, Carol A. B., and Jennifer Hackney. 2000. *Gender Issues in Ethnography*. Thousand Oaks, CA: Sage Publications.

Whyte, William F. 1943. *Street Corner Society*. Chicago: University of Chicago Press. ❖

# Chapter Five

# Writing Fieldnotes

This chapter is about writing fieldnotes, the data of ethnographic research. Writing fieldnotes is necessary to the successful conduct of field research and is a part of research that anthropologist Clifford Geertz (1973) and others refer to as *inscription*. The inscription of fieldnotes is a time-consuming activity that requires commitment on the part of the researcher.

In some ways it can be both easy and exciting to do the observational work of ethnography. To gain entrée into and be accepted by members of a setting, to engage in the type of focused observation characteristic of ethnography, to feel the first stirrings of belonging and acceptance—these are the exhilarations of field research. But writing fieldnotes is its necessary drudgery.

In this chapter, we discuss what fieldnotes are, the process of writing them up from observations and from earlier inscriptions such as jotted notes, and what constitutes good and useful as opposed to inadequate and not very useful fieldnotes. Since we live in a computer age, the various uses of the computer in generating and using field research are also discussed at various points. But first, we place fieldnotes in the historical context of early anthropological research and the case studies of the Chicago School.

Fieldnotes have been used in qualitative social research for decades, perhaps generations if one counts traveler and missionary precursors to anthropology and sociology. Anthropological ethnographers such as Bronislaw Malinowski wrote about their encounters with "natives" in the field as they went about collecting kinship and economic data, also inscribing some of their (not always positive) opinions about these natives and their cultures (Emerson 2001d, 7). Malinowski wrote in 1922 that in fieldnotes

> belong such things as the routine of a man's working day, the details of his care of the body, of the manner of taking food and preparing it; the tone of conversational and social life around the

village fires, the existence of strong friendships or hostilities, and of passing sympathies and dislikes between people; the subtle yet unmistakable manner in which personal vanities and ambitions are reflected in the behavior of the individual and in the emotional reactions of those who surround him. (quoted in Emerson 2001d, 7)

University of Chicago sociologists collected fieldnotes as part of their set of case study methods, using them along with survey, documentary, and interview data. As Emerson notes, field research was an "optional component of the case study approach" rather than the sole method. He adds that even in case studies that relied extensively on observation, such as Nels Anderson's *The Hobo* (1923),

> the primary value of direct contact and observation lay in allowing the researcher to see for him or her self rather than in providing access to subjective meanings or perspectives. (Emerson 2001d, 12)

The use of fieldnotes in the late nineteenth and early twentieth century was not particularly self-conscious or reflexive; the relationship between what the observer saw and what he wrote down was seemingly obvious. It was not until the movement toward postmodernism in academia began in the late 1960s and early 1970s that the issue of representation (see Chapter 1) emerged as an issue, and thus the issue of fieldnotes—since fieldnotes, as contemporary scholars point out, are one form of representation. It is not just the finished ethnography that is a representation of the field, the fieldnotes are a prior representation of it. As Geertz says,

> The ethnographer "inscribes" social discourse; *he writes it down.* In so doing, he turns it from a passing event, which exists only in its own moment of occurrence, into an account, which exists in its inscriptions and can be reconsulted. (Geertz 2001, 67, emphasis in original)

In his discussion of fieldnotes as the inscription of thick description, Geertz set the epistemological framework—and indeed practical standard—for fieldnote writing in the coming decades of qualitative research.

## Fieldnotes as Inscription of Thick Description

To reiterate, fieldnotes are inscriptions (written representations of what has been observed), and they are, ideally, thickly descriptive. Contrast, in Box 5.1, a thin with a relatively thick (lots more could be written down!) description of the ROTC building on a university campus. The researcher is entering the building in order to conduct an ethnography of the student lounge, which is upstairs in the building. Thick descriptions take account of context, including season of the year, time of day, weather, buildings, and anything else of relevance for "setting the stage" of the setting.

---

### Box 5.1

## Thin and Thick Description of a Campus ROTC Building

***Thinly Descriptive Fieldnotes***

I walked into the ROTC building and asked someone for directions to the student lounge, and went upstairs.

***Thickly Descriptive Fieldnotes***

The ROTC building, as I approached it, looked as if it were built in the 1920s out of native stone. Above the door that I was approaching a Roman eagle was carved, wings outspread. The door had a pane of glass in the center, and on the glass was taped a typed list of (many) rules of conduct to be observed in the building, a list I did not read but decided I would read carefully when I came out later.

As I entered, I observed much upon the walls. To the left were glass cases that stretched from about waist height to head height (of a six footer) and contained many sports trophies and photographs. To the right, photographs in frames adorned the walls: displays of the faces of white men (mostly) in uniform, grouped, seemingly, according to rank, with the leader or commander at the top of the frame. That list of typed rules appeared in several more places on the walls. . . .

---

Thick descriptions are based on attending to as much detail as possible in the setting—"Write down everything that you see or hear going on" is what we tell students, although we acknowledge that writing down everything that you see or hear is as impossible as seeing and hearing everything that is going on. The observer sees and hears within horizons of meaning, which encompass geographical and social location, and observational choices as well. To illustrate these horizons of meaning we use Warren's research on the steps of the campus building where she works, steps that serve as both entry and exit points, and as smoking areas for the students and workers who come in and out of the building (see Box 5.2).

Social location also shapes what kinds of things are noticed within the setting and thus what gets into fieldnotes. In group studies of inter-action in public and semipublic places, students attend to different dimensions of that interaction. One student might be fascinated by the apparent spatial rules of waiting at a bus stop or riding on a bus, noting which standing and seating places were occupied and which left open. Another might take note of conversations, writing down what she heard people talk about in a crowded deli. What is observed in ethnographic settings is likely to be a variation of what is observed in everyday life that, in turn, is the outcome of biographical experiences.

Emerson, Fretz, and Shaw (1995), whose *Writing Ethnographic Fieldnotes* is the major sociological discussion of the issue, give a vivid

---

**Box 5.2**

### Smokers' Steps: The Process of Writing Fieldnotes

On these steps, where smokers gather to smoke and chat with one another, fifteen minutes of observation can result in ten or more double-spaced pages of fieldnotes. I have also found that writing jotted notes while I observe to prompt my memory later prevents me from observing for the full fifteen minutes, because in the act of looking down to jot notes I lose moments of observation. And I have found that in the few minutes it takes to go up in the elevator from the ground floor of my building to the seventh I have already forgotten some of the details of what I just observed.

What I see and hear as I observe the steps depends upon where I am: standing close to the building looking out, sitting on one of the steps—a lower or higher one, a right or left one—or beyond the steps, at the side of the pathway that leads to the road. Thus, what is seen and heard depends partly on geographical location—where the observer is at any given moment. Furthermore, once settled into a location, there are many things going on, so that choices are made of what to observe within the ongoing flow of interaction. As I sit on the top step and observe and watch and listen to the smokers do I also attend to the passers-by, and if so, until what point—the end of the steps, the end of the path, the street beyond? Do I watch an interaction all the way through, or shift my attention to different parts of the setting as I alternately look up and around, and look down to write my jotted notes?

What I see and hear also depends partly on social location—where I come from in the cultural scheme of things. As a late-middle-aged professor, I notice students in a fairly undifferentiated manner—they are identified by me by their backpacks, their casual clothes, their youth. But I have found over the years of having my students observe campus settings that *they* make fine distinctions between students that I cannot, literally, "see." While I can differentiate roughly between graduate students (leather book bag, somewhat less casual clothes), they can differentiate between freshmen, sophomores, juniors, and seniors from cultural clues built into clothing and demeanor that are invisible to me.

---

depiction of differences in fieldnote descriptions of checkout lines in grocery stores. While all three examples they provide of such notes are thickly descriptive, each attends to different features of checkout lines. They note that one set of fieldnotes

> describes the line *spatially* in terms of individual people (particularly physical appearance and apparel) and their groceries as laid out before being rung up. (1995, 6)

In another,

> The observer describes moving through the line as she experienced the process on a moment by moment basis, framing her accounts of others' behavior as she received, understood, and reacted to them. (1995, 7)

And a third,

> In these notes the observer initially writes himself into a prominent role in the line but then he moves himself offstage by spotlighting another character who says and does a number of flamboyant things as he waits and then gets checked out. This express line becomes a mini-community. (1995, 8)

The first set of fieldnotes reflects the noticing of spatial relations, physical appearance, and apparel; the second focuses on temporal sequences; and the third presents interactions and personalities. That said, the reader may wonder whether there is any right way to write fieldnotes, or, if fieldnotes vary with horizons of meaning, is there any way to differentiate between well- and badly done fieldnotes? Yes: well-done fieldnotes are those written as soon as possible after the events in the setting have transpired, and for which as much time as is needed has been taken. The fieldworker, to write thickly descriptive fieldnotes, has to make a commitment to thick rather than thin description, to sooner rather than later fieldnote writing, and to taking a good deal of time to write the fieldnotes. Technical assistance, from jotting notes to using computers, can help (or sometimes hinder!) the process of writing fieldnotes.

## Time and Memory in Fieldnote Writing

No matter what one has observed within horizons of meaning, the inscription of these observations in fieldnotes requires holding them in memory. A few settings—mainly those in which writing itself is normative behavior—lend themselves to writing notes while observing. A college classroom is a setting in which the presence of someone writing on a lined tablet will not be attended to as out-of-place. However, typical behavior in a college classroom also includes focusing one's eyes on the instructor rather than gazing around at others, so that the observational behavior of an ethnographer in the classroom might seem odd.

Even where taking full fieldnotes in the setting is possible, it is not necessarily desirable, since it is virtually impossible to take notes while looking downward, and continue to observe closely. But neither is it necessarily desirable to take *no* notes in the setting, since relying solely on memory can result in large gaps in thick description. The general advice to the field researcher is to take brief jotted notes in the setting. These jotted notes may be taken overtly—in front of the members—in settings where such behavior does not seem odd, for example a court-room or a classroom. Where any writing might seem disruptive or odd (for example in a bar), notes can be jotted down on a small pad after retreating to a bathroom or other private place.

Sometimes, both strategies are useful in the same setting. When observing court hearings during Warren's mental health court research, she would jot down notes because this behavior was not unusual among courtroom-audience participants that included witnesses, other students, and so on. But in the backstage areas of the setting—judges' and attorneys' offices, for example—taking out a notepad and jotting down notes would have been both disruptive and difficult, since in those areas so much going on left no time to stop and write. Thus, memory alone had to be relied on to inscribe backstage interactions and talk.

Noting and remembering becomes more problematic as the setting becomes more complex and time spent in it greater. In the smokers' steps example, the setting is a public one, with interaction in public places the focus. Fifteen minutes or five hours on the steps would yield observations of similar kinds of interactions, the kinds observed by Goffman in *The Presentation of Self in Everyday Life* (1959) and other works. In the mental health court, in contrast, the complexities were much greater, starting with different subsettings that ranged from the courtrooms (2) to the judge's chambers (1) to the district attorney's and public defenders' offices (1 of each)—and these are just a few examples. Observation sessions could be a few hours or an entire working day at the court. What is best for the memory work of fieldnotes in these different kinds of settings?

In the smokers' steps research, Warren found that a half hour of observation followed by an immediate retreat to her computer upstairs was optimum for memory together with continuity of observation. For the mental health court, Warren alternated observing for whole days with observing for mornings, afternoons, and parts of mornings and afternoons. Since her drive back to her office from the court took from 30 minutes to an hour, this was the minimum time elapsed between observation and fieldnote writing. Although the mental health court fieldnotes were as thickly descriptive as possible under these conditions, there were definite memory problems by this time, especially with respect to sequence. After observing in complex settings for a relatively long period of time, what tends to be forgotten first is often sequence—you may recall what happened reasonably well, but not necessarily when it happened in connection with other happenings in the field. Computers and other technical aids can, however, help with the problems of time and memory.

## Computers and Audiotapes

Before the computer era, fieldworkers wrote their fieldnotes by hand on lined pads, or later, typed them with manual and then electric typewriters. Both these forms of inscription make it difficult to alter the content or sequence of fieldnotes, although strategies were developed, such as leaving the left-hand page of a bound notebook blank for later entries and remembered insertions (Warren 2000). Computers, however, facilitate the addition and rearrangement of inscription when something once forgotten is later remembered. In addition, audiotaping fieldnotes for later transcription can be useful in situations where it is impossible to write full notes immediately after observing.

In Warren's study of a psychiatric hospital for children and adolescents in Los Angeles (1983), the drive to and from the facility was one-and-a-half hours each way. Though it did not occur to her at the time, she could have used a tape recorder to record oral fieldnotes as she drove to and from the hospital. Then, later, these fieldnotes could have been transcribed using a computer together with a tape player controlled by a foot pedal (somewhat misleadingly called a "transcription machine"). Although this process is more time-consuming (counting the time taken to speak and then to transcribe the speech) than ordinary fieldnote writing, it is useful in those cases where the "dead time" of driving leads to forgetting some, or much, of what was observed earlier. As with all use of technology in the car, such as cell phones, this strategy has its dangers; if you try it, remember it is the driving, not the recording of notes, that is your primary task.

The dissemination of computer technology during the past three decades has helped enormously in writing fieldnotes (for other uses, see Chapter 9). It is a rare student—and an even rarer professor—who does not have access to a personal computer, or at a minimum, one provided by a computer lab in her academic institution or workplace. Once out of the field, the qualitative researcher makes a beeline for the computer, to get the fieldnotes down on paper as quickly as possible using whatever word processing program is preferred. The ability, when using computers, to move text and add materials is very useful for field researchers as one memory is retrieved and unlocks another. Visual representations of the field, such as the spatial relations between people waiting at a bus stop, can be prepared using computer software as well. And multiple copies can easily be made, preparing the way for coding and analysis (see Chapter 9).

## Preparing and Labeling Fieldnotes

Researchers use many strategies to prepare and label their fieldnotes. Some researchers prepare several sets of documents, one set a thick description of the setting, another an account of researcher responses—emotional and otherwise—to what went on, and the third an analytic commentary, noting conceptual ideas and connections as they occur. Other researchers prepare one narrative, in which reactions and analytic points are bracketed off from the descriptive text. For example, we return to Warren's Smokers' Steps:

### Smokers' Steps Fieldnotes, October 22, 2002

there is a lone smoker on the steps as I walk out into the crisp, almost cold fall afternoon air. She [YWF] is sitting on the second step from the bottom, to the right as I exit . . . she is about 5'3" and 190 lbs, long blond hair, no jewelry or makeup, no glasses, wearing jeans and a tucked-in white cotton shirt, thin and somewhat dirty white sneakers on her feet, white socks showing. She is drinking a coke from a can, and reading a hardback book placed on the step between her legs and feet [I wonder if she is a student or a janitor? No backpack, but a hardback book; looks like the "uniform" of the women janitors in this building].

Useful shorthand for writing fieldnotes are abbreviations such as "YWF," which means "Young White Female," abbreviations that make it unnecessary to write this kind of phrase out fully each time a stranger appears in the fieldnotes. Some researchers object to these gendered and racial characterizations, finding them stereotypical; however, what we first notice about strangers in everyday life tends to be their embodiment—as women or men, race, age, height, weight, and clothing—and this is what we then also first notice about strangers inscribed in our fieldnotes. Note that social class and university membership are also implicit in this excerpt; there were various "markers" of social class and student or janitor status in this observation, but these were not as apparent as gender and age. Similarly, if you observe a man and a woman with a small child in your setting, rather than assuming that they are a family, describe them as a man and a woman with a small child [presumably a family]. Although abbreviations are not as "technological" as computers and audio recorders, they are among the techniques that make fieldnote writing go somewhat more smoothly than otherwise.

## Keeping Track of Fieldnotes

Computers are also useful in keeping track of fieldnotes. One of the horror stories of ethnography is the one about a young ethnographer who went to the field for three years. On his return, he loaded his box of handwritten fieldnotes into his Volkswagen, stopping at a store to pick up a few groceries. As he was in the store the Volkswagen was hit by another car, exploded, and burned up, destroying the box of carefully taken notes with the car. Although this story may be apocryphal, the message behind it is not: you don't want to put an enormous amount of time and effort into fieldnotes only to have them disappear.

We both write our fieldnotes on our computers, saving to a disk (see Box 5.3). Once finished with the batch of notes, we make a hard copy, and also make a backup copy from the disk to the hard drive. Periodically, every few months and definitely at the end of a fieldwork phase, Karner also backs up her entire set of fieldnotes and project materials to a CD as well. Thus we end up with multiple copies of our data: disk, hard copy, hard drive, and CD. Since keeping track of documents involves being able to find them as well as not losing them, it is important to make your labels for these materials clear, so you can remember what they were called and how to find them again. There are almost as many ways of organizing fieldnotes as there are researchers doing fieldwork. What is most important for you is to find an organizing strategy that is meaningful to you and fits with the software and hardware you are using.

---

### Box 5.3

## Organizing Your Fieldnotes

**Warren says:** On my computer disk and hard drive I use terms for the setting (Smokers' Steps, SS), fieldnotes (FN), the number of the notes (1 for first, and so on). So I have: SSFN1.txt. I put the hard copies in file folders labeled the same way as I label the outside of my disks: FNSS1–5, for example. This works for me. If you take more than one set of notes, for example, you might reverse the order: SS (Smoker Study), FN (Fieldnotes), R (Reaction Notes), A (Analytic Notes) for three sets of files; SSFN1, SSR1, SSA1.

**Karner says:** My primary organizing tool for research materials is the use of the directory structure on my hard drive, which I supplement with backup copies to floppies while the project is in progress (I use a separate floppy for each subdirectory) and then final backup to a CD at the completion of phases of fieldwork. I begin with a directory for each project, then a subdirectory for fieldnotes, subdirectories for observation locations, and then separate files for each observation. I use a word processor that allows for longer file names so I can be as descriptive as I desire. So, my computerized system of organization looks something like this:

C:/Research/VA project/observations/family therapy/3Oct.doc

C:/Research/VA project/interviews/staff/psychologist-1.doc

C:/Research/VA project/interviews/patient/John Smith Interview1.doc

C:/Research/VA project/notes/identity issues.doc

I also create notebooks for my hard copies that are organized in the same directory structure, using dividers and color-coded notebooks (blue for fieldnotes, red for staff interviews, green for patient interviews, etc.)

Computers are also useful for assembling materials other than narrative fieldnotes for your study. If you have a scanner, for example, you can scan in relevant documents, such as a magazine article on the different policies universities have regarding smoking in, outside of, and around buildings. Visual records of your settings can also be scanned (or taken with a digital camera) and stored on your computer or a CD. Of course, it is important to remember that your organizing system and computer are tools for completing your research—if your organization process gets too complex you will have to make and keep lists of where all your files are and how you may have used abbreviations!

## What Fieldnotes Look Like

What should these thickly descriptive computer-saved fieldnotes look like? First, they should be fully narrative (see Box 5.1) rather than terse and listlike. Second, they should be contextualized as to time and place. If you are not able (as the noted anthropologist Margaret Mead was and many are not) to take note of the minute-by-minute timing of things, at least take note of what time you entered and what time you left the field. If you are working as a lone researcher, you might include this information at the beginning of each set of notes. However, if you are working as part of a research team, where colleagues will be reading each other's accounts, it can be helpful to put together a "face sheet" form that should be filled out for each set of notes (see Box 5.4). This allows each person to get a quick overview of the notes just by looking at the face sheet. Whether you chose to embed this information in your notes or in an attached face sheet, it is crucial to have it documented so that you will have as full (or thick) a context as possible within which to analyze your field data.

For example, Warren's fieldnotes on the smokers' steps begin and end: "I walked out of the building on to the steps at 10:05 a.m. . . . I went back inside at 10:35 a.m." They have a heading and a context:

### Smokers' Steps Fieldnotes, October 14, 2002

I walked out of the building onto the steps at 9:03, just after the time, as I have learned, that the janitors get their second break. The weather was windy, cold and overcast, discouraging the enjoyment of smoking or doing anything outdoors on the steps. Two smokers (YBM and YBF) were standing with their backs to the building, shoulders hunched, nobody on the steps in the wind [the dedication to smoking must be considerable to come out here in this weather in order to smoke].

As this extract shows, fieldnotes are a cumulative enterprise; the ethnographer learns more and more about what goes on in the setting as time passes. By the time of this observation, two months into the

---

**Box 5.4**

## Sample "Face Sheet" for Fieldnotes

### Public Utilization of Green Space Project

Fieldnotes completed by:

| | | | |
|---|---|---|---|
| _____ | John Smith | _____ | Peter Tu |
| _____ | Betsy Hernandez | _____ | Margaret Chou |

Observations site:

| | | | |
|---|---|---|---|
| _____ | Memorial Park | _____ | University Park |
| _____ | Veterans Park | _____ | City Zoo Park |

Location of researcher within site:

Time entered the field: _____    Time exited the field:_____

Subjects observed:

Activities observed:

Team notes:

---

research, Warren had learned that student-smokers appeared on the steps during the minutes between classes, janitors during scheduled work breaks, and professors and administrators more or less whenever they wanted to (highlighting both social class and bureaucratic frameworks for interaction on the smokers' steps). By then, she had also learned some of the social types: which smokers were janitors, which students, which professors. As part of the university and the building, Warren was already a member and before starting the research had a stock of knowledge on which to draw, which was also displayed in her notes:

### Smokers' Steps Fieldnotes, November 4, 2002

> . . . as I leave the doorway, I see a familiar trio sitting on the steps: Chrissy, the MAWF [middle aged white female] secretary in my department, together with the two secretaries from the Other Department (YWF1 and YWF2) she often smokes and talks with. They are all smoking, C on the top left step, YWF1 to the right of her on the next step down, YWF2 to the left of her (from where I stand). I say, "hi," they all turn their heads in unison and say "hi," then go back to their animated conversation. I hear the word "thermostat turned down to 68 degrees" in a tone of indignation from one of the three [I feel the same way about this interoffice memo]. I pass the trio and head down the path. . . .

One thing *not* to put in fieldnotes is the real names of people you encounter during your research. In public or quasi-public settings from beaches to university campuses you will encounter both strangers and people whose names you know. "Chrissy" is not the real name of the smoker on the steps. Although some fieldworkers use real names in fieldnotes and change them when writing for publication, because of the legal issues discussed in Chapter 2, we believe it is wiser for names to be changed at the point of fieldnote writing. Although fieldworkers often use *pseudonyms* with the same first letter as the real name—pseudonym Chrissy for the real name Cathy, for example—not doing so is even more protective of confidentiality than same-letter pseudonyms. When using pseudonyms, many researchers keep a separate log of the actual names and the pseudonyms locked up in a safe place, as memory may or may not hold for a long, complex project. However, should you chose to do this, we remind you once again of the cautions discussed in Chapter 2.

A finished fieldnote set, thickly descriptive, resembles an essay or narrative with a heading, a beginning, a middle, and an end. Although there are different ways to write fieldnotes, the most effective way, we believe, uses many of the narrative conventions, including the use of correct grammatical forms, full sentences, paragraphing, and the use of quotation marks for statements that are rendered close to verbatim. All these requisites for fieldnotes are debated among qualitative researchers, but the use of quotation marks for verbatim speech is probably the most contested.

The argument against the use of quotation marks in notes and publications for verbatim speech is that it is not really verbatim: the speech is heard, interpreted, remembered, and inscribed, but there is a lot of "slippage" away from verbatim during this process. The observer may mishear, misinterpret, or misremember, yet still use quotation marks to represent verbatim speech. Although slippage is clearly inevitable, the use of quotation marks is in our view preferable to eliding speech; thus, "The YWM leaned over to the YWF and said, 'are you going to class today? I'm not going, I don't want to walk over there in the rain'" rather than "The YWM asked the YWF if she was going to class today and said he was not going because of the rain." Trying to recapture talk verbatim encourages the researcher to include more thickly descriptive details.

Fieldnotes, and sometimes published writing, often include maps and other visual aids for understanding and visualizing the setting (see Gubrium [1975], for example). A researcher who is writing about interaction in a library may draw a map of the library—its stacks, reference desks, student study desks, and so on—and may also include the placement of various students and employees at various times in the stacks or at the desks. Warren often mapped the engagements and encounters between smokers and others (see Box 5.2) on the steps. A map can serve as an organizing structure for locating your remembered observations as well as a way to easily reference the spatial locations of observations in your notes.

As we noted above, a set of fieldnotes resembles a story, with a beginning, middle, end, and many pages in between. With a computer, the researcher can add remembered details to the narrative at any point, while initially writing up the notes or at a later time. Disk and hard drive copies of your notes can be single-spaced, while we recommend that hard copies be printed either single- or double-spaced, with wide enough margins for you to make comments as you read and reread your fieldnotes. As important as writing fieldnotes is, the reading and rereading of them is of equal importance.

## Reading Fieldnotes

Fieldnotes are the qualitative research equivalent to quantitative researchers' "raw data." Quantitative researchers take numbers and turn them into statistical tables, while qualitative researchers take fieldnotes, interview transcripts, images, or other documents and turn them into further inscriptions. But between inscription and reinscription is the reading and rereading of fieldnotes, always by the ethnographer, and sometimes also by others, whether team field research supervisors or course work instructors. Reading fieldnotes is a stage in ethnographic research; it is also an epistemological issue in relation to the audiences for our writing.

It is a truism of qualitative research that it is less linear in process than quantitative research. In quantitative research, the researcher has a research design with theory, hypotheses, quantitative methods, quantitative analysis, and write-up of findings (see Chapter 1). In ethnography, the researcher enters the field and takes notes, reenters and takes more notes, reflects and analyzes, continues in the field, writes up some thoughts—and so on, in an overlapping circle of activities. But there are still some rough stages between entrée and leaving the field. At the end, you will have a (we hope large) body of fieldnotes, some already partially analyzed, to read and reread.

Why all this reading and rereading? At the time you inscribed the first, tenth, or seventeenth set of notes, you were becoming more and more familiar with the setting—but not yet with the connections between the setting and concepts from your discipline. On reading or rereading, these connections may emerge. Christine Robinson, for example, recorded innumerable instances in her notes of conversations among lesbians in the Brownville community that went something like this: "Great to see you here today! We really missed you at the last potluck," or "Where's Ann? I haven't seen her for a long time," or "We were sorry you couldn't make it for the party last week, we had a lot of fun." As her Ph.D. research supervisor, Warren read these fieldnotes and marked them, in the margins, "social control," because these kinds of comments seemed to indicate members' interpretations of past and present, and attempts to influence future, behavior. At the time, Warren was doing research on Cub Scout activities, and had noticed many of the same kinds of comment by members of the scout community (while lesbian and Boy Scout groups may be substantively different, in formal terms, such as the activities of social control—see Simmel [1950]—they appeared pretty much identical). In the end, everyday life social control (an important issue in 2000s sociology) became the focus of Robinson's (2003) ethnography.

Without thickly descriptive fieldnotes, conceptual connections cannot be made in this manner. Although Robinson's research interests were not focused on greeting rituals, she did write down what she heard (and she heard socially controlling rituals over and over again in many places), not just what was already of interest to her. She did not remember the greeting rituals, either, since they were not important to her until she conceptualized them as an aspect of social control. But she had made a commitment to writing and reading fieldnotes, did so diligently, and reaped the conceptual rewards of her diligence. Thus, the fieldworker should always read and reread her own notes even if there is no supervisor to also read them. Rereading notes throughout and after the process of fieldwork can lead to a chain of new insights that further shapes the inscription of ethnographies.

## Writing the Other, Inscribing the Self

As inscription, fieldnotes are intended to describe what anthropologists call the Other—other cultures, other meanings. But since they are inscribed by selves, they also reflect those selves. This is clearly true where fieldnotes are routinely read by other people

(Warren 2000). But it is also true where the notes are likely to be read only by the fieldworker. Emerson, Fretz, and Shaw argue that the stance from which fieldnotes are written is shaped in part by the *"intended or likely audience,"* which is generally "herself as a future reader" (1995, 44). The possibility of legal action in relation to ethnographic fieldwork (see Chapter 2) may also make the inscription of fieldnotes attentive to the possibility of unwanted audiences (Warren 2000).

As Sanjek (1990, 34) comments, fieldnotes reveal about the writer "the kind of person you are" both pedagogically and personally. Thus, they reflect back to the reader the writer's pedagogical and personal self, as well as those others whose inscription is their ostensible purpose. In the pedagogical context, novice and student fieldworkers may worry about fieldnotes "not being done well": skimpy or verbose, unfocused, or not looking at the "right" things (Jackson 1990, 27). In a personal context, "Fieldnotes can reveal your childish temper" (Jackson 1990, 22).

One possible consequence of the fear of audience reaction is the censoring of notes, especially those that might or will be read by others. Emerson, Fretz, and Shaw suggest that if a student is afraid of the responses of supervisors to what she writes, the student researcher should produce one set that includes all the material of interest, and another in which it is censored; the censored set of fieldnotes goes to the supervisor (1995, 222). Several of our students in field methods classes have admitted that they have turned in censored fieldnotes and kept uncensored ones (Warren 2002, 88). Censored materials include those involving the other, and those involving the self.

Generations of sociologists and anthropologists have indicated censorship of fieldnote materials that might cast discredit on "their people," perhaps an incident of sexual harassment, perhaps the "embarrassing or illegal activities of poor urbanites" (Obbo 1990, 291). Fieldnotes taken in contexts where the fieldworker, supervisors, and members of the field setting are all known to one another may be censored for gossip or other linkages of personal behavior with identifying characteristics, which would then have made the notes themselves into a form of gossip (Warren 2000, 189).

But fieldnotes inscribe the self as they inscribe the other, so that censorship of the self may occur as it relates to the field. Beyond "childish tempers," fieldworkers may want to conceal aspects of self that might be discrediting or stigmatizing. In earlier decades, this was often the case with qualitative sociologists who studied lesbian or gay subcultures. But even today, some lesbian or gay graduate students who intend to continue into academia may conceal their sexual identities as they write supervised fieldnotes about lesbian or gay others, fearing problems with hiring and tenure (Warren 2003).

At times, rather than censoring, the ethnographer writes about himself for the fieldnote audience. As supervisors of fieldnotes, we have found that students use them to communicate directly with us, as in the following example from a student's research on a group home for delinquent boys:

> Jack [one of the boys] got defensive, but that only makes sense. It makes sense that he would want to retain the attitude so as to appear consistent. In other words, retain the *fake* attitude as a way of showing off for Colin [another inmate]. Consistency would mean his attitude was real, not just performance. (Sorry I am low on detail here. Am I lacking?). (Warren 2000, 194)

This note was more like an analytic memo than thick description. In response to it, Warren asked the student to avoid glossing over the specifics of interaction by using words such as "defensive," and tell the reader what was said and done by Jack to lead the writer to that conclusion.

Sometimes—indeed quite frequently—students write about various aspects of themselves in their fieldnotes as they observe and react to interactions in their setting. One student, as she wrote about the ethnicity, clothing, and appearance of members of the Hispanic health care setting she was observing, also marked her own:

> Maria wore a red blouse and "skort" . . . splashed with bright yellow, pink and orange tropical flowers. I felt that she looked typically colorful and Hispanic, while I in my cobalt blue and white striped sweater and denim jeans looked typically pale and conservatively Anglo. (Warren 2000, 195)

In their fieldnotes, students have—either purposely or as part of the way they write—given us all kinds of information about themselves: sexuality, ethnicity, clothing, appearance, self-confidence or a lack of it, and life events. Although there are very few examples of communication of the self via notes in the published literature, there are a few. Here is an extract from anthropologist Don Stull's notes during his team field research in Garden City, Kansas:

> No one but me tries to set and keep common agendas. But then I think everyone looks to me to play that role. Then again, maybe I am just too anal. . . . I am getting surly in my dealings with other team members. (quoted in Erickson and Stull 1998, 33)

Reading and writing fieldnotes are the keys to successful ethnographic research, whether the research is done alone or as a member of a team. If the researcher is either a team member or doing research supervised by an instructor, an external authority is insisting on those notes. If, however, the fieldworker is not supervised by anyone, no external prompt pushes writing these notes. As we said in the beginning of this chapter, writing thickly descriptive fieldnotes is time-consuming and requires a commitment on the part of the researcher. Do not rely on your memory of events instead of writing fieldnotes—and do not rely on your memory of your fieldnotes instead of reading them. They are as important to your qualitative research as are the transcriptions of qualitative interviews, discussed in the next chapter.

## Suggestions for Further Reading

Emerson, Robert M., Rachel I. Fretz, and Linda L. Shaw. 1995. *Writing Ethnographic Fieldnotes.* Chicago: University of Chicago Press.

Sanjek, Roger. 1990. *Fieldnotes: The Makings of Anthropology,* 34–44. Ithaca, NY: Cornell University Press.

Van Maanen, John. 1988. *Tales of the Field: On Writing Ethnography.* Chicago: University of Chicago Press.

Warren, Carol A. B. (2000). "Writing the Other, Inscribing the Self." *Qualitative Sociology* 23 (Summer): 183–200. ❖

# Chapter Six

# The Interview

*From Research Questions to Interview Questions*

The second major qualitative method, used together with fieldwork or by itself, is research interviewing. Today we are all familiar with different types of interviews: the job interview, the medical interview prior to physical examination, the psychiatric interview, the journalistic interview seen on television. Other types of interviews share with the research interview the intent to get to know the interviewee better, but the purposes of that *getting to know* are different. In the job interview, the employer wants to fill a position. In the medical or psychiatric interview, the case history taker wants to arrive at a diagnosis. In journalistic interviewing, the interviewer does, like the research interviewer, want to use the interview to contribute to a body of knowledge. But the body of knowledge developed by the journalist is generally of the storytelling or whistle-blowing kind, while that of the social scientist has conceptual or theoretical import.

Research interviewing is a special kind of conversation in which the interviewer questions the respondent on a topic of interest to the interviewer, and of some relevance to the interviewee. There are several types of research interviews, including the survey interview, which will not be covered in this chapter since it is part of quantitative rather than qualitative research. One type of qualitative interview is the oral history approach, in which respondents are questioned in the context not so much of their individual biographies but as witnesses to the historical events that occurred during their lifetimes. In this chapter we will be covering the qualitative interview, sometimes called the *in-depth* or *intensive* interview, which is focused on the meanings that life experiences hold for the individuals being interviewed.

Interviews typically involve one interviewer and one respondent, but other forms include the focus group, in which one interviewer questions more than one respondent. Interviews may be conducted face-to-face, over the telephone (Shuy 2002), or on the Internet (Mann and Stewart 2002). We will confine our discussion, in this chapter and Chapter 7, to the qualitative face-to-face research interview with one or more respondents. As Kvale describes it, this type of interview is

> a conversation that has a structure and a purpose. It goes beyond the spontaneous exchange of views as in everyday conversation, and becomes a careful questioning and listening approach. . . . [It] is not a conversation between equal partners, because the re-searcher defines and controls the situation. The topic of the inter-view is introduced by the researcher, who also . . . follows up on the subject's answers to his or her questions. (Kvale 1996, 6)

Research interviews today are often single events, with the inter-viewer interviewing a respondent only once. Interviews can also be part of longitudinal research designs, in which they are used to trace the development of social meanings over time. In Warren's work on schizophrenic women in the late 1950s and early 1960s (Warren 1987), the eight interviewers interviewed 17 women and 16 of their husbands for up to three years (with a follow-up interview for some 12 years later), at intervals ranging from weekly to monthly. These interviews showed the changes in the women's understandings of their psychiatric diagnosis and mental hospitalization from admission through discharge.

Interviews in one form or another have been used in many ways and in many places and times. The origin of the interview, like that of field research, is sometimes traced to the journeys of Herodotus (Bailey 1995, 7) or the dialogues of Socrates (Kvale 1996, 21). Its mod-ern origins, however, are more commonly located in the social reform studies of the nineteenth century. In the 1830s, for example, Harriet Martineau interviewed women and men throughout the United States, concluding that there was some similarity between the lives of women and of slaves at that time (Reinharz and Chase 2002, 222). Martineau was also an early participant observer in the lives of American women (Bailey 1995, 7). These and other nineteenth-century qualitative and reformist studies in the United States and Europe formed the back-ground to the development of the Chicago School.

## The Chicago School and the Development of the Interview

The Chicago School continued the traditions of urban social sur-veys and reform politics in their case studies of the early twentieth cen-tury. Interviews were used, together with quantitative social surveys, documents, and fieldwork, to illustrate the local conditions of the times, and to suggest what might be done to ameliorate those conditions. Early Chicago methods texts distinguish between what we now call qualitative interviewing and interviewing done with a questionnaire or schedule (Platt 2002, 36). Pauline Young, in a discussion of interviews published in 1939, recommended that the interview be based on "a considerable degree of rapport . . . [and] the mutual discovery of common experiences" (quoted in Platt 2002, 36). Young also discussed the value of the interview:

> The personal interview is penetrating; it goes to the "living source." Through it the student . . . is able to go behind mere outward behavior and phenomena. He can secure accounts of events and processes as they are reflected in personal experiences, in social attitudes. (quoted in Platt 2002, 36)

The focus of sociological research shifted after World War II to the quantitative survey interview and away from fieldwork and qualitative interviewing, with several major studies of the armed forces. While the primary concern was still finding out about and ameliorating social conditions—at first, the condition of the armed forces—the methods were increasingly quantitative rather than qualitative, applied rather than historically based. Although qualitative interviewing remained as a major method in anthropology, it was overshadowed in sociology by survey interviewing until at least the 1980s. Several textbooks on qualitative interviewing in the social sciences were published in the 1990s (Arksey and Knight 1999; Kvale 1996; Weiss 1994), while a major *Handbook of Research Interviewing* (Gubrium and Holstein 2002) was published in the early 2000s. From the Chicago school until today, sociologists have explored important issues in qualitative interviewing, beginning with the question of when to use qualitative interviews instead of, or in addition to, other methods.

## When to Use Qualitative Interviews

Qualitative interviews may be conducted as part of ethnographic research, as part of a larger research design, or as the sole method of a study. The decision to do an interview study, or to have an interview component in a larger study, is based on the kind of research questions you wish to answer. As a rough rule of thumb, if you are interested in behavior and interaction, use the ethnographic method; if you are interested in biography and accounts, use the interview method; if you are interested in both, use both methods.

The use of multiple methods is illustrated by Karner's (1994) study of inpatient Vietnam veterans diagnosed with post-traumatic stress disorder (PTSD). In this longitudinal research project, Karner employed ethnographic observation and qualitative interviews. She observed the activities of a Veterans Administration hospital unit for the treatment of combat-related PTSD and the various therapeutic activities that took place there, which included small therapy groups, educational classes, recreational activities, formal and informal discussions between staff members and veterans, and the veterans interacting among themselves in unstructured activities. Karner was able to raise issues or ask questions in the small therapy group she observed, giving her access to the opinions and insights of the veterans as they talked. This component of her study, similar to an informal focus group (see below), allowed Karner to focus on behavior and interaction, whereas in the later stages of her project she began a sequence of intensive interviews collecting the veterans' biographical accounts. By using multiple methods, Karner was able to contrast what was *said* (accounts) with what was *done* (behaviors) by the veterans and staff. This contrast provided a much broader understanding and thicker description than had she employed only one method.

What sets the interview apart from the other kinds of conversations inevitable in field research is its formal structuring: the development of a set of specific questions to be asked of respondents, the selection of respondents, and the audio- (or sometimes video-) taping of the interview. It is these elements of the interview-as-conversation that require the separate consideration of an interview study component, or interview study, as part of human subjects IRB review. We will deal with these issues in the rough time order in which they generally occur: conceptualizing the topic, framing the research question, developing the specific questions, the IRB review, deciding on the interview format, sampling respondents, and planning the interview. In Chapter 7, we will discuss the process of interviewing as social interaction and speech event, what happens after the interview, and transcription. The subject of analyzing interview transcripts will be discussed in Chapter 9, together with the analysis of fieldnotes, images, and other documents.

## From Research Topic to Interview Questions

Many interview researchers, like ethnographers, select topics because of some biographical connection; they want to find out how other people have thought or felt about, or handled, some particular issue or problem. For example, Shirley Hill (1994) was interested in sickle-cell anemia because of experiences within her own African-American community with the disease. Other researchers—especially those in research teams, and sometimes students in classes—are assigned interview topics by supervisors, instructors, or granting agencies. Karner and Hall (2002), for example, were asked by their funding agency, the Administration on Aging, to design and conduct a study that would systematically document the service insights of staff members of community service organizations.

Whatever the topic of the interview, a general research question, or set of research questions, should be framed from it: how do "other women" get involved with married men, and what adaptations have they made to their situation (Richardson 1985)? How do African-American mothers handle the medical, economic, and emotional problems associated with raising a child with sickle-cell disease (Hill 1994)? What is it like for an older woman to be married to a younger man (Warren 1996)? From these general research questions the interviewer develops a set of 10 to 15 specific research questions. Examples of specific research questions can be seen in Boxes 6.1 and 6.2. The questions in Box 6.1 may seem vague, and those in Box 6.2 rather mundane, but both sets of questions elicited a wealth of narratives. In Box 6.1, question 3, for example, was designed to elicit information about whether the couple rented or owned a home, if the home was owned by the woman (which it generally was), and who moved in with whom (generally the man moved in with the woman). Questions such as number 10 in Box 6.1 are typically asked at the end of an interview in case there is something on the respondent's mind that the interview has not yet elicited.

---

### Box 6.1

#### Interview Questions for a Study of Older Women and Younger Men

1. When did you first meet [name of spouse or cohabitee]?

2. How did it go between you at first?

3. When and where did you first live together?

4. When did you get married?

5. How is being married to . . . ?

6. Do you have or are you planning to have children?

7. How do you get along with her/his family?

8. How about her/his friends?

9. When you think about the future, how does it look?

10. Is there anything else you would like to add?

(Warren 1996)

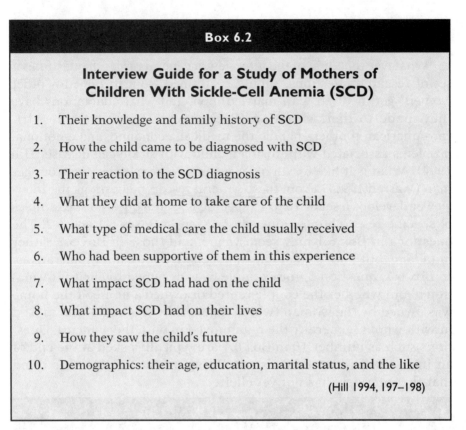

**Box 6.2**

**Interview Guide for a Study of Mothers of Children With Sickle-Cell Anemia (SCD)**

1. Their knowledge and family history of SCD

2. How the child came to be diagnosed with SCD

3. Their reaction to the SCD diagnosis

4. What they did at home to take care of the child

5. What type of medical care the child usually received

6. Who had been supportive of them in this experience

7. What impact SCD had had on the child

8. What impact SCD had on their lives

9. How they saw the child's future

10. Demographics: their age, education, marital status, and the like

(Hill 1994, 197–198)

Interview questions have to be developed prior to submitting a research proposal to IRBs, since these committees will want to know what you are going to ask the respondents. The level of specificity necessary to satisfy the committee may vary by institution. The interview guide that Karner was required to develop for the IRB process at a Veterans Administration hospital that was unfamiliar with and somewhat reticent about the use of qualitative methods can be seen in Box 6.3. However, Box 6.3 represents only the first of a four-page listing of interview topics for the proposed six hours of interview time, and thus one quarter of the material insisted on by the Veterans Administration hospital IRB.

## Face Sheets

Rather than asking about demographic information such as gender, age, and occupation in the interview, you might, instead, develop a face sheet for that purpose (see Box 6.4) for the respondent to fill out as you set up your tape recorder. This face sheet should have a code keyed to the same code on the audiotape you will use for the interview (much more infrequently, you may be using a videotape), and on the transcript of the interview (more on this later).

**Box 6.3**

## IRB Interview Guide for Study of Vietnam Veterans With PTSD

I will be following the format of intensive interviewing, which is more like a guided conversation than a formal questionnaire. I will be interested in three main areas of the veteran's life experiences: childhood, Vietnam, and post Vietnam. I will ask the veterans, in broad general terms, to describe their experiences and how they felt at the time. The veterans will be able to answer these open-ended questions with as much specificity as they wish. I will follow up with elaboration probes when appropriate, such as "What do you mean by . . . ?" or "How did that make you feel?"

My main purpose will be to elicit the veterans' memories and understandings of their experiences. I will be using the topics listed below as a broad guideline for the material to be covered. These topics are not inclusive; rather they will be used to facilitate an open dialogue between the veteran interviewee and myself.

**Interview Series Topics:** During the first session, I will be attempting to get acquainted with the veteran. I will answer any questions about the study that he might have and give him a general outline of how the series of interviews will proceed.

### Basic Demographics and Current Situation

(1) Date of birth

(2) Sex

(3) Race or ethnic background

(4) Current marital status

(5) Number of previous marriages

(6) Number of children, sexes, and ages. Do any *live* with him?

(7) Age at time of Vietnam tour

(8) Was he drafted or did he enlist? If enlisted, rationale

(9) Length of tour

(10) Main military duties, in and out of country

(11) Branch of service

(12) Date of tour

(13) Was he wounded in combat

(14) Length of total military service

(15) First memory of arriving in Vietnam

(16) How does he remember his tour (briefly)?

(17) In general, how did his service in Vietnam impact his life?

(18) How often does he think about Vietnam?

(19) Does he think that most people understand what Vietnam was like?

(20) What is the greatest misunderstanding about Vietnam?

(21) Has he visited the memorial in Washington, DC? Under what circumstances?

(22) Does he read books or see films about Vietnam? Why or why not? Are any of the portrayals accurate? Did he find any of them emotional or moving? In what ways?

(23) Does he feel comfortable talking about Vietnam?

(24) Does he speak of Vietnam often? If so, to whom?

(25) How did he come to be in the PTSD unit? Is this his first time

(26) Is he service connected for PTSD? If yes, at what percentage? If no, does he have a claim pending?

(In equal detail, the IRB proposal goes on to list topics for each of three main areas of the veteran's life experiences: childhood, Vietnam, and post Vietnam, Karner 1994, Appendix A.)

There are several things to notice about this face sheet. In a study of people who might include the transgendered, the researcher would include something like "other" as a third category along with M and F; doing so in *this* study would just seem odd. Warren's ordering of M before F is also commonplace in the social sciences (look at any survey you receive); thus, she kept this ordering because to do otherwise might introduce unnecessary error by causing women to check the M box and vice versa. Since this was the face sheet for a study of older women married to younger men (Warren 1996), the exact age was important. Where the specific age is not so crucial, but some idea of age is necessary, the interviewer may use age groupings for the respondent to check (i.e., 18–25), with the parameters of the age grouping set by the likely ages of the respondent. With older populations, it is more useful to ask for birth dates rather than age, as one's date of birth does not change over the years and is more likely to be remembered and reported consistently.

---

**Box 6.4**

### Demographic Face Sheet for a Study of Older Women/ Younger Men

Your gender   M _____   F _____

Your age _____

Current marital status _____

Dates of any previous marriage(s) _____

Number and ages of children _____

Education—Highest level attained: _____

Occupation _____

Ethnicity/race _____

---

Although (to get at social class) Warren asked about education and occupation, she did not ask about income; people are often reluctant to disclose or truthfully report their income. Warren surmised that she would get enough information from the qualitative interviews on income differentials to avoid asking for income on the face sheet. Marital status, previous marriages, occupation, race, and ethnicity were left open (without response categories) on the face sheet so that the respondents could define these as they saw fit. Also, you will see in many older studies that religion was routinely included in demographic data collection, but is often omitted today; Warren did not see religion as something she wanted to explore with respondents and so omitted it.

## Questions, Prompts, and Probes

If some questions are deemed problematic or disturbing, they should be left until the end of the interview; the easiest and least disturbing questions should come first. This is because of the expectation, seen throughout the literature on qualitative interviewing, that some degree of rapport will develop between interviewer and respondent (more on rapport in Chapter 7); a respondent who might be reluctant to answer a particular question upon first meeting the researcher might be more willing to do so after an hour or more of conversation. McCracken suggests that interviews begin with "grand tour" questions that sketch out the terrain to be covered (1988, 35). This overviewing function can also be served by the face sheet that has been filled out and handed in to the interviewer, who can then refer to it and ask questions from it: "Oh, I see you have been married four times; can you tell me about the ages of your previous husbands?"

In addition to the relatively small number of planned questions for the qualitative interview, the researcher must be prepared to probe for clarification or prompt for additional details. Because the use of prompts and probes depends on the respondent's narrative, they are difficult to specify in advance. This is also true of the additional questions that arise as the respondent tells his story. McCracken gives an example of the use of probes and additional questions in interviewing:

> [one] device is to repeat the key term of the respondent's last remark with an interrogative tone
>
> (Respondent: "So me and my girlfriend decided to go out and get wrecked."
>
> Interviewer: "Wrecked?"
>
> Respondent: "Yeh, you know, really, really blasted").
>
> If these techniques are not effective, the interviewer can be more forthcoming ("What do you mean 'blasted' exactly?") but not more obtrusive ("Do you mean 'intoxicated'"?). (1988, 35)

We will return to the issue of prompts and probes in the next chapter, when we discuss the interview process in greater detail.

Questions that are obtrusive or "lead the witness" should be avoided in the qualitative interview. Interview studies that are based on leading—or even bullying—respondents have been criticized as promoting untruthful answers. In the influential mid-twentieth century Kinsey reports on sexual behavior, for example, pressure was used to get respondents to "admit" to sexual practices:

> It became necessary to say, with firmness, even vehemence, and yet always with kindness, "Look, I don't give a damn what you've done, but if you don't tell me the straight of it, it's better that we stop

this history right here. Now, how old were you the first time that this or that happened?" Surprisingly, in not a single case did a person refuse to continue. (quoted in O'Connell and Layder 1994, 132)

Fifty years later, the use of such tactics casts doubt on Kinsey's findings:

Considered in the light of research into social conformity and the way in which people tend to comply with researchers who are perceived as authority figures, this makes Kinsey's figures on levels of sexual activity look . . . suspect. (O'Connell and Layder 1994, 132)

The alternative to leading the witness is the phrasing of questions that have as little content as possible. Rather than "Didn't that make you feel awkward?" use "How did that make you feel?" The first form of the question assumes that the respondent felt a certain way (awkward), while the second form assumes that she had a feeling. If the narrative that elicited "How did that make you feel?" would lead any competent observer to believe feelings were involved—for example the respondent has just described how her husband rejected her—then the second form of the question would be appropriate. Where feelings might not be at issue—for example the respondent has just described a dinner with her husband—you might use something like "How was that?"

The purpose of qualitative interviewing is the elicitation of narrative stories from the respondents that indicate the meanings they give to those aspects of their life-world relevant to the interviewer's topic. Such a purpose requires the pre-interview development of questions as a general guide, but it also requires flexibility in using, adding to, deleting, expanding, or in other ways changing the substance or order of these questions. This emergent aspect of the qualitative interview, like the emergent features of ethnography, makes the letter-of-the-law fulfillment of IRB review procedures somewhat problematic. Although the interviewer plans to use probes and additional questions when necessary, she cannot plan in advance what these probes and additional questions will be (as seen in Box 6.3).

## The IRB Review

Your instructor may have obtained an agreement from your institution's IRB that your interviewing is part of your training rather than an independent research project. Or you may have to prepare and submit your interview plan to your IRB with the help of your instructor. Either way, it is important to remember the three principles of human subjects protections discussed in Chapter 2: informed consent, confidentiality, and avoiding harm.

Informed consent generally requires that you present your interviewees with a letter describing the purposes of your research and its institutional sponsorship (as we noted in Box 2.3 of Chapter 2).

Assuring confidentiality requires that although you may—and probably will—know the identity of your respondents (thus you cannot promise anonymity), you will not publicize the names of your respondents, or so many identifying details that they could in fact be identified. Thus you will use codes, rather than names, to identify respondents on transcripts, audiotapes, and face sheets, keeping a master list of names and codes in a locked file, to be destroyed at the end of the research project.

There are some types of respondents, and some topics or questions, that IRBs may not permit you to get involved with. "Protected classes" of people who cannot be interviewed without great difficulty include children and minors, and institutionalized populations such as prisoners. These people are presumed to be unable to provide free and informed consent, children because consent resides with their parents (and will have to be obtained from their parents), and prisoners because they are confined involuntarily and thus cannot truly consent to or refuse anything. Your instructor will let you know, if you are doing interviews, what kinds of people you are going to be permitted, by your institutional IRB, to ask questions of the respondents—and what topics and lines of questioning you may pursue.

Combinations of topics and populations are particularly problematic for researching with qualitative interviews (e.g., adolescents' sexuality). That is not to say that no social scientist, ever, will be able to interview adolescents about their sexuality, just that the IRB review process is likely to be long and cumbersome, permissions from parents difficult to obtain, and the outcome uncertain. In studies of nonspecial populations that aren't particularly controversial, there may still be specific questions that an IRB will not approve for the researcher to ask, or will want reworded.

Additionally, IRB proposals generally expect the researcher to provide information about any potential harm that might come to the respondent as a result of participating in the interview. This can include even minimal "harm" such as talking about psychologically stressful events like combat or rape. In attempting to get approval for such a project, a researcher should have some sort of support available for distressed interviewees or at least a procedure to follow should the need arise. For example, in Karner's interviews with the Vietnam veterans (1994) where she proposed to discuss stressful events in their lives, she identified staff volunteers on the PTSD unit who agreed to provide counseling support for any veteran who might feel the need during or after the interview. This procedure assured the IRB committee and she received approval.

## The Format of the Interview

Thus far, we have been considering interview dyads (two people) consisting of one interviewer and one respondent. This will most likely be your situation if you engage in face-to-face interview research for your methods course. But there are other possibilities for interview formats; some include more than one interviewer, and others more than one respondent. Although the Bay Area study (Warren 1987, and see Chapter 1) used eight interviewers, these interviewers did not interview in pairs or groups; indeed, with the exception of focus groups and evaluation studies, we are unaware of any studies in qualitative interviewing that use more than one interviewer at the same time. There has been some discussion of triadic interview situations, in which there is one interviewer and two respondents, perhaps a married couple (this form is commonplace in clinical interviewing related to marital counseling). At times, also, what starts out as a dyadic interview situation comes to involve other people, particularly where interviews are done in private homes where spouses and children can wander in and out.

### Interviews With Dyads and Triads

In sociology, two-person and three-person groupings are often referred to, respectively, as dyads and triads. Holstein and Gubrium have explored the dynamics of interviewing two people together, in one instance an elderly married couple that lived in a nursing home(1995, 67–78). Although the focus of the life-history interview was Don, the husband, "As the interview unfolded, it soon was apparent that Sue did not much like Don's version of things because it did not include her" (Holstein and Gubrium 1995, 67). Sue, then, began to direct the interview toward parts of Don's life that included her. Following Don's description of his early life and move to Florida, Sue says, "[Sarcastically 'Why don't you tell her that we got married in the meantime? I'm part of it, too, you know'" (1995, 68). Later in the interview, after Don has described various aspects of their life in the Depression, Sue again intervenes:

> [Chuckling] "Just listen to him. In the meantime we had three more children." [Sarcastically] "Remember that?" (Holstein and Gubrium 1995, 68)

It is clear from this interview, and from clinical interviewing with couples, that the story told in an interview with one person in a marriage will differ not only from the story told by the other person, but also from the story told by both together. In her classic study of working-class families, sociologist and clinician Lillian Rubin decided to interview wives and husbands separately because I was interested in understanding the way each experiences the marriage relationship and his or her role in it. . . . [T]he perceptions of husband and wife are not necessarily congruent, and . . . both perspectives are necessary for understanding the reality of a marriage. . . . [W]omen tend to discuss their feelings about their lives, their roles, and their marriages more freely when men are not present. (1976, 10–11)

Interestingly, triadic issues with interviewing may arise even if the married-couple interviewees are not co-present. In the Bay Area research, with one interviewer interviewing both spouses individually over a period of time, spouses sometimes sought access to confidential information about the other. Mr. Sand was disturbed when he found out that the male interviewer had not shared information with him about Mrs. Sand:

He asked me if I had talked to his wife that day and when I did not answer at once he repeated the question and I finally told him that I did. . . . He told me that . . . I knew things about what was going on at the hospital with his wife, and I didn't tell him a thing about it. He brought this up a few times. (Warren 1987, 266)

## Focus Groups

Interviews with one or two interviewers and a group of people are called focus groups, and are common in communications, program evaluation, and market research. Although only a few social science research studies used focus groups during the 1980s, by the late 1990s there were over 200 (Morgan 2002, 142). Focus group interviewing for other purposes tends to be highly structured, focused on the product to be sold, program to be assessed, or media event to be analyzed. Social science focus group interviewing tends to be less structured, focusing, like qualitative interviewing in general, on the participants' rather than the researcher's meanings and interpretations (Morgan 2002, 146–147). Focus group interviewer David Morgan describes his "ideal focus group":

The ideal group would start with an opening question that was designed to capture the participants' interest, so that they themselves would explore nearly all the issues that a moderator might have probed. Then, just as the allocated time for that question was running out, one of the participants in the ideal group would spontaneously direct the others' attention to the topic for the second question by saying something like, "You know what really strikes me is how many of the things we're saying are connected to . . . ." (Morgan 2002, 148)

Focus groups offer a data collection strategy that allows for the involvement of a larger sample in a shorter amount of time. They are a highly efficient means of collecting informational data that is not of a sensitive nature. For example, what services would parents like to see in their neighborhood parks? How satisfied are students with their educational experience at a particular college? What are some ideas for increasing efficiency in an organization or business? In focus groups with two interviewers, one researcher usually takes the lead and asks most of the questions, while the other researcher may play a more supportive role—noting "talking points" on a blackboard, introducing prompts or probes, and interjecting other questions infrequently.

What is said in focus group interviews will differ from what is said in dyadic ones, just as dyadic interviews differ from triadic. Dean Wright (1994) interviewed adolescent boys about their attitudes and behavior toward girls of their own age. These boys, in the individual interviews, were quite understanding about girls' expectations for male-female relationships. However, when the same boys were interviewed as a group, they were much less sensitive and bragged about their dominance over girls. In her veterans study, Karner (1995) found great variation in the men's presentation of self as strong and tough in unit groups to emotionally distraught in the dyadic interviews. If you wanted to study how context might influence behavior or narrative, then focus groups can provide an ideal setting and format.

Your choice of interviewing people one by one, in pairs, or in focus groups will depend on the kind of talk you expect to elicit. As Rubin (1976) has shown, if you interview married couples about their marriages, you are likely to get different responses from the wife, the husband, and in a joint interview situation. Your choice in this case would depend on your research questions: Do you want to be able to compare husbands' and wives' views of marriage? Do you want to see how the couple interacts as well as hear what they have to say? Or, as in the case of the adolescent boy focus group, above, do you want to compare responses across different interview formats? Whatever you decide about how many people to interview at one sitting, your next task will be to decide what the parameters will be for respondent selection in terms of age, gender, class, and other social statuses.

## Sampling Respondents

Qualitative sampling strategies have a different underlying logic than the strategies used by quantitative researchers: what is called theoretic rather than random sampling. Random sampling is used in positivist, quantitative research, to ensure the generalizability of findings to the populations from which the sample was drawn. Theoretic sampling, by contrast, seeks in respondents only the criteria specified by the research questions: African-American mothers in Shirley Hill's study, home care workers in Karner's (1998a) research, or first admissions of white women with children to Napa mental hospitals in Warren's study of *Madwives* (1987). Within the context of theoretic sampling, the researcher has to decide the number of respondents she will interview (which may change as the research progresses), what types of respondent to interview (using criteria such as gender, age, and class), and how to locate specific respondents using these criteria.

## Number and Type of Respondent

If you are a student or employee, the number of respondents you will interview may be pre-set by the instructor or research design; we both require students in one-semester classes to do 10 interviews for a qualitative interviewing paper. Published research on one type of respondent (e.g., "older women" or veterans with PTSD) may be based on as few as 15 or as many as 100 or more respondents. The original *Madwives* (1987) research was based on thousands of interviews, but with fewer than 50 people, including 17 wives, 16 husbands, and a variety of psychiatric hospital personnel. By contrast, Diane Vaughan (1990) interviewed 103 people for her book on *Uncoupling*, and Carole Brooks Gardner (1995) interviewed more than 500 respondents for hers on public harassment, including minority and nonminority women and men.

The social characteristics of the people interviewed will depend on the research questions that you have derived from your topic. When Shirley Hill (1994) decided to study the caregivers of children with sickle-cell disease, she chose to sample African-American women (since African Americans are the main sufferers with sickle-cell in this country, and women the main caregivers). She was also interested in economic barriers to care, so she sampled lower-class families. These were the only restrictions she put on her sample, which she sought from among personal acquaintances and others associated with the hospital-sponsored sickle-cell anemia caregivers' self-help group. Diane Vaughan, who wanted to study the experience of divorce and other kinds of uncoupling, interviewed "young and old, male and female, gay and straight, married and living together" (1990, 197).

Since the topic you have chosen for your interview research may have some biographical importance to you, it is likely—and may be a good thing—that there will be similarities between you and your respondents. There is a considerable literature, for example, on the gender of interviewers and respondents; although with some topics this may not matter, with other topics it may matter a lot. In interviewing men who had been recently divorced, Terry Arendell found that from the initial point of contact, the interview became a proving ground for masculinity and a site for the exercise of male dominance displays against ex-wives (and sometimes against all women). (1997, 342)

These men immediately "took charge" of the interview topic and attempted to "place" Arendell as married or unmarried, available or not, male basher or nice girl (Warren 2002, 96). Interviews between matched interviewers and interviewees will elicit one kind of interaction and narrative, whereas a very different interaction and narrative may emerge between an unmatched dyad. It might seem that interviews with divorced men, from the Arendell experience, would go better if it were a man doing the interviewing—but then again, they might not.

## Finding Respondents

A common means of finding people to interview involves locating a social setting in which they can be found. Just as Hill found her African-American mothers at a SCD support group, Karner often works with local organizations to access her respondents. By locating her veterans' study on an inpatient unit of a Veterans Administration hospital, she had many willing participants who looked forward to the interviews as something to break the boredom of institutional life. When studying homecare workers, Karner (1998a) was able to solicit interviewees through the homecare agency, which also provided a location for the interviews. In her study of nursing home aides, Karner employed the same strategy of gaining access through cooperating institutions (Karner et al. 1998).

However, finding actual respondents to interview within the parameters the researcher has set up, without the assistance of a cooperating organization, can be a daunting task. Vaughan (1990) describes her first strategy for trying to obtain respondents to interview concerning uncoupling. She sent 100 letters to individuals and couples selected from newspaper divorce listings one to five years before the research started: "Four responses trickled back . . . but no one agreed to be interviewed" (1990, 198). Warren had a similar lack of response when she attempted to find elderly people to interview who had had electroshock therapy. Warren posted flyers in nursing homes and other places where elderly people were present, and in psychiatrists' offices and hospital waiting rooms, but to no avail.

The only way Warren eventually found her interviewees—and the main method used by Diane Vaughan—was through snowball sampling. This term refers to the process of accumulating interviewees from within interlocking social networks, beginning with an initial contact. Richardson used a similar strategy. She says:

Finding "other women" to interview was not difficult. . . . I announced my research interest to nearly everyone I met—conferees, salesclerks, travel acquaintances, and so on. Women I met in these different circumstances volunteered to be interviewed or put me in contact with women who were involved with married men. (1985, x)

Most discussions of sampling for interviews presume that the respondents obtained will be strangers; this is even reflected in the title of one of the leading textbooks on qualitative interviewing, *Learning From Strangers* (Weiss 1994). However, the topic of interviews is often of mutual interest to both respondent and interviewer, and especially when snowball sampling is used, the interviewer finds herself interviewing within her own and interlocking social circles, as Richardson (1985) did with some of her respondents. Sometimes, as in Esterberg's (1997) ethnographic and interview study of a lesbian community, the researcher finds herself studying friends and acquaintances, co-members of the same groups or communities. At other times, as in Warren's research on electroshock, although electroshock had no biographical relevance to her (she had obtained a grant, with others, to do the study), the snowball sampling technique with which she found respondents meant that she was interviewing the relatives of friends and colleagues.

From the point of view of obtaining interview data, interviewing nonstrangers sometimes may mean that respondents do not answer our questions in detail, because as we have heard many of them say, "Why are you asking me that? You know all about that!" But sometimes more than the interview is at stake. Shifting from a purely sociable or personal to a research agenda may have consequences for the researcher's social relationships as well as for the data gathered. Interviewing people with whom one is familiar may take unexpected turns and have unexpected consequences. For one thing, respondents may be annoyed at being asked questions that they know the interviewer knows the answer to but is trying to get on tape "for the record" (Harkess and Warren 1993). In addition, the topic of the interview may bring tensions into the relationship between interviewee and interviewer.

When Warren was doing interview research on electroshock therapy with elderly psychiatric patients, she interviewed one of her friends concerning the psychiatric hospitalization and planned electroshock treatment for her mother. During the interview, this respondent became very upset with both herself and Warren, accusing Warren of accusing her of abusing her elderly mother with electroshock. The interview questions did not give her that impression—they were quite bland—but her prior knowledge of Warren as a sociologist and critic of institutional psychiatry did. This episode had a negative impact on the friendship for some months after the interview, even after the friend's mother had been discharged from the hospital without receiving ECT.

## Planning for the First Interview

Once respondents have been identified and have agreed to be interviewed, it is time to set up an appointment with them. As a courtesy, respondents should be consulted as to what date, time, and day of the week is convenient for them, and what kind of place they would like to be interviewed in. It is difficult enough to get respondents to make and keep interview appointments; if you also ask them to come to campus (with the search for parking and similar problems), you are making their job and thus yours all the more difficult. You may also not want to interview respondents in their homes, especially in the case of male-female dyadic interviews. Often a public place is the best choice, such as a table at the library or a quiet cafe or bookstore that does not mind you interviewing at one of their tables or, in nice weather, a park bench. Sometimes the respondents may ask you to come to their workplace or office for the interview, and that is often a very good choice, especially if the interview is about their work.

In selecting a place (see Box 6.5) for the interview, you will want to choose a location that will maximize the respondent's physical comfort as well as your own. Also keep in mind that you would prefer that the location be quiet and generally free of distractions. You will want to be able to sit comfortably for an hour without being interrupted. A table is also helpful for placing the recording device between the two of you as well as for taking notes. Privacy is also key to conducting a good interview. When selecting a time for the interview, make sure that your respondent will have enough time to talk without feeling hurried. We have also found that it's best to avoid mealtimes, as you do not want your interview curtailed by hunger. Avoiding mealtimes also saves you from having to negotiate invitations to join respondents for meals. In addition, you should select a time when you are *sure* that you can arrive on time. It is important for you to be there when you said you would.

---

### Box 6.5

### Keys to Selecting Good Interview Locations

- Convenient for the respondent
- Comfortable and safe
- Quiet and free from distractions
- Private

---

Your preparations for the interview will include both yourself and your technology. When you first meet the respondent, how you present yourself and what you say are significant in helping the respondent crystallize his or her perception of both you, as an interviewer, and the experience of the interview as well. Therefore it is important to pay more attention than you usually might to specific details, common amenities, and cultural sensitivities. You will want to present yourself as an interested listener: empathetic, trustworthy, polite, nonjudgmental, and professional. However, you generally do not want to be perceived as an authority figure (do not wear your power suit) or as someone completely alien (from a different class, culture, or with dissimilar values). Try to dress somewhat like your respondents, but more conservatively. It is important for your respondents to feel that you can understand them and their attitudes, beliefs, and values, or they will not feel comfortable sharing them with you.

Your dress should be appropriate to the situation. If you are interviewing members of a biker gang, for example, it makes no sense to go to the interview in a suit and tie; the reverse may be true if you are interviewing attorneys. A rough rule of thumb is that your dress should not echo the respondents'—do not dress as a biker if you are not one—but should respect their choices. Thus, a sports coat might be appropriate for a man interviewing an attorney, and jeans and a t-shirt for a man interviewing a biker. Your demeanor should be unfailingly polite; although a calm, nonjudgmental demeanor will probably work with both bikers and attorneys (at least, work better than confrontation and hostility!), a looser demeanor might work better with the bikers and a tighter one with the attorneys.

Although some interviewers (and ethnographers) use videotape, most published interview research is based on audiotape. Be sure that you have good quality, pretested audio equipment: a recorder with two sets of fresh batteries and an electrical cord, and an adequate supply of tapes (twice as many as you think you need). Take along a selection of 30 and 60 minute tapes, starting with a one-hour tape and moving to a half-hour tape if the one-hour one runs out. The recorder can be of any size, but must always be visible to the respondent as well as to you to ensure that it is still functioning. Be sure to test your equipment thoroughly before the interview, at least once at the site where you are going to be doing the interview, to see if you are going to plug in the recorder or use the batteries, and to situate it and test for sound pickup. The most common interviewing situation is for a respondent and an interviewer to be across from each other at a medium-sized table, with the recorder and microphone placed between them to record both questions and answers.

Arrive at your first interview (and each subsequent one) at least 15 minutes before the prearranged time to set up your audiotape equipment—and to ensure (generally) that you are waiting for the respondent rather than vice versa. You will want time to construct your interview environment. You want to sit close enough together so that your respondent can easily see any notes you have so you do not seem deceptive. You want to be comfortable; you want privacy; and you want to be free from as many distractions as possible. Keep these things in mind when first sitting down and constructing the interview environment. It is very disruptive to the flow of talk if you need to readjust things midway through.

For an interview with someone you don't know, wear a name tag so that the respondent can identify you; you might even want to hold up or have on the table a larger sign with your name or the project title on it (not the respondent's as is done when a stranger is being met at the airport). When the respondent spots you, get up (if you have been sitting), smile, and introduce yourself. How you introduce yourself is important—use Mr., Ms., or Mrs. when addressing the respondent unless the respondent asks you to call him or her by another name or title. Showing respect can be key, especially if you are somewhat younger than the respondent. When saying your name, do not use titles. For example:

> "Hello, Mrs. Doe. I'm Jane Smith and I'm one of the interviewers for the Diabetes experience project. It's very nice to meet you."

Make sure the respondent is seated comfortably across from you, giving him or her time to settle in (stowing purses, coats, etc.) as you make pleasant small talk about the weather or the traffic. When the respondent is comfortable and gives you eye contact, it is time for the formal interview to begin.

You should begin by explaining the purpose of the interview. Respondents who believe in the importance of the research and especially its relevance to their own situation are more attentive and provide more productive interviews than those who are uninterested. So remember that in telling them about the interview project, you are, to some extent, informing them about its importance. You should keep the explanation as clear and concise as possible—be sure to stay away from jargon and other big words. Be simple and straightforward. For example:

> This interview is part of a study to see how well the Sunshine Day Care is working for the people that use it. We are trying to find out if people are satisfied with the services so we will know what to change in the future. We are also looking at different types of experiences with caring for older persons so we have some questions that ask about your experience of caring for your elderly relative.

Also be sure to allow respondents to ask any questions they may have or voice any concerns. Take any concerns expressed seriously and answer them fully. You want the respondent to feel listened to, even before starting the formal interview.

At this point you are ready to ask the respondent's permission to turn on the tape recorder. You might also tell the respondent that he or she should feel free to turn the recorder off at any time if there is something that he or she would rather not have recorded. We have never had this happen, but it offers the respondent some sense of control. Another thing you might try is enlisting the respondent's assistance in making sure the recording light stays on so you can explain why you will be checking periodically (especially if you have a recorder that silently runs out of tape like Karner does). After you have the go-ahead to begin recording, you can give the respondent the consent form to sign, with a copy for each of you to keep, so that you will have a record of any comments that are made about the form. Then present the respondent with the demographic face sheet, if that is how you have decided to get basic information about gender, age, and so on (see Box 6.4). You should have your list of questions (show the respondent if she asks to see them) in your hand, and a lined pad and pen or pencil to take notes. Your interview has begun.

### Suggestions for Further Reading

Gubrium, Jaber, and James Holstein. 2001. *Handbook of Interview Research: Context and Method.* Thousand Oaks, CA: Sage Publications.

Kvale, Steinar. 1996. *InterViews: An Introduction to Qualitative Research Interviewing.* Thousand Oaks, CA: Sage Publications.

Rubin, Irene, and Herbert Rubin. 1995. *Qualitative Interviewing: The Art of Hearing Data.* Thousand Oaks, CA: Sage Publications.

Weiss, Robert S. 1994. *Learning From Strangers: The Art and Method of Qualitative Interview Studies.* New York: Free Press. ❖

# Chapter Seven

# The Interview as Social Interaction and Speech Event

$\mathbf{A}$ survey interview and a qualitative interview may look alike, with prepared, trained interviewers asking questions and recording answers. But for the qualitative interviewer the interview is not only a method, it is a social interaction of the very type that qualitative methods were designed to study! Thus, the qualitative interview as social interaction has been the subject of numerous methodological analyses over the past few decades, beginning (from the standpoint of the interview process) with issues of rapport and trust, and ending with the epistemology of interview data.

The qualitative interview has also been studied from a sociolinguistic perspective as a speech event, since it consists of talk between two native speakers, or various combinations of native speakers, non-native speakers, and translators (Briggs 2002; Mischler 1986). The presumption in this chapter is that of an English-speaking interviewer and an English-speaking respondent. The complications that arise when the interviewer and respondent speak different languages (the interviewer is not fluent in the respondent's language, or a translator has to be used) are beyond the scope of this chapter—and of most student research.

In this chapter, we explore the interview, and its aftermath, as social interaction. We then consider the challenges of transcription, or taking a speech event and turning it into text. Finally, we take a look at the epistemology of the interview: how qualitative researchers have interpreted the interview as a source of data and of sociological knowledge. Since interview transcripts will join fieldnotes and other texts as the subject of analysis (in Chapter 9), it is important to understand what kind of data they represent.

## The Interview as Social Interaction

Discussions of the interview as social interaction—and indeed speech event—have taken place at least since the Chicago School. As Vivien Palmer said in 1928,

> Any interview constitutes a social situation between two individuals; it is a process of continuous, spiral interaction in which one person's response to the stimulation of another in turn becomes the stimulation for another response. (Palmer 1928, 171)

Although this more than 70-year-old perspective on the interview as a social situation is still at the heart of contemporary definitions, many of the other ideas about interviewing proposed by Palmer and other Chicago School researchers are quite different. Unlike many of today's qualitative interviewers, for example—especially feminist ones—Palmer advised the research interviewer to maintain an objective "detachment as a scientific investigator" throughout the interaction (1928, 175). Today some qualitative sociologists, particularly feminists, recommend a more participatory role for the interviewee.

The interview as social interaction, like other social interactions in everyday life, can range from disastrous to mutually rewarding, depending on the talkativeness of the respondent, the topic of the interview, the functioning of the audiotape, and the interview process itself. Some respondents may not want to talk very much and give brief "yes" or "no" responses, something that occurs when the respondent does not really like to talk any of the time, is intimidated (perhaps because of class disparities), or would prefer to avoid the topic. Although most interview topics are of mutual interest to respondent and interviewer, some topics may be interesting but uncomfortable to the respondent. For example, Hackney (1996) was able to obtain interviews about body and weight among overweight acquaintances and friends, but once they were in the interview they wanted to say as little as possible about the matter and could hardly wait for the interview to be over. Not all topics contribute to interview rapport, as we saw in Chapter 6 in the discussion of Terry Arendell's interviews with divorced men.

The importance of functioning, good audiotape equipment was also stressed in Chapter 6, together with pretesting of the equipment (if possible) at the site of the interview. An interview may go very well, with a talkative respondent interested in the topic, but if it is not recorded it is not, from the point of view of the interviewer at least, a good interview. When Warren interviewed gay men in the late 1960s for her dissertation (Warren 1972), she had not pretested her recorder at the site (an otherwise empty classroom of a university campus) and found when she went to play back the interview that there had apparently been no electricity coming from the outlet into which the tape recorder had been plugged. Karner had an experience where the tape itself was defective, and even though the recorder had been pretested and was working well, when she switched to a second (faulty) tape it no longer recorded. Ideally you will not have such serious technical problems when you do your interviews, since no matter what the social process of the interview, if it is not recorded—if the interviewer has to rely on jotted notes and memory—it is much less useful.

The interview process has been studied as a social situation with a beginning, an unfolding or natural history, and an ending. Preparations for the beginning of the interview were discussed in Chapter 6, including the use of the face sheet, the setting up and turning on of the tape recorder, and the polite greeting rituals that generally precede the formal interview. This social situation has been analyzed from several perspectives: the development of rapport early in the interview between respondent and interviewer so that the respondent will offer thick, richly detailed narrative accounts; the social characteristics of respondent and interviewer; and the biographical situation within which the respondent is being interviewed (e.g., whether she is very busy or has time on her hands). The interviewer's decision to use dyadic, focus group, or other interview formats was considered in Chapter 6; in this chapter we discuss what happens if other people enter into dyadic interviews.

## Rapport, Truths, and Telling Accounts

The development of *rapport* between interviewer and respondent has been an important theme in discussions of both survey and qualitative interviewing in the decades from the Chicago School (Palmer 1928, 172) until the 1980s. The purpose of establishing rapport was to find out truth; without rapport, problems of untruthfulness and evasion would, it was feared, occur. In the 1920s Palmer indicated that the purpose of the interview is to elicit the respondent's "experiences and attitudes as they actually have occurred or exist" (1928, 173–174). Similarly, in the 1980s, Jack Douglas said that his "ideal goal" in interviewing "is the revelation of the complete truth about human life" (1985, 95–96). From a different perspective, we see interviewing as a means to facilitate the telling of individual accounts within the specific context of an emergent speech act. Thus, there is always "truthfulness" in the interaction that is reflective of broader social truths even though the actual information conveyed may have a limited intersection with any empirical reality. We will discuss this further when we turn our attention to the epistemology of the interview.

Establishing rapport—whether to elicit truths or accounts—is still an essential component in successful interviewing. Indeed, how to establish and maintain rapport with respondents was the subject of discussion during the six decades between Palmer and Douglas. Palmer proposed in the 1920s that rapport would be broken if the interviewer talked too much, suggesting the use of body language instead:

> Gestures, the nod of the head, smiles, facial expressions which reflect the emotions narrated are . . . very important. They also aid the interviewer in escaping pitfalls; if the response is put into language it can more often lead to disagreement and misunderstandings which break the *rapport* between the interviewer and his subject. (1928, 171–172, emphasis in original)

Some 60 years later Douglas argued that the key issue in rapport is warmth, something that he says "is not my trump card. . . . But . . . can be learned" (1985, 106). We would argue, in contrast to Douglas, that respect (from which warmth may also follow) is the essential component of building rapport—respect for the respondents and respect for the knowledge and perspectives they have to offer.

First impressions, Jack Douglas reminds us, are lasting impressions, and putting the best foot forward from the very beginning is potentially a vital determinant of everything that follows (Douglas 1985, 82). If first impressions are "too bad," he further cautions, "everything that follows . . . may not follow at all" (1985, 81–82). Further into the interview, a respondent's voice tones, gestures, or silence might indicate a breakdown of previously established rapport. Under such circumstances the interviewer might, for example, change the order or type of questioning until the respondent seems more comfortable, or re-engage in small talk (Douglas 1985).

Interviews are like conversations, but they are not the same as social conversations. How much to interject into the discussion and how much self-disclosure about one's personal life the interviewer will make must be carefully thought out. Karner had a student who felt that she was conducting some wonderful interviews. She believed that her "technique" was to share a lot of her own opinions and experiences to build rapport. When it came time to analyze her data, she found she had substantially less data than her classmates to work with and that none of her respondents had provided any information that was contradictory to the views she had espoused, rendering her data problematic. Balancing rapport and what sociologists refer to as active listening is as important in interviewing as the research questions themselves.

Active listening is also recommended in past and contemporary discussions of how to generate (and not subsequently destroy) rapport between interviewer and respondent. As Rubin and Rubin (1995) point out in their textbook on qualitative interviewing, the interview is as much about listening as it is about talking, and the first thing an interviewer has to be is a good listener. A good listener is an active and attentive listener. Interviewers with this skill do not expect the recorder to pick up everything for them while their mind wanders; instead, they listen carefully to everything the respondent says, in both words and body language, and respond accordingly.

Active listening lets respondents know that you are interested in what they have to say, and that you are not just there to collect data for your own research needs—it is a demonstration of your respect for what insights they have to offer. A good listener, and thus a good interviewer will use both nonverbal (nodding and eye contact) and verbal ("I see," "oh yes," "ah, that makes sense") encouragements while listening. Using the open-ended question format discussed in Chapter 6, ideally, will reduce any "ego threat" so that the respondent will feel comfortable in answering honestly and in a straightforward manner. It can be wise to emphasize that there are no "right" or "wrong" answers. In spite of this, some respondents may need reassurance that they are answering the questions correctly or in a helpful and interesting manner. Comments such as "you are doing fine" or just nodding and saying "good" can help alleviate apprehension. These gestures demonstrate a respect and concern for your respondents that can help build a sense of trust and rapport.

Some researchers argue that the rapport has to be exactly right, not underrapport but not overrapport either. Underrapport might lead to untruths or refusal to answer or short yes or no responses. Overrapport, however, might lead to the respondent trying to please the interviewer with a socially desirable answer rather than a true one—that is, telling the interviewer what she wants to hear (like Karner's student discussed above). Palmer suggests that a "detached attitude" can guard against overrapport "distorting the story of the person interviewed, against causing him [the respondent] to express himself in terms of the interviewer" (1928, 175).

Another issue with the idea of rapport is that discussions of it are based entirely on the interviewer's determination that it has or has not occurred. In an interview between sexologist Alfred Kinsey and "an older Negro male" the following exchange occurred:

Kinsey . . . inquired if he had ever "lived common law."

The man admitted he had, and that it had first happened when he was fourteen.

"How old was the woman?" [Kinsey] asked.

"Thirty-five," he admitted, smiling.

Kinsey showed no surprise. "She was a hustler, wasn't she?" he said flatly. At this, the subject's eyes opened wide, he smiled in a friendly way for the first time, and said, "Well, sir, since you appear to know something about these things, I'll tell you straight." (quoted in O'Connell and Layder 1994, 131)

From Kinsey's point of view he had established rapport with this respondent by showing he "knew the score." O'Connell and Layder question this interpretation:

> Why did [Kinsey] not consider the possibility that the man was exaggerating the age difference, or that the smile and wide-eyed "Well, sir" could have been a straightforward mockery of Kinsey's rather transparent line of thought? (1994, 131)

Did Kinsey achieve overrapport so that the respondent told Kinsey what he wanted to hear? Or did Kinsey underdevelop the rapport, resulting in mockery? As readers we are generally left with only the interviewer's assessment of whether he or she has established rapport or is being subtly mocked or manipulated. Rapport might be more appropriately conceived of as the basis for telling accounts, rather than truths. Without some sort of rapport, very limited telling will occur. With rapport, a rich textural accounting can unfold. This most often occurs when researchers approach potential interviewees with respect and genuine interest.

We offer an excerpt from an interview sequence Karner conducted (see Box 7.1) that demonstrates the complexity of rapport and truth even further. In interviewing men diagnosed with PTSD, she found:

> Telling about traumatic memories was a process of revelation of the self to the self and to others. Veterans often recounted their experiences in an emotionally stressful, contradictory, and fragmented manner that undermined their credibility and thereby maintained both a truth and a secret. Moreover, the aftermath of trauma is always expressed, if not in words, then in actions or symptoms (van der Kolk 1988). The veterans' nonverbal process of retelling was manifested in their hypermasculine pursuits of

---

**Box 7.1**

### Self Accounts and Truths

This excerpt from Karner's "Medicalizing Masculinity: Post Traumatic Stress Disorder in Vietnam Veterans" (1995, 58–60) illustrates how *truths* shift and evolve with each telling of self. Karner writes,

In the *first interview*, Ramsey spoke, with great regret and sorrow, about the individuals he felt he had killed needlessly. He recalled having remorse at the time and he contrasted that to other soldiers' joy in killing. Ramsey unfolded his story in contradictions, first mentioning what happened and then claiming that he could not have done it. "I should've if I was like somebody else that was brought up different than me and didn't have any feelings about human life then I would have come back bragging and said 'Oh I killed somebody today.' You know as though I'd marked the little part on the helicopter you know that I got a kill today." Ramsey also mentioned during the initial interview that he had "kind of went off the deep end, the

## Box 7.1 (Cont)

extreme opposite of being a very sheltered Christian—I went to the extreme opposite!" However, he gave closure to each event narrated by withdrawing from the aggression and willfulness of the event. He mentioned what happened and then concluded with "I feel so guilty." At various times during the interview, Ramsey paused to ponder, "I don't know if you call it murder or kill, I don't know for sure, at times I call myself a murderer." He contemplated the appropriate label for his behavior and could not accept either word.

During the *second interview* [two days later], Ramsey told some of his stories from the perspective of Scott, the other door gunner in his helicopter. "I tell you, I had a problem with that. I didn't go back and brag about it with the other guys. The other guys would brag about it. . . . It wasn't any problem for Scott, because Scott had done a lot of killing. . . . He whooped and hollered." Then Ramsey mentioned later in the second interview, "I didn't perceive myself as being someone who could kill somebody and then laugh about it and feel good about it." He paused briefly, then added, "I didn't." Ramsey was still narrating through negations. He had forgotten the candor of his first interview and, when pressed to talk about the time when he had killed a woman and the child in her arms, he could not. Ramsey talked around the event and tried, but ended with "I can't come out and say it."

The telling of traumatic memory was inhibited by its lack of language but it was also a process much like the construction of a puzzle. The veteran gave clues in multiple ways, all but telling without telling, while he remained unable to speak of it directly. Approximately six weeks later, during the *third interview*, Ramsey had become much more vocal. He had been able to tell his stories in "trauma group" and now had a language to help him integrate them within himself. Ramsey began by disclosing, "Well, I wasn't telling myself exactly the truth because I really enjoyed killing that woman. . . . because I was so angry about my friend being killed." Later he broadened his statement, adding more pieces to the puzzle, "I've learned just to go ahead and tell the truth that I enjoyed killing." The main focus of this interview became Ramsey's desire to kill. . . . He spoke of his enjoyment and euphoria in Vietnam, being able to kill at will. . . . Ramsey had decided that his feelings were acceptable in light of the rationale that he only wanted to "put to death people who deserve it." When asked directly if he would kill again, Ramsey answered ambiguously, "I wouldn't admit that, there's no way I'd admit that." Ramsey had started to let some of his traumatic experiences unfold. From his narrative, it seemed that he had mentally placed all the times he had felt like killing within his Vietnam experience. Thus when his combat memories began to unravel, his other, similar memories came to the forefront as well.

During the *fourth interview*, about a month later, Ramsey was willing to address one more element of his traumatic experience. In all the earlier interviews, he had identified the death of his friend Mike as the impetus for his entire excessive combat killing.

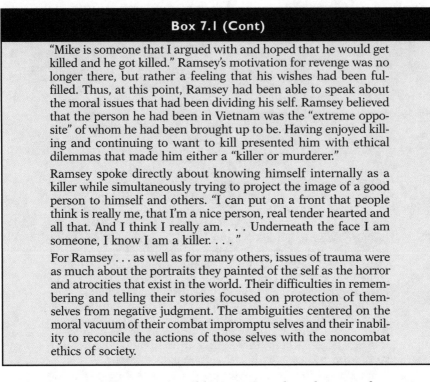

**Box 7.1 (Cont)**

"Mike is someone that I argued with and hoped that he would get killed and he got killed." Ramsey's motivation for revenge was no longer there, but rather a feeling that his wishes had been fulfilled. Thus, at this point, Ramsey had been able to speak about the moral issues that had been dividing his self. Ramsey believed that the person he had been in Vietnam was the "extreme opposite" of whom he had been brought up to be. Having enjoyed killing and continuing to want to kill presented him with ethical dilemmas that made him either a "killer or murderer."

Ramsey spoke directly about knowing himself internally as a killer while simultaneously trying to project the image of a good person to himself and others. "I can put on a front that people think is really me, that I'm a nice person, real tender hearted and all that. And I think I really am. . . . Underneath the face I am someone, I know I am a killer. . . . "

For Ramsey . . . as well as for many others, issues of trauma were as much about the portraits they painted of the self as the horror and atrocities that exist in the world. Their difficulties in remembering and telling their stories focused on protection of themselves from negative judgment. The ambiguities centered on the moral vacuum of their combat impromptu selves and their inability to reconcile the actions of those selves with the noncombat ethics of society.

drinking and drug use, recklessness, and outbursts of anger, whether the veteran consciously willed it or not. Lives became the texts of expression (Greenspan 1992, 146). (Karner 1994, 216).

As qualitative researchers, we understand that social truths about selves and knowledge emerge in the interaction of the speech act. Even if the respondent, like Ramsey (Box 7.1) believes he is telling the truth, his account may vary considerably from that of some observer and even from his own other tellings. Thus the notion of truth, much like the issue of accuracy of internet web pages that we discuss in Chapter 8, can be set aside to some extent. Rather the actions and the accounts that emerge or are given provide the "texts of expression" that constitute social data that can be analyzed. From this perspective, all interview responses do contain both a "truth and a secret." And even outright, obvious lies may contain social truths and useful data.

As reflected in many past and present textbooks on qualitative interviewing, the ideal interview is one in which rapport is established and a rich narrative emerges. The ideal interview is also on a topic of mutual interest to researcher and interviewee (Kvale 1996). Many individuals are quite willing to talk and will agree to be interviewed. As the Rubins state,

At a basic level, people like to talk about themselves; they enjoy the sociability of a long discussion and are pleased that somebody is interested in them. . . . [Y]ou come along and say, yes, what you know is valuable, it should not be lost, teach me, and through me teach others. (Rubin and Rubin 1995, 103)

Indeed, we have both had students doing interviews as part of ethnographic observation studies, where respondents continue to offer the researcher insights long after the formal interview ceases. If a researcher takes the time to express genuine and respectful interest, respondents will often want to make sure that the interviewer understands fully. Other times, however, talking does not come so easily. Strategies and issues related to maintaining the flow of talk during the interview include impromptu prompts, respondent resistance, and emotional content. (See Box 7.2 for a brief summary of such techniques.)

---

### Box 7.2

## Comments for Eliciting Rich Narrative Accounts

**Impromptu Prompts**

(Permission to take time to think)
*I know it is a complex question and you might want to think about it . . .*
(Clarifying difference between spouse caregiving and illness caregiving)
*I know that some people see caregiving as just part of being a spouse, but I wonder if there are some things that you find yourself doing now, that you didn't do before . . .*
(Clarifying if the respondent understands the question)
*Does that make sense?*

**Respondent Resistance**

(But you already know that . . .)
*Yes, you are right, but I need to ask you "for the record."*
(Didn't you already ask that?)
*Yes, this does sound similar, but it is a different question.*
(Oh, I really don't know . . .)
*I realize this question may be difficult to answer without some thought.*
Or
*I don't have to know exactly, but what is your best guess?*
(I don't know the future, how could I know?)
*Well, of course nobody knows for sure, but given the ways things look now, what do you think or what is your best guess?*
(I'm really not sure . . .)
*Can you tell me what it is about the question that you're not sure of?*

**Emotional Content**

(If respondent seems emotionally overcome . . .)
*I can see that this is difficult for you; would you like to take a moment?*

---

**Impromptu Prompt.** In the process of conducting an interview, you may find that in spite of all your planning and preparation, one or more of your questions is not eliciting the information you are seeking.

There are a variety of possible reasons for this challenge, but it is up to the researcher to respond to it. If a response is not offered, it may be that the question requires thought and the respondent merely needs some time to think. An interviewer may prompt: "I know it is a complex question and you might want to think about it." The interviewee will probably let you know if that is the case or if there is a need for clarification. Furthermore, this prompt gives the respondent permission to pause and think. The second option might be to further clarify the question you've asked, or ask if the question makes sense. You can easily say, "Does that make sense?" For example, "I know that some people see caregiving as just part of being a spouse, but I wonder if there are some things that you find yourself doing now, that you didn't do before . . ." would be a way of clarifying a question about different kinds of care.

**Respondent Resistance.** Sometimes you may be conducting an interview with someone who may seem hesitant to answer. Though we will talk in greater detail below about resistance due to perceived threat to self, here we will cover the less problematic kinds of resistance. There are many forms of resistance to answering the interview questions. One comment you might hear is, "Didn't you already ask that?" or "You already know that, why are you asking?" Always begin by agreeing with the respondent: "Yes, you are right, I do know that, but I need to ask you 'for the record'" or "Yes, this does sound similar, but it is a different question."

At some point, the respondent will undoubtedly say "I don't know" to one of the questions. Very seldom is it that the respondent really does not know; more often it is that he needs a minute to think. So you might respond with: "I realize this question may be difficult to answer without some thought." Again, you are giving the respondent permission to think about the answer and acknowledging that it is a challenging question. If the respondent is still reticent to respond, you may say, "I don't have to know exactly, but what is your best guess?" This is especially helpful if you are asking about when something long ago occurred. Or if the hesitance comes from being asked to estimate something in the future, you can answer: "Well, of course nobody knows for sure, but given the ways things look now, what do you think or what is your best guess?"

"What do you mean by that?" is another sensitive respondent response. The interviewer should treat this as a simple request for clarification. The problem is to communicate the meaning of the question without suggesting an answer and without changing the meaning of the question. If the respondent does not understand the question, you can ask: "Can you tell me what it is about the question that you're not sure of?" Perhaps it is just the wording or language usage that is confusing, or the respondent may not be sure of the referent.

**Emotional Content.** Some questions will invoke an emotional response. Every interviewer should be prepared for this to occur—even if you don't think you are asking emotionally stressful questions. A graduate student of Warren's was interviewing a biracial man about the experience of being biracial when it became clear that the topic itself caused him distress about his ambiguous identity and place in the world. Since almost any topic can be emotionally charged for someone, you will need to be sensitive to this possibility. If the respondent is overcome by emotion or starts to cry, you need to set down your pencil and give him or her some time. You might offer to postpone the rest of the interview for another time: "I can see that this is difficult for you; would you like to take a moment? Or we could finish the rest of the interview another time." Usually, if given a moment, respondents will want to continue—but you need to acknowledge their pain and give them the choice. It is best not to marshal them through the interview if it becomes obvious that they are upset.

Much like being a good conversationalist, there is an art to eliciting rich narrative accounts within the speech act of interviewing. And interviewing, like the rest of social life, does not always go smoothly, but it is seldom disastrous. As with observation and writing fieldnotes, your comfort level will increase with practice, and the more interviews you conduct, the better you will be at facilitating thickly descriptive responses.

## The Interview Topic and Participants

The interview, like field research, involves an embodied researcher of a particular appearance, gender, race, and age; one or more respondents with their own social characteristics and a topic that may be of interest to both participants but a threat to one. No matter what the previous understandings or initial rapport, and no matter who is doing the interviewing, certain topics, or even certain questions or subtopics within a general topic, may stymie the interview process. Adler and Adler discuss an interview with a drug dealer's "old lady" that had to be terminated because of her discomfort:

> we thought that she liked and trusted us and that, as a graduate student in cultural anthropology, she understood and respected academic research. However, as soon as the interview began, we realized that she felt uncomfortable discussing the drug trafficking of her friends: She ducked our questions, feigned sleepiness, and avoided direct answers. We politely left and lost all future access to her. (2002, 525)

Perhaps because the Adlers were focusing on illegal activities, their withdrawal from the situation was the appropriate response. If, however, the topic was one without legal ramifications, a skillful interviewer might use the respondent's reticence to redirect the questions to uncovering the source of discomfort. For example, "I know this is an uncommon experience, but if you could help me understand why some people have such a hard time talking about it—that would really help my research." The interviewer can "talk around" the topic and focus on the interviewee's approach and emotional response to the issue. Another approach might be to ask about the differences between those who are willing to talk about the topic and those who are not. If the interviewer broadens the reference group (using "some people" or "other people" rather than "you"), the interviewee is given some emotional and personal distance from the topic and may be much more comfortable talking around his or her own experience.

As we saw in Chapter 6, both survey and qualitative interview researchers may seek to "match" respondents on such characteristics as gender and race in order to (they hope) maximize rapport. This matching theory of rapport has not always been the dominant one. In many of the early Chicago School texts, the gender of the interviewer was often left unspecified; given the focus on interviewer "objectivity," it presumably did not matter who did the interviewing. But when gender was mentioned it was the male interviewer who was preferred, because of his greater presumed empathy, friendliness, and authority (Warren and Hackney 2000). This preference lasted at least until Kinsey's studies in the 1940s and 1950s; as O'Connell Davidson and Layder note, "Kinsey's assumption that women would tell the truth about their sexual lives to male interviewers now appears as dated" (1994, 130). By the 1970s and 1980s, women interviewers were presumed to be the empathic "sociability specialists" who could extract the truth from women and men informants (Warren and Hackney 2000).

Social class, as well as gender, may affect the social situation of the interview as it is read through the bodies of the participants (demeanor, accent, dress, and so on). The social class of the interviewer as well as the respondent has been at issue during the decades of twentieth-century interviewing. Kinsey, for example, refused to

> employ women, Black people, or people with Jewish names. . . . because he believed that "only WASPs [White Anglo Saxon Protestants] . . . could interview everybody." (O'Connell Davidson and Layder 1994, 130)

Although the Kinsey research team considered matching interviewers with respondents on such features as class, occupation, and race, they concluded that "The qualities of the interviewer, not his sex, race, or personal history, were the important variables" (O'Connell Davison and Layder 1994, 130). Today researchers would probably attend both to the "matching" of social statuses and the personal "qualities" of potential interviewers before hiring them.

Respondents of lower social status and education may be reluctant to talk with someone they perceive as an authority figure—or they may feel obliged to talk with the authority figure but give monosyllabic answers. Respondents of higher social status and occupation may be reluctant to talk with an interviewer not because they have nothing to say but because they do not have enough time to say it in, such as the physicians interviewed by Grace DeSantis (1980). People who are just busy may not be able to find the time to be interviewed, or if they are interviewed, hurry to get the interview over. In the Bay Area study, some of the women did not want to be interviewed in the post-hospital phase of the study because they did not want to be reminded of the stigma of ex-patienthood, while others were willing but were busy with housework and childcare (Warren 1987).

The issue of "matching" interviewers to respondents based on social characteristics raises similar issues to those of incorporation of the fieldworker we discussed in Chapter 4. Much as the stranger fieldworker faces different challenges to incorporation than the member fieldworker, interviewers that are matched confront issues that differ from those an unmatched interviewer will meet. Furthermore, matching is not a fixed or static position (Naples 1996); it is fluid and permeable as individuals become acquainted with each other and find some commonalities and differences. In interviews about children, parenthood of both parties may be more important than similarity with regard to race or age. De Andrade (2000) found that even as a member of the ethnic community she sought to interview, respondents continually questioned her background and connections as her status was evaluated and negotiated during her fieldwork. A related and important issue is the ability to grasp the meaning of whatever is being said by the respondent. Zinn (1979, 159) was an early proponent of the notion that "minority scholars" could "ask questions and gather information that others could not." However, DeVault (1995) warns that interview talk can reveal racial-ethnic dynamics that are not necessarily explicit but can be understood, even by an unmatched interviewer of a different race, through careful and active attention.

Although the interviewer may have decided on the format of the interview, actual interviews may involve a range of people other than those originally planned for. This is especially true of situations in which the interview takes place in a household or at a place of work. Children needing their mother's attention frequently interrupted the Bay Area ex-patient interviews. Interviewers may or may not regard such interruptions negatively; although they break the flow of narrative, they also provide opportunities to observe the life-world of the interviewee. In her informal interviews with Mexican immigrants, Pierrette Hondagneu-Sotelo says that she "observed daily family interactions and conflicts, participating in meal and meal preparation, viewing television and videos, and talking with informants" (1994, xxi). She was particularly interested in noting the differences between interview accounts of the division of household labor and what actually occurred (including her own "research bargain," as a woman, of helping with food preparation). Heying Zhan's (2000) interviews with individual family members in rural China were regularly interrupted by other members of the family as well as neighbors who would come to join in the conversations. Since Zhan's interest was in intimate family caregiving duties and expectations, the public nature of the interview situation, she found, compromised her responses considerably. Given the cultural norms of the villages, she was unable to hold any private interviews.

There is a range of interview social situations and interactions as wide as that of everyday life. At one end of the continuum is the ideal interview described by Rubin and Rubin (1995); at the other, the interview in which only monosyllabic responses are obtained. The monosyllabic-response interview is probably worse from the interviewer's point of view than a refusal, since she has invested considerable time (and perhaps money) in the process without a usable narrative. Failure to obtain a "good" (narratively rich) interview may reflect defects in the training, preparation, or approach of interviewers, but it may also (or instead) reflect the social situation of the respondent at the time of the interview.

The end of the interview occurs at some point after the asking of the last question or probe by the interviewer, perhaps question 10 in Box 6.1 (Chapter 6): "Is there anything else you would like to add?" From such questions the interview tends to wind down, with shorter answers and longer pauses leading to comments from either the respondent or the interviewer such as, "Well, that is probably about it for now." Sometimes respondents are eager, and sometimes reluctant, to end the interview; in fact, it is not necessarily easy to determine when an interview is over and ordinary leave-taking rituals begin. In practice, interviewers often see the end of the interview as the turning-off of the tape recorder; a point at which another phase sometimes begins, that of after the interview.

## After the Interview

From the interviewer's point of view, once all questions are asked and the audiotape is turned off, the event is complete and it is time for leave-taking rituals. Some interviewers, however, do recommend a period of what Kvale calls "debriefing" after the interview:

> At the end of the interview there may be some tension or anxiety, because the subject has been open about often personal and emotional experiences and may be wondering about the interview's purpose and how it will be used. There may perhaps also be feelings of emptiness; the subject has given much information about his or her life and may not have received anything in return. (Kvale 1996, 128)

From the point of view of the respondents, the end of the interview may be a welcome relief, or something to prolong if possible, and anything in between. Respondents vary from extremely busy people who have squeezed in a half hour to respond hurriedly to questions to elderly or isolated people who are lonely, desire company, and do not want the interviewer to leave (of course these responses may also be situational, with the same people busy at some times and not at others). In research Warren did with some colleagues and graduate students on the period after the interview, we found that respondents' behavior varied depending on their life circumstances, once the tape recorder was turned off (Warren et al. 2003). Some, at that point, seemed willing to say things they had not said on tape; for example, when Harkness (2003) videotaped pawnbrokers they expressed sympathy for their customers. Once the videotape was turned off, they expressed stigmatizing views of those same customers. Comments such as these, though not recorded, should be detailed in your fieldnote descriptions.

Other respondents sought to continue the conversation with the interviewer once the recorder was turned off rather than proceeding to leave-taking rituals. If you are receiving pertinent information and want to continue, you should ask if it is okay to turn the recorder back on. In other cases, respondents just want to engage the interviewer in more balanced conversation. This was true in many of Weibold-Lippisch's interviews with the caregivers of recently deceased elders, who wanted to talk about their experiences more, get advice and referrals, or ask about the experiences of others in the same situation (Warren 2001). The point is for you, as an interviewer, to be sensitive to the cues given by the respondent as you are packing up to leave, and perhaps be willing to give a little more of your time if debriefing seems needed. Diane Vaughan took time after her interviews to talk with the respondents about the interview itself, in order to "help them make the transition from the interview, with its focus on the past, into their present life" (1990, 200). Eventually, however, the interview *does* have to come to an end.

After the respondent has gone, you should spend some time writing up notes about the context and conduct of the interview, either where you are (in a cafe, say), or as soon as possible after you return to your home or to campus. You should write down everything you can remember about the context of the interview: where it took place, how the respondent was dressed, looked, and behaved before, during, and after the interview, any body language that would not be captured on tape, and your interpretation [set off in brackets like these] of the respondent's appearance, demeanor, and body language. If you interviewed the respondent in his or her office, home, or other space (and it may be safe to interview respondents at home under some circumstances, say, if the respondent is a relative or friend), describe these places in some detail. As we saw in the ROTC building example (see Chapter 5), physical context can say a lot about social life.

## Transcribing the Interview

The issue of transcription—how to get the interview speech event into the form of a written text—has been the subject of discussion since the Chicago School researchers used the method on a large scale. In the days before audiotape recording of interviews, the interviewer was advised to jot down notes during the interview to use as memory prompts later, and to write out the interview from memory as soon as possible, before it has "gone cold" (Palmer 1928, 177). This is essentially the same advice that is delivered today with regard to fieldnotes (see Chapter 5). Interviewers were advised to try to make their written transcriptions reflective, so far as memory permitted, of the respondent's own words:

> If the interview is reported in the first person, in the actual phrases and language used by the informant it will furnish better data. . . . When the research worker makes the report in his own terms, when he translates the expressions of the informant into his own language or summarizes them in trite generalizations or common concepts, he . . . has so transformed the original narrative that it has lost its exactness. (Palmer 1928, 176)

The use of audiotape equipment in interview research came into use during the 1950s and 1960s; indeed, the interviewers received machines halfway through the Bay Area project (Warren 1987). Today, audiotaping is seen as a necessity for the transcription of interviews, whether the research is by teams or individuals. In large-scale funded studies, transcription may be done for you; your coded audio- or video-tape is whisked away from you to a transcriber who then returns a textual copy to you and/or to your supervisor. But most students, both undergraduate and graduate, will have to transcribe their interviews themselves. And this is a good thing to do: if you did the interview, you are able to visualize the physical setting, remember what the respondent said if parts of the tape are unclear, and above all, relearn by relistening to what the respondent said.

Some academic departments have tape players with foot-pedal devices (misleadingly called transcription machines) available to you that can be used in conjunction with a computer to help you with transcription by not requiring you to move your hands from keyboard to audio device. This will help. But even with this help, transcribing interviews is an extremely time-consuming and labor-intensive task—which is why it is often done so unsatisfactorily by hired hands (who also do not have access to memories of the interview). It may take four to six hours to transcribe a one-hour interview, or even more. It is important to transcribe everything that is said during the interviews, including your own questions and probes, because, as Mishler (1986) notes, an interview is a speech event as well as a special type of social interaction—thus, the contextual entirety of the dialog needs to be included. It is also important to transcribe everything the respondent says, including things that do not seem important or relevant to the topic, because what seems irrelevant at one stage of interviewing might seem much more relevant at a later time. And it is also important to preserve the narratives—the voices—of your respondents.

Although these are the general principles of transcribing, it is well known that even the most diligent and motivated of transcribers will leave things out. For example, you are interviewing an adolescent about his standing in his peer group. At one point he "digresses" to a lengthy description of a Simpsons program that probably has some connection in his mind to what you have just asked him about what the peer group is wearing this semester, but has no relevance in yours. The best thing to do is to transcribe the entire episode—you may, on rereading, see the connections that the adolescent was making—but at least put in parentheses what was going on ([“here Respondent M3 talked for 15 minutes about a Simpsons episode”]) rather than just simply skipping over the strip of talk ([. . . .]).

There is some hope among researchers that the tedious typing process of transcription may someday be a thing of the past. The innovation of digital recorders that with expanded memory cards can now record hours of dialogue coupled with advancing technology in speech-to-text software may lead to a decline in hours spent at the keyboard. Karner has had one student who has experimented quite successfully with this approach. Halbert (2003) used a digital recorder to conduct impromptu interviews with individuals attending informal music events. He spoke with a number of different individuals, with a variety of speech particularities, was able to input the digital recording (through a USB port) to his computer and run a speech-to-text program on it. This program then generated a lengthy textual document, which Halbert read through while listening to the recording. Halbert estimates that the software is about 85 percent accurate, misinterpreting punctuation, capitalization, slang, speech idiosyncrasies, and homonyms most commonly used. While proofreading, he edited the materials to denote speaker (interviewer or respondent), enter punctuation, and assure accuracy. It took him an average of less than two hours to fully transcribe and format a one-hour interview, and that, Halbert claims, included the time it takes to download the audio into the computer!

Whether you have gone digital or are still using a foot-pedal transcription machine, the accuracy of the final transcript is essential. Although the transcription of interviews has been undertaken by generations of researchers and is a vital step in qualitative studies using interviews, "it does not yet appear to be standard practice for qualitative researchers to consider transcription quality prior to their undertaking the analysis of textual data" (Poland 2002, 630). Although transcription is supposed to generate a verbatim record of what has been said (transcriptions often cannot communicate how it has been said), even the most careful researchers generating their own transcriptions have identified lapses in their capturing of "the original language and flow of the discussion" (Poland 2002, 632). Poland points out that seemingly minor details, such as the placement of a period or comma, can change the meaning of utterances. He comments,

> "I hate it, you know. I do" carries a different meaning from "I hate it. You know I do." Although the original meaning and intent *may* be clear from the intonation and pacing of speech in the audiotape, it may be much less so in the transcript. (2002, 632; italics added)

Other problems in verbatim transcription include turning run-on talk into sentences, identifying occurrences of respondents' quoting other people, and the mistaking of words for other similar words. Poland (2002, 632) gives examples from his own transcriptions in which the word "consultation" was substituted for "confrontation," and "an evaluation model" was translated as "and violation of the model." Transcribers typically check for errors and omissions in their work by going backward and forward on the tape; this process can itself generate omissions by not going backward or forward far enough and thus missing parts. Poland's example reads:

> in one case "I lost a very close friend to cancer" should have read "I lost a very close friend to lung cancer." The omission of the word "lung" was significant given the focus of the study on smoking cessation. (2002, 632)

Transcription by hired hands can generate even more problems in the text than transcription by researchers concerned with accuracy, either because of carelessness or its opposite. Poland describes a case in which a transcriber "(a legal secretary) took it upon herself to tidy up the discussion so it would *read* better, just as she would have been expected to do with dictated correspondence at work" (2002, 633; italics in the original). As Poland (2002) notes, verbal interactions are quite different than written statements, and can look quite messy when they appear on the printed page.

There is some debate in the literature over the ethics of tidying up respondents' speech in transcription. Some researchers worry that lower-class or minority respondents may be made to sound inarticulate or linguistically incompetent if their words, pauses, grammar, and so on are transcribed verbatim. If protection of human subjects requirements have been adhered to, the respondents would not be stigmatized as individuals for their language, but as members of a particular class or ethnic group. Other researchers worry that if vernacular, grammatical errors, and other features of speech are "tidied up" in the transcription, then some of the original meaning of the talk will be lost. Poland suggests a compromise: not changing talk to protect respondents at the point of the transcription but doing so at the point of publication, taking "care that what is removed does not appreciably alter the meaning of what was said" (2002, 634).

What should not be lost in the interview transcript are the specific questions asked. In quantitative survey research questions are supposed to be asked in the same way to all respondents, although this tends to be impossible in practice (Suchman and Jordan 1990). Although in qualitative research you start out with a list of questions approved by your IRB, there is no epistemological barrier to changing the order or format of questions, and this might be done in any given interview. And probes and supplementary questions will be different for different respondents. Thus, although it might be tempting to transcribe only the respondent's answers, the interview is a particular type of speech event involving questions and answers, and the questions are as important as the answers—they are what elicit the narratives.

After the first interview and the first transcription, review what has gone on in order to make any necessary changes for your next interview and transcription. Was the café you met in too noisy? Change the locale. Did it take six hours to transcribe a half-hour interview? Try to find one of those foot-pedal machines or consider going digital. Continue this review process with each subsequent interview. If two respondents raise their eyebrows and pause at question number 3, look at this question again to see what might be puzzling or confusing about it, and perhaps try asking it another way. At the end of this process you will have a body of interviews, transcribed and ready for analysis, that represent an accumulation of knowledge not just about the topic but about the process too. You are ready to analyze your data; but before you do so, it is important to consider the epistemology of the interview in order to understand what kind of data it generates.

## Epistemology of the Interview

In the literature on the epistemology of the interview from the 1970s to the 2000s, there has been an ongoing debate over the kind of knowledge generated by interviews: can interview data be used for interpreting social life that occurs outside of it? There is a continuum of perspectives on what kind of knowledge can be legitimately generated from qualitative interviews, beginning with the "camera" theory of knowledge espoused by positivists (see Chapter 1). This view is in some ways echoed in our discussion of rapport, since rapport has been framed as necessary to the elicitation not only of answers but also of truthful answers from respondents. Whenever methodological discussions turn to the idea of truth (truth about behavior, true opinions, etc.), the camera theory of knowledge is in operation.

The other end of the continuum is the radical opposite of this camera theory of knowledge generating truth. This radical opposite is the belief that since the interview is a form of social interaction, it can generate knowledge only about the interview, not about anything beyond it, and certainly not truth. A radical interpretation of Arendell's (1997) interviews about divorce with divorced men would, for example, see it as saying nothing about the men's divorces, but everything about the interaction between Arendell and the men. Obviously most qualitative interviewers do not share this extreme view; otherwise they would not be doing interviews in the first place.

In the middle of this continuum—where we and many other qualitative researchers feel most comfortable—is the position that interviews can tell us about the social interactions of the interview, but they can also provide accounts of circumstances outside of it. In Holstein and Gubrium's terms, the interviewee is not merely a "vessel of answers" from which truth can be ladled by the interviewer. They note:

> Meaning is not merely elicited by apt questioning nor simply transported through respondent replies; it is actively and communicatively assembled in the interview encounter. Respondents are not so much repositories of knowledge—treasuries of information awaiting excavation—as they are constructors of knowledge in collaboration with interviewers. (Holstein and Gubrium 1995, 4)

This notion of collaboratively constructed knowledge positions the interview as a social interaction, a speech event, and also (still) about a particular topic of interest to the interviewer (and ideally to the respondent also).

As we mentioned in Chapter 1, although ethnographies and interviews are both qualitative research methods that seek to understand the meanings of social life to respondents, they have epistemological differences. Ethnographic research is based in observation of interaction in what has been called the ethnographic present. Interview research can be focused on the present, past, or future of the respondent, but it cannot be focused on behavior (see Box 7.3). The data gathered by interview methods are accounts of behavior, biography, TV watching, or whatever the interviewer is interested in; they are not reflections of behavior. Although some behaviors—notably sexual behaviors (O'Connell Davidson and Layder 1994)—have been made the subject of interviewing, this is only because observation of such behaviors is private and virtually precluded, not because of a belief that accounts of conduct are preferable to observation of it. For example, see a discussion of the confusion of terms, accounts, and behaviors (Warren 2002) with one of the interviews of one woman in the Bay Area study that we include in Box 7.3.

Proceed with caution, always, when claiming or encountering the claim that accounts of behavior reflect actual behavior, especially behavior involving cultural taboos, stigma, lawbreaking, or moral outrage. Such behavior may be "forgotten" or may be lied about to the interviewer. Although the Kinsey researchers were very concerned to ferret out negative lies—denying sex behaviors—they were unconcerned about the possibility of positive lies—claiming sex behaviors that they had not engaged in (O'Connell Davison and Layder 1994). Both negative and positive lies about behavior are more than possible in interview research.

---

**Box 7.3**

## Accounts of Behavior in Interviews

As this example demonstrates, if Messinger and Warren had taken the interviewees' account at face value, they would have misinterpreted both the meaning of the term "homosexual" for her as well as what kinds of behaviors were being referenced. Warren (2002, 98) writes,

> In the Bay Area Study, sociologist and interviewer Sheldon Messinger talked approximately twenty-five times between November 1957 and July 1958 with "Kate White" (Messinger and Warren 1984). Among the "delusions" that precipitated Kate White's diagnosis and hospitalization was the idea that she was "homosexual," and her husband was homosexual too. In the commonsense meanings of the 1950s (and 2000s for that matter), homosexuality referenced same-gender erotic preferences, attraction or behavior. But, taking the interviews with Kate White as her story, it became clear that what she was talking about was not desire or eroticism but social role: she wanted to work outside the home, and men did that, so perhaps she was homosexual. During her hospitalization, her husband had enjoyed keeping house and taking care of the children, a woman's place, so perhaps he was also homosexual. For Kate White, homosexuality referenced gender roles, not sexual desire (in fact she was having an affair with a man at the time).

---

The epistemology of the interview is important to the interviewer because one's position on this continuum of interaction determines what one feels justified in doing with the data. A survey researcher who defines respondents as vessels of answers need not pay attention to the social circumstances under which these answers were ladled out, as long as they *were* ladled. In practice, of course, survey researchers are not so naïve about the process of interviewing (Suchman and Jordan 1990). A researcher who holds the radically opposite point of view, that the interview as a social interaction cannot reflect any realities outside the interview, will either not do interviews or analyze them only as interviews.

The middle-ground position is that interview-grounded knowledge can be used as data about social life, but with two caveats. First, the knowledge gained from the interview is the outcome of a situated encounter between embodied interviewer and respondent and does not consist of the ladling of answers out of a respondent by an interviewer. Second, the knowledge gained is in the form of accounts of social life, not of observed behaviors or truths. If you want to find out what people do, it is necessary to observe. If you want to find out what people *say* about what they do, what they *say* they believe or value, what they *say* their opinions are, then the interview method is ideal. Those of us who take the middle ground are willing to use interview transcripts as accounts of the other, subject to these caveats, and analyze them as such.

Now that you have completed your interviews and understand them as emergent speech acts, you are ready to contemplate the analytic promise of your data, which we will discuss in Chapter 9. First we will turn our attention to the additional forms of data relevant to qualitative researchers that we will address. In Chapter 8, we will look at visual and narrative data that can be found in magazines, historical documents, photographs, and on the Internet.

## Suggestions for Further Reading

Gubrium, Jaber, and James Holstein. 2003. *Inside Interviewing: New Lens, New Concerns*. Thousand Oaks, CA: Sage Publications.

Holstein, James A., and Jaber F. Gubrium. 1995. *The Active Interview*. Thousand Oaks, CA: Sage Publications.

———. 2003. *Postmodern Interviewing*. Thousand Oaks, CA: Sage Publications.

Mishler, Elliott G. 1986. *Research Interviewing: Context and Narrative*. Cambridge, MA: Harvard University Press.

Spradley, James. 1979. *The Ethnographic Interview*. International Thomson Publishing. ❖

# Chapter Eight

# The Textual and the Visual as Qualitative Data

*Documents, Images, and the Internet*

In addition to observed social worlds and the talk of interviews, sociologists may seek data in the media: in the printed word and in visual images, in magazines and newspapers, videos and film, and historical documents, and on the Internet (including Web sites and chat rooms). There are several ways in which sociologists study media, including quantitative (and sometimes qualitative) studies of media consumption by, and the impact of media on, audiences (Becker 2002), ethnographies of how media are constructed, and qualitative analyses of the cultural meanings of media representations. Our focus in this chapter will be on using media as data for studying culture, and on the creation of media—as in photo-elicitation—to explore meaning and experience.

The qualitative study of media representations may be interdisciplinary (including the humanities as well as the social sciences) and is sometimes referred to as cultural studies or cultural analysis. Within sociology, the term *culture* refers to the material and nonmaterial social artifacts and representations that surround us, from TVs and computers to the structure of language and the proscriptions and prescriptions of gender roles. Qualitative researchers who focus on such social artifacts are interested in analyzing them in roughly the same way as other qualitative sociologists observe social groups or interview respondents.

Cross-cultural and trans-local comparisons can also be made by using documents, something that can be useful in an increasingly global environment. Local newspapers from the midwestern, eastern, and western states can be compared for the political perspectives they espouse. American magazines can be compared with Japanese for what they say about the place of ethnic features in contemporary fashion, that is, providing you know Japanese! Or they can be analyzed visually if you do not know the language. One of the problems in doing cross-cultural research is addressing the issue of language. But at your stage of research, as an undergraduate, you will be able to find mountains of material to use for cultural analysis in the language of your choice.

Documents of many kinds can be used for qualitative research, including public documents published by local and national government bodies. Other documents useful for sociological research are magazines and newspapers, which can be analyzed for both their editorial content and their advertising. Magazines and newspapers can generally be found easily on the shelves (and in the microfilms, for earlier years) of public libraries. Some (such as the *New York Times*) can be found in all or in part on the Internet. Although many other kinds of documents can be studied by qualitative researchers, everything from minutes of business meetings to legal statutes, we will focus mainly in this chapter on magazine advertising.

## Magazine Advertisements as Data Sources

The use of advertisements as data sources has a fairly long history in qualitative sociology. Erving Goffman, whose observational studies of everyday life and of total institutions have been read and used by generations of researchers, also wrote one of the first cultural analyses in qualitative sociology, *Gender Advertisements* (1979). In this work, instead of studying the presentation of self in everyday life, or interactions between mental hospital staff and patients, Goffman studied the ways in which women were represented in magazine advertisements during the 1970s. This tradition has been continued by many qualitative sociologists and other social scientists and historians, including Susan Bordo in her books *Unbearable Weight* (2003) and *The Male Body* (1999).

The study of magazines, both articles and advertising, is interesting and useful for cultural analysis because what is depicted in these sources are often the cultural ideals to which the media and the marketplace would like us all to aspire. Magazines cater to virtually every category of person and interest, from the large-circulation magazines for women or adolescent girls to small-circulation magazines directed at particular interests, leisure pursuits, sports, or sexual orientations. And countercultural "zines" direct their adherents' attention to the culture by publicizing transgressions of it.

Why are these marketing and media-linked representations of culture important to qualitative researchers? First, they are an easy-to-access source of data in a research era in which regulations on human subjects can hamper face-to-face forms of qualitative research. Second, they are not just easy to access; they are a rich source of data on idealized cultural representations on, for example, the type of body and appearances marketed to, and thus often sought by, teenage girls or boys, or adult women or men. Although it is not possible to prove the impact of these representations *on* culture, we can study them as representations *of* culture.

## Studying Gender and Culture

Qualitative sociologists are increasingly interested in the study of various aspects of culture, including gender. Many studies of magazines and advertising have followed Goffman's lead and analyzed the representation of gender in magazines aimed at adolescent or adult women. In *Unbearable Weight* (2003), Bordo looks at the content of magazine and other print advertising, both in the late twentieth century and in earlier decades. She notes, as have many other feminist scholars, that the feminine ideal body, although somewhat variable over time, is a site of intense social control. This control is sometimes direct, for example, as in enforced sterilization, but it is often indirect, operating through media representations. As Joan Brumberg also shows in her book *The Body Project* (1997), since the 1920s the ideal body for women has been slender. The details vary: Representations of the 1920s flapper show an elongated neck, overlarge head, and flat chest; the 1950s girl has breasts that are pointed and rigid, her slim waist encircled by a tight belt, her hips hidden under a flaring skirt. But the requirement for slenderness remains the same.

As Bordo (1999, 2003), Brumberg (1997), and other scholars of the culture of gender have shown, the means proposed for attaining the ideal woman's body include dieting (since the discovery and publication of the measured calorie in the early twentieth century), exercise, pharmaceuticals (diet pills and aids), and increasingly, plastic surgery. One way to attain the modern ideal figure—slim, muscular, and big breasted—is to have breast enlargement surgery. And the youthfulness as well as the slenderness of the magazine-advertisement ideal has to be maintained, again through diet, exercise, pharmaceuticals, and cosmetic surgery.

Magazines aimed at teenage girls—such as the long-lived *Seventeen*—have been a major source of data for a decade of cultural studies. The advertisements and articles in these texts illuminate the relationship between gender and culture through the representation of ideal and non-ideal bodies. In addition, because these and other magazines are designed to sell products—the magazines themselves, and the products advertised in them—they further illuminate the relationship between culture and the economy. Brumberg describes the treatment of menstruation (how to handle it in relation to products, how it is interpreted culturally) as an example:

> In a 1989 issue of *Sassy,* a lively and sometimes irreverent magazine for adolescents, the editors (all women in their twenties) shared personal stories about menarche and menstruation. As if they were sitting in a private bedroom sipping diet sodas, they swapped "menstrual nightmares" about what it was like to leave a puddle of blood on a chair, or to struggle to find the right opening for a tampon. These stories of embarrassing personal moments were honest and funny, but they all focused on issues of personal hygiene because that is the language we use in America for talking about such things. (1997, 52)

While *Seventeen, Sassy,* and other teen magazines are aimed at adolescent girls in both their articles and advertising, advertising aimed at boys has also been of interest to cultural analysts. Some scholars turned their attention during the late 1990s to advertising and other representations of men's bodies. Women in advertisements often appear in relation to men and the private sector—as domestic functionaries, doing cooking or laundry; as goddesses, preparing the face and body for cosmetic perfection; or as companions. Men in advertisements, by contrast, appear in scenes: at the helm of a boat, in the midst of a corporate deal, busy and successful in the public realm. These are generalizations, of course, and exceptions can readily be found: advertisements that show older people wearing trendy GAP clothes, a woman in a business meeting, or (very rarely) a man doing the laundry. But pick up any magazine at, say, your doctor's office and flip through it; we think you will find that the generalizations made by Bordo, Brumberg, and others reflect the majority of contemporary advertisements in mainstream publications for adult women as well as adolescent girls, from *Good Housekeeping* to *Cosmopolitan.*

In addition to magazines aimed at particular genders, age-groups, and ethnicities, magazines cater to various interests from stamp collecting to tennis to sports. Newspapers, as well as magazines, are useful sources of still other topics, for example, the way in which crime stories unfold in the media. We are all familiar with the journalistic search for "background" when a particularly heinous murder has been committed. We can all trace the ways in which journalists look for clues in the murderer's past for his present conduct: "John Smith's eighth-grade teacher said that he was always a loner and kept to himself." In Barry Glassner's recent *The Culture of Fear: Why Americans Are Afraid of the Wrong Things* (2000), he traces the presentation of crime through the lens of the media. His cultural analysis juxtaposes other forms of evidence (crime statistics, neighborhood studies) to demonstrate how the media frames and presents events in fear-engendering ways. Glassner, countering the depiction of "road rage" presented by

ABC's newsmagazine *20/20* as all around the average person "everywhere you drive, waiting to explode," states,

> Big percentages do not necessarily have big numbers behind them. The dramatic "up more than 50%" statistic in the AAA study derived from the difference between two relatively modest figures: the number of traffic incidents that involved major violence in 1990 (1,129) compared to 1996 (1,800). An increase of 671 incidents in fifty states over seven years is hardly "a growing epidemic" (*USA Today*'s description of road rage). Nor does it warrant the thousands of stories about road rage that appeared in print and on radio and television—coverage that helped produce the 671 figure in the first place. The AAA derived their estimates from newspaper, police, and insurance reports, all of which are influenced by hype. The more talk there is about road rage, the more likely are newspaper reporters, police officers, and insurance agents to classify as examples of it incidents that they would have ignored altogether or catalogued differently in the past. (Glassner 2000, 5)

Magazines (and newspapers) are also useful for exploring change over time, something that the researcher may not be able to do with ethnographic or interview research, particularly over longer time spans. In her analysis of how courtship and dating rituals have changed, Bailey (1989) traced advice about courtship and dating in magazine articles and advertisements. She also examined college handbooks, textbooks, etiquette books, and "advice columns" in newspapers and magazines. From these sources she was able to map the shift from the family-monitored courtship of the late 1800s to industrialized, urban dating patterns of the mid-twentieth century.

> In the calling system, woman took the initiative. Etiquette books and columns were adamant on that point: it was the "girl's privilege" to ask a young man to call. Furthermore, it was highly improper for the man to take the initiative. In 1909 a young man wrote to the *Ladies' Home Journal* adviser asking, "May I call upon a young woman whom I greatly admire, although she had not given me the permission? Would she be flattered by my eagerness, even to the setting aside of conventions, or would she think me impertinent?" Mrs. Kingsland replied: "I think that you would risk her just displeasure and frustrate your object of finding favor with her." (Bailey 1989, 20)

Using the discussions of the era provides examples of the contemporary norms as well as any debates about them. Many magazines, like *Seventeen* for example, have had seven decades within which to compare trends and differences, as well as similarities, in the representations of gender and age: appearance, clothing, sexuality, etiquette, occupational and educational concerns, dating, courtship, and cigarette smoking. All of these can be studied in the 1940s as well as the 1990s. But how do we best find them? The answer is related to which magazines we sample from, and then which issues of the magazine we use for data sources.

## Sampling From Magazines

Although random sampling is seldom used in qualitative sociology (because the purpose is not statistical generalization to larger populations, but rather, the identification of themes or patterns), it is important to be thoughtful and systematic in your choice of data sources. If you just grab whatever magazines are available on the table of your physician's office, your selection of advertisements or editorials to study will reflect an unknown variety of audiences to which these magazines are aimed, from young women to Christian readers to car enthusiasts. Your analysis—what you can do with such data—will suffer greatly without an understanding of the purpose and context it was created within. Do some research to determine what ranges of magazines are likely to have advertisements that reflect your interest.

Once you have identified the range of magazines, the next question is what specific magazine or magazines should you study? Match your magazine choice to the topic you are interested in: *Seventeen* if you are interested in young women and change over decades; perhaps *Sassy* if you are only interested in the past 15 years. Then, which issues of the magazine? If you are interested in comparing the decades from the 1970s through the 1990s, then you might consider looking at all copies of monthly magazines from 1970 to 1999. If your time frame is longer, you might want to sample fewer issues, say every other month, or four per year. The point is to balance a fair amount of coverage, systematically selected, with a reasonable workload.

Comparisons are often fruitful and quite interesting, so you could choose to compare magazines aimed at young females with those targeted to young males—if you can find any aimed at young males. Most people could probably name *Seventeen* and perhaps a couple of other girls' publications, but not anything for young men—so that your first cultural discovery is that most magazines for adolescents are for females. Furthermore, they are for females in a male world; the advertisements in them, and the content, tend to focus on appearance, hair, body, makeup, and other aspects of cosmetic feminine allure. But you could probably compare *GQ* with *Cosmopolitan* for a cultural exploration of advertisements that appeal to both male and female readers.

Your final choice is which advertisements to analyze from the magazine issues you have selected. At this point, use theoretic sampling to identify those advertisements that most exemplify the themes you are looking for. In this type of sampling, the opposite of random sampling, you look for texts or images that epitomize the broad themes you have identified. If, for example, you want to make the point that advertisements in men's magazines generally show the men alone, in some leisure, adventure, or business setting, or with a woman, but rarely in male pairs, find advertisements that exemplify each of these images, but also be sure that, if you do find an unusual advertisement, you include it for contrast. If you want to make quantitative points, you are going to have to count all the advertisements in the issue (e.g., if you want to find out what percentage of household labor advertisements feature women versus men, or what percentage of advertisements featuring males are set in adventure contexts). You are also going to have to tell the reader, methodologically, how you decided to distinguish a household labor advertisement from one that is not, or an adventure context advertisement from one that is not.

To illustrate this point further, think about the claim that sex sells. Since the 1950s at least, when cars were advertised with young women in the picture, both laypersons and scholars have made claims concerning the sexuality of the advertisements (e.g., see Kilbourne 2000). If you want to study the sexuality of advertisements, you are going to have to decide what constitutes sexuality: what, in the images you see in the advertisements, can be regarded as sexy or sexual. Think about the possible elements of sexiness: gender and age—a youthful, slim, attractive appearance; body—how much is revealed or concealed, and how; pose—how provocative, but what constitutes provocative? Eyes—can eyes be sexy, and if so how—by the outlining of makeup? by the narrowing of lids? What, if any, are the borderlines between sexual and sensual, and does it matter? Is long hair sexy? On men? Nowadays one might also be able to ask, is there actual sexual behavior apparently going on in the advertisement? How far are you going to take your definition of sexual? In the early 1990s, cultural analysts accused the makers of Camel cigarettes of employing sexual imagery in their advertisements. The prominent image associated with the brand was Joe Camel, whose features they said resembled a penis and a scrotum. The company was blamed for targeting young consumers via this sexualized imagery.

Finally, if you are doing comparisons over time, you will note that the definition and extent of sexiness as displayed in advertisements changes over time. One body part that was extremely important in Victorian times, for example, was the arm. The outline of women's legs was covered to the ankle with long skirts, but the arm, although covered by long sleeves, was outlined by clothing, and the outline could be seen! As a consequence, you will see a great deal of attention paid to sleeves and cuffs in fashion magazine advertisements of the 1890s, something you would probably not see for the 1980s. And we no longer think that if we do not cover the legs of pianos and other furniture, men will get so sexually aroused that they might attack the women present or perhaps even the furniture itself!

## Historical Documents: Voices From the Past

This discussion now brings us to primary historical documents. As with magazines, a great deal of historical material can be culturally analyzed and used for comparisons over time and across space between different societies or nations. Historical documents can most generally be found in college or university libraries, sometimes in special floors or buildings set aside for rare documents or collections of books and documents, or archives. A research librarian at one of the branches of your college or university library is the best source of information on easily available historical documents. Primary historical documents can also be found on the Internet.

What makes a document historical? If you are going to do historical research as part of your training in qualitative sociology, your instructor will probably tell you where the dividing line is between what is and is not historical. Warren, for classroom purposes, chose 1970 as her dividing line, so that her students must find documents earlier than that date for their papers. Karner, on the other hand, takes a more project-specific approach to designating what is historical. This sounds somewhat arbitrary, and in some ways it is. From a common-sense perspective, everything prior to this moment is past, and thus in a way historical—and yet we regard the last minute or two, or last week, as the present. We would all agree that the 1400s represent the historical—but how about the 1980s? Again, your instructor will provide guidance in time boundaries.

What makes a historical document primary? Although the matter is not always so clear-cut, in general, a primary document is one generated during the time period of interest. For example, if you want to study seventeenth-century Puritan sermons, your primary documents are copies of the original sermons, not books or articles written about the sermons in later years. Later books about sermons (or anything else historical) are referred to as secondary sources. Qualitative sociologists who do historical research use primary sources as data, and secondary sources for background information.

The farther back in time you propose for your study, the more difficult it generally is to find primary documents. So, in practice, we both encourage our students to do research with documents from the mid-nineteenth to early twentieth centuries. This is a good period for analysis because there is a wealth of materials from this time period, and yet it is far enough in the past that cultural differences, as well as similarities, can be seen. For example, in Brumberg's study of body projects, she traces the cultural history of causal theories of, and treatments for, acne. Today considered a result of hormonal activity, acne was thought by many nineteenth-century physicians to be a consequence of "'sexual derangement' such as masturbation or promiscuity . . . or . . . impure or lascivious thoughts" (Brumberg 1997, 64).

Although Brumberg used female adolescents' diaries as well as physicians' accounts as sources of data on the meaning of acne, she had access to far more medical journals and texts than diaries. Using historical documents as a source of data means that we tend to hear certain kinds of voices rather than other kinds. The further back we go in the past, the smaller the proportion of people who could write; thus we expect to find documents from those kinds of people who could write—generally upper- rather than lower-class people, educated rather than not, in professions that emphasized writing, and men rather than women. Also, only certain kinds of documents have been preserved through time; others have either been thrown away, become lost, been burned accidentally or purposely, or in other ways been rendered unavailable. Upper-middle-class men as well as women in ancient Rome were literate, because soldiers wrote to their wives and the wives wrote back. But only the soldiers' letters were preserved, because in the culture of the times what was important was the public world of men, the military battles that carved out empires—not the domestic world of the wives who wrote back.

In the example of acne treatment from Brumberg, some of the voices heard from the nineteenth century were those of physicians, then known as "dermatovenereologists" because of the presumed association between acne and sexual thoughts and behavior (Brumberg 1997, 63). These "experts" wrote for the *Journal of the American Medical Association* (a journal that is still going strong) and for other disciplinary publications. Less likely to be heard from the past are the voices of the parents of adolescents with acne, or the adolescents themselves, although Brumberg did have access to a few diaries. And the further back we go in the past, the scarcer the voices of anyone but the experts: the only voices you will hear will be those of physicians, theologians, and lawyers, going back as far as the philosophers Aristotle and Plato in ancient Greece.

Historical documents, then, provide for the qualitative sociologist particular representations of culture: not the idealized, market and media representations found in magazines and newspapers, but expert, often medical, religious, or legal perspectives. As an example of this difference from the late nineteenth century, take the issue of corsets for women. If you look in the pages of women's magazines from the era, you will note innumerable advertisements for all kinds of corsets, which nipped the waist in (the purchaser hoped) to the 16 inches proposed as the ideal. These advertisements encouraged the reader to purchase and wear corsets. But if you look in the pages of medical journals during the same time period, you will see something different: many physicians were concerned and discouraged women from wearing corsets. They wrote that corsets damaged the women's internal organs by pushing them downward into other parts of the abdomen. Women's lungs were compressed so that they could not breathe; some of them could not even get up off the sofa. A few physicians, however, were willing to cooperate with the corset wearer by surgically removing ribs—something that is reputed to have been done by popular culture "stars" within the last decades of the twentieth century.

What is striking and interesting about qualitative research based on historical documents is the interplay of continuity and change in our culture. If you look at American women's magazines from the eighteenth century, for example, you will see many of the themes still present in contemporary magazines: the focus on fashion, on body image, and on attracting and keeping men, for example. But the content of these themes will have changed significantly: from long sleeves and intricate embroidery to spaghetti straps; from wasp-waisted with spine thrown forward to thin and muscular; from virginal and retiring to sexually experimental and actively seeking dates.

Sampling from historical documents is somewhat different than sampling from twentieth-century magazines and newspapers because of the differential preservation of texts, and the actual rarity of some of them. Students usually begin with a topic they want to study historically, for example, nineteenth-century prison reform. Since this particular topic is quite a large one, it could be narrowed down to the United States (some historical studies are Anglo-American, but to go much farther than England the student will have to know other languages). It would even be possible to study prison reform in one state if that state had a good deal of interest in the topic, as did, for example, Pennsylvania and New York.

What kind of documents would you find for such a topic? You would find several types, among which proceedings of commissions of inquiry or other bodies given the task of investigating prison conditions and suggesting reforms would probably be most fruitful. Such texts are generally found in the government documents sections of university and other libraries. You can also find monographs written by prison reformers through the general catalogs of libraries, for example, those of Franklin Benjamin (*Prison Science Versus Prison Discipline: Reminiscences of Six-and-Thirty Years,* 1900) or Elizabeth Fry (*Observations, on the Visiting Superintendence and Government of Female Prisoners,* 1827). Of additional interest might be Oscar Wilde's writings from prison as well as on prison reform (*De Profundis,* 1907). University and museum libraries often have a wealth of both well-known and little known, underresearched documents such as Wilde's prison reform materials.

Prison reform is one of innumerable fascinating historical topics; gender is yet another. There are many ways to study gender historically, including some of the cultural studies work already mentioned, such as *The Body Project* (Brumberg 1997). Warren's research on aging in premodern Western society shows her interest both in the general interpretation of aging by experts of the times, and the specific issues of gender within aging. For this research, Warren drew from various kinds of texts, including advice and self-help treatises and manuals from ancient Greece and Rome into the Enlightenment (Warren 1998).

Warren found throughout the centuries certain themes common to the philosophical and medical discussion of aging. In contrast to the romantic notion that "in the old days" people revered the elderly, she found that this was not the entire story. Aging, and the elderly, were viewed in Western culture ambivalently at best, and with hostility at worst. Listen to a seventeenth-century description by Sir Francis Bacon of the old:

> dry skinn'd and impudent, hard bowelld, and unmercifull; bleare ey'd, and envious; downlooking, and stooping . . . trembling limbs, wavering, and unconstant, crooked finger'd, greedy and covetous, knee trembling, and fearefull, wrinkled and crafty. (quoted in Warren 1998, 23)

Warren found that old or aging women were even more liable to this kind of commentary than old men, since the cessation of menstruation during menopause was seen by premodern physicians as a kind of toxicity. Here are some first-century (male) descriptions of old women:

> your back is bent like a yard-arm lowered, and your grey fore-stays are slack, and your relaxed breasts are like flapping sails, and the belly of your ship is wrinkled by the tossing of the waves, and below she is full of bilge-water and her joints are shaky. Unhappy he who has to sail still alive across the lake of Acheron on this old coffin-galley. . . . Even if you smooth the skin of your many-trenched cheeks and blacken with coal your lidless eyes and dye your white hair black and hang round your temples curly ringlets crisped by fire this is useless and ridiculous. (quoted in Warren 1998, 27)

Contemporary women still attempt, 2,000 years later, to disguise the signs of aging by cosmetics and hair preparations, and are also derided for doing so, or criticized for not doing so. We, as students of culture ask ourselves, why the gender continuities? Some theorists find the answer in the concept of patriarchy—but this is another story that we will return to in Chapter 9 when we discuss the position of women in the 1950s.

## Sampling Texts

As in the example of ethnographic research, some topics provide easier access than others in doing historical research. Getting into a mental hospital is more difficult than sitting at a bus stop, and studying thirteenth-century Irish monasteries is likely to be more difficult than studying nineteenth-century American prison reform. In terms of historical time, the closer the period you are interested in is to the present, the more materials will be available. We often suggest studies of the late nineteenth century to students because in this time period there was a great deal of interest in public hearings, documentation, and the gathering of statistics, both in America and in Europe. There are some topics, for example in the sociology of medicine, for which eighteenth-century documents can be found easily enough to make projects feasible for undergraduates. But it is difficult to study periods much earlier than the mid-eighteenth century without special research and language training, especially for the pre-Enlightenment era in Europe when the language of choice for published work was often Latin.

There are topics for which you might find one or two or a few documents, but no more. Warren has among the papers on her desk a brief medical journal article published in 1787 that describes a form of sex-change operation on a young child, but this is the only such article she has ever seen or read about; and so, for a qualitative sociologist, there is not much to be done with such rarities.

Historical documents can be found in rare book collections and other libraries here and there, locatable through card catalogs or browsing. But there are also systematically collected (although not always fully catalogued) archives and collections of books, often left as a group to a library. Spencer Rare Books Library at the University of Kansas, for example, contains archives from the Irish Republican Army, and also from the personal library of a man named Brodie, who left his mostly eighteenth-century collection of eclectic books to a relative, who in turn gave them to Spencer (*http://spencer.lib.ku.edu/sc/irish.htm*). Another assemblage of interest might be the Wilcox Collection (also at the University of Kansas, *http://spencer.lib.ku.edu/kc/wilcox.htm*), which purports to contain one of the largest compilations of left- and right-wing United States political literature from 1960 to the present. Many such rare and varied collections are accessible to undergraduate researchers. If you are interested in doing qualitative research with historical documents, the best place to start is with the research librarian at your local library.

The most important thing to remember about historical document research is to be flexible; sometimes you can start on one topic with historical research, and as you browse, end up with something else entirely. One of the reasons for this might be the paucity of documents in your local area for a given topic (interlibrary loan may be too slow for a semester's project), while another may be that in some old volumes all kinds of articles and essays are bound together. Warren found the article on the sex-change operation while looking through a volume to which she had been directed through a card catalog entry on "Eyes." So, following all available leads may be the best strategy in historical research.

## Images in Qualitative Sociology

What can sociologists do with visual images? The use of images has a long history within social research. From the pencil sketches and water-color drawings of premodern travelers to the more modern photographic technology of still and moving pictures used by early anthropologists, images have played an important role in conveying culture and experience. Contemporary visual sociologists (for example, see *http://sjmc.cla.umn.edu/faculty/schwartz/ivsa/Links.html*) categorize images in three primary ways: subject-produced; researcher-created; or preexisting. Drawings, paintings, photographs, film, or video may be made by the research subjects, made by the researcher either about the subjects or to show the subjects, or already in existence in a visual archive somewhere, perhaps a research library. Each of these categories of images can be subjected to Marcus Banks' three sets of questions for analysis (Box 8.1) and/or may be used to facilitate open-ended interviewing called photo-elicitation. We will discuss each of these types of images and their uses within qualitative research below.

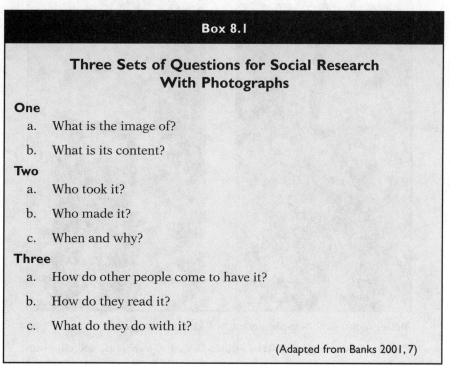

**Box 8.1**

### Three Sets of Questions for Social Research With Photographs

**One**

   a.   What is the image of?

   b.   What is its content?

**Two**

   a.   Who took it?

   b.   Who made it?

   c.   When and why?

**Three**

   a.   How do other people come to have it?

   b.   How do they read it?

   c.   What do they do with it?

(Adapted from Banks 2001, 7)

*Subject-produced* images are an insightful way of having individuals collect data about their life worlds with limited direction or interference of researchers. In field observation and qualitative interviewing, usually the data collection is directed, for the most part, solely by the researcher. Though a relatively recent shift, "there has been a move by critical and interpretative visual anthropologists, visual ethnographers, and visual sociologists, to reflexively *engage* with those they study" (Prosser 1998, 102). For example, Worth and Adair (1972) taught filmmaking to their Navajo subjects and asked them to visually depict their culture, traditions, and rituals. Chalfen (1974) used a similar approach with eight groups of children aged 5 to 16 from different socioeconomic backgrounds. He asked each group to "make a movie" and then documented the processes by which they created their "socio-documentary." Damico (1985) had schoolchildren take photos as a means of understanding the racial composition of their worlds. Ziller (1990) asked subjects to document "meanings of self" in various contexts (war, peace, country, culture) and life events (release from prison, relationships).

*Mother of two sons. Auto-photograph by Viktoria Gotting, 2003.*

More recently, Milligan (2003) has used photographs of home restoration to understand how homeowners make choices about change and preservation of older structures. Rae (2003) also had urban co-op owners document the changes that they had made to their residences since gaining ownership of the building. Additionally, Caroline Wang has been a strong proponent of what she calls "photovoice," which she defines as

> an innovative methodology that puts cameras in the hands of rural women and other constituents who seldom have access to those who make decisions over their lives. As an educational tool, the practice of photovoice has three main goals: (1) to empower rural women to record and reflect their lives, especially health needs, from their own point of view; (2) to increase their collective knowledge about women's health status; and (3) to inform policymakers and the broader society about health and community issues that are of greatest concern to rural women. (Wang, Burris, and Xiang 1996, 1391)

In his work Good Company (1982), Douglas Harper portrays the circumstances and experiences of tramp life in images and text.

Grounding her approach in a feminist epistemology, Wang and Burris contend that "photovoice allows people to document and discuss their life conditions as they see them"(1994, 171). In *Participatory Video: Images That Transform and Empower*, White (2003) provides an overview of the work of numerous individuals and organizations who use subject-produced visuals in their work as applied sociologists—that is, work that is intended to bring about positive social change.

In other research, *sociologists create the images* through still or moving photography as a visual ethnography. This approach has a long tradition in anthropological documentary photography (e.g., see Bateson and Mead 1942). Within sociology, visual methods did not emerge until the 1960s, when sociologists began using camera and video in an ethnographic manner. Douglas Harper (1982), a visual sociologist, used his camera as one method of studying modern-day tramps. Howard Becker says that Harper's photographs contain, and express, ideas that are sociological in their origin and use, and thus may not be as transparent to an immediate reading as other photographs. For instance, the photograph of a man shaving needs to be seen in context, as Harper points out, as evidence that refutes the common notion that these men are bums who don't take care of themselves and don't share conventional standards of decorum. As he says, when we see these men with a two-day growth of beard we should realize that that means that they shaved two days ago. (Becker 1995)

*Heather hums quietly to Helen.*

Similarly, Cathy Greenblat (2004) has documented the lives of individuals with Alzheimer's disease in an institutionalized setting. In *Alive With Alzheimer's*, her black-and-white images document that Alzheimer's sufferers are still capable of living and thriving, albeit in a new and different manner. Given the disease process, individuals with Alzheimer's disease are less able to tell their experience in narrative or interviews. Thus, Greenblat's choice to employ the methods of visual sociology gives expression to an experience that could not otherwise be captured and communicated. In a work in progress, Greenblat further explores the meaning of age and the forgotten worlds of institutions in "Tales of the Asilo" (2003). In this visual ethnography of a Mexican old age home, Greenblat uses her camera to document the experiences and relationships that occur in this isolated space.

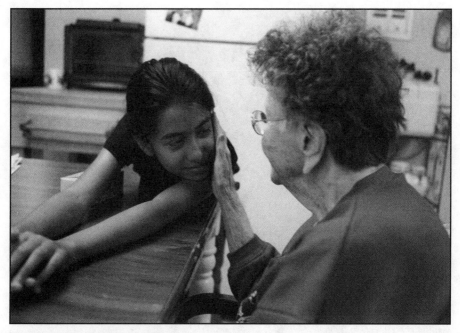

*Anna caresses Melissa's cheek.*

Finally, some research relies on *preexisting images,* such as photographic archives, postcard collections, photoblogs, and family snapshots, to understand various aspects of social life. These images can be "useful for 'backward mapping' but often lack important contextual information such as the relationship between the photographer and the subject, why a photograph survived when others did not, and the photographer's intention in making the image" (Prosser and Schwartz 1998, 122). If you are working with images from an archive or collection, they can be approached much like the historical documents that we have discussed above, and they have the same limitations as other forms of history.

Kumin (2003) is currently engaged in a fascinating study of early images of nineteenth-century Brazilian Indians. She found the initial drawings that were made in the field by the first outside explorers of these tribes in an archive in Switzerland. Using these field images, she is able to identify how the images were reconstructed to match Victorian gender assumptions for public consumption in printed volumes. For example, in one original drawing, a woman was engaged in hunting activities, yet the published image shows the woman in a more passive pose, carrying supplies behind her male partner, while all the remaining elements of the image match the initial drawing.

*Visiting the church in Asilo.*

Judith Friedman (2003) studies postcard images to understand what aspects of local environment and community are deemed important enough to celebrate in this format. In addition to postcards collected by individuals, archives such as the collection of historic Texas postcards are available online through the University of Houston Libraries (*http://info.lib.uh.edu/sca/digital/texpost/histexpc.htm*). Other cultural images can be found in museums, such as the mourning stamp collection at the National Museum of Funeral History in Houston, Texas. This unique museum also has the group photographs of early funeral directors' conventions (where Karner was surprised to note the presence of women) as well as the Smithsonian's collection of mourning photographs. The Library of Congress American Memory Project is an excellent Web source of historical images of all kinds (*http://memory.loc.gov/ammem/collections/finder.html*). These images provide an interesting insight into the "backward mapping" of communities and social rituals.

A new and emerging site for image collection is the Internet, which we will talk more about later in the chapter. Here we want to mention the opportunity that the World Wide Web provides for individuals to document their lives and share their images. Wakeford and Cohen

(2003) have begun to study the growing trend of photoblogging, where individuals use their digital camera phones to take pictures of the various activities of their day and post them directly to a photoblogging site, such as *http://photoblogs.org.*

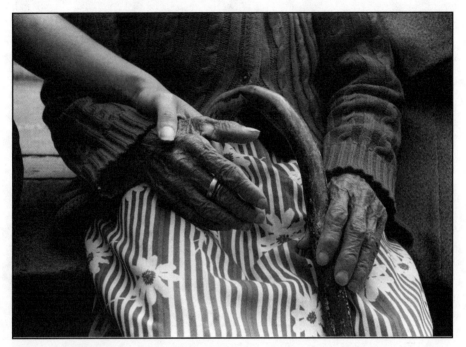

*Moments of tenderness in Asilo.*

> People have kept chronological diaries, journals, and logs for eons. Blogs are the next permutation of this. "Blogs" evolved from "Web logs," which were nothing more than personal journals published on the web for all to see. Blogs have grown quite a bit since the early days (the late 1990's) and now may offer several interactive and multimedia features depending on what the author wants to share. (*http://photoblogs.org/faq*)

Photoblogs are photographic Web logs that are updated regularly and maintain some chronological structure. Some photobloggers include diary-type text, while some may just have captions with their images. On most sites, discussion and feedback from viewers is encouraged, and some sites contain a running dialogue (like an Internet discussion board) between author and viewers. This type of visual log, which is unmediated by researchers and offers a representation of individuals' sense of themselves, is a relatively untapped yet potentially rich opportunity for social research. Sociologist Danah

*Postcards can reveal what was considered unique about the city and worthy of promotion. This postcard shows off the bath houses and beach resort area of Galveston, Texas.*

Boyd has a bibliographic listing of blogging sites on her page (*http://www.sims.berkeley.edu/~dmb/blogging.html*), which cites a number of resources for budding young blog researchers.

## Using Visual Images as Prompts

While photographs can be analyzed as reflections of various social scenes, they can also be used as visual "prompts" during qualitative interviewing or as part of a set of qualitative methods. One term for this kind of strategy is *photo-elicitation*. Initially described by Collier (1967), photo-elicitation is a "very simple variation on the theme of open-ended interviewing" (Harper 1994, 410). The researcher assembles photographs selected on the basis of their potential significance to interviewees. The photographs are then "shown to individuals or groups with the express aim of exploring participants' values, beliefs, attitudes, and meanings, and in order to trigger memories, or to explore group dynamics or systems" (Prosser and Schwartz 1998). Photo-elicitation can be accomplished with subject-produced, researcher-created, or preexisting images. Sometimes photo-elicitation is used in the context of a focus group, where images are presented to elicit memories, narrative accounts, and discussions.

In exploring historic photographs of a 1914 tent city near the mining town of Ludlow that was subsequently attacked by the Colorado militia, Margolis (1988) sought to more fully understand the remaining images by comparing them with other data. Using the photographs as elicitation devices, Margolis sought to find any living residents who had been in the area at the time of the attack. One particularly poignant image showed a lone tent left standing with the caption, "Typical miner's family fearlessly facing the guns of the militia" (Margolis 1988, 45). However, when interviewing Emma Zanetell, an 89-year-old woman who had lived in the tent city, Margolis learned of a different meaning of the image.

> "That's my tent," she exclaimed, "I'm there sick in bed." The story emerged that, a day or two before the picture was made, she had given birth to twins who died. Her husband and relatives had gone to Trinidad to bury the babies, leaving the tent colony undefended. While they were gone, the militia tore down the tents and burned them. Two soldiers came into Emma's tent; one told her to get up so they could set fire to her tent. Too sick to move, she overheard the other soldier threaten to kill his companion if he harmed her. Mercy, not fierce determination, explains why . . . one tent [was] left standing. (Margolis 1988, 45)

Images can provide a means to remember and retell experiences that interview questions alone might not elicit.

Using visual methods as a complement to other qualitative approaches, Radley and Taylor (2003) employed subject-directed image making as a catalyst for better understanding the patient recovery experience in a hospital ward. They requested that postsurgery patients take 12 pictures of anything on the ward that was (positively or negatively) significant to them, then used the images in two photo-elicitation interviews—one interview as soon as the images were developed and then again a month after the patients had left the hospital. Box 8.2 includes an example of the patients' images and their reasons for selecting that aspect of their recovery for inclusion.

The images themselves are mundane—beds, windows, shower rooms, and bathrooms. Yet the meanings the patients attached to the images, or how they "read" them, to use Banks' term (Box 8.1), yielded "something that was already in the experience of the patients, things about which they might not have spoken beforehand or could not easily speak about in an interview" (Radley and Taylor 2003, 90). For example, one characterized a picture of a clock as "time stands still" and another referred to a picture of the stairs as "escape route." The patients' photographs offered nonpatients a new perspective on the ordinary objects and spaces on the hospital ward. In the act of photographing and explaining their images, patients "articulated into significance" the unseen experience of the "sites, sources, and channels of treatment and care" (Radley and Taylor 2003, 92). Taking a more general theoretical stance, the hospital researchers proposed that "the anesthetic device of medicine extend beyond the actual drugs used," and in the hospital context "the person dulls his or her senses against the stimuli of the medical setting and the interventions that it supports" (Radley and Taylor 2003, 94). The patients' photographs and narratives bring to light the "onslaught on the whole sensorium" of the hospital experience, which reinforces passivity and compliance (Radley and Taylor 2003, 95).

---

**Box 8.2**

### Images of Recovery
### "Sites, sources, and channels of treatment and care"

Twelve images by a 48-year-old woman patient taken on the eighth day after her surgery:

| Image | Reason for Photographing |
|---|---|
| 1. Chair next to bed | I was looking forward to sitting on it |
| 2. Window in ward | I looked out to a lovely view |
| 3. Bathroom & toilet (looking in) | I was left in there struggling after the operation |
| 4. Bathroom & toilet (looking out) | I was left in there struggling after the operation |
| 5. Bed in 4-bed room | It made me feel good |
| 6. TV room | I had space and was able to cool down |
| 7. View from window in TV room | [no comment] |
| 8. Fish tank in dayroom | It was very calming |
| 9. Shower room | An effort and long awaited |
| 10. Restaurant downstairs | Went with boyfriend |
| 11. Notice board | I could see from my bed and noted slanted writing |
| 12. Name details on bed | My name was spelled wrong at first |

(From Radley and Taylor 2003, 92, 84)

---

## Sampling Visual Images

How a researcher chooses which images to select or compose for a study is influenced by the research questions and the overall research design of the project. If, for example, you have decided to give your subjects cameras, the images produced constitute your sample. This means that your sampling decisions occur when you select the subjects or settings (which we discuss in Chapters 3 and 6), rather than with the photographs. Likewise, if you are working with preexisting images, for instance in a photographic archive, your sampling frame will follow the topic of interest and what materials are available. You will then develop a systematic approach, balancing the need for coverage with a feasible workload, as we talked about earlier.

For example, Jerome Krase (2002) studies what he calls "ethnic theme parks": urban areas that have become recognized as part of the immigrant tourist industry. Over the past three decades, Krase has studied and photographed a wide range of internationally recognized ethnic neighborhoods where one finds ethnic festivals and other spectacles. Often these neighborhoods and events are listed in city guidebooks, reinforcing ethnic stereotypes as well as the "authenticity" of ethnic experiences. Krase has documented Chinatowns as well as other ethnic theme parks around the globe. We include three of his photographs, within which you can see that he has used the symbolic, architectural boundary marker of the entrance gate as one thematic means of image selection.

Researcher-made images call for reflexivity and careful thought. In choosing to construct the images—whether by taking photographs or making videos—the researcher recognizes

*Chinatown in Philadelphia.*

the added complexity introduced when making images in the course of conducting research . . . [and also feels] compelled to consider issues regarding "empowerment" (of subjects), and "ownership" (of data and findings), especially in regard to photographs. We accept that making pictures can be a threatening act (amply demonstrated by the metaphors photography invokes: we "load", "aim" and "shoot") that yields an artificial product, an artifact of the idiosyncratic relationship among photographers and subjects, the medium, and the cultural expectations it generates. (Prosser and Schwartz 1998, 119)

Visual images communicate powerful messages that can be immediate and direct. How a researcher selects and constructs the images that will be included in the study, at each point in the process, allows for possible manipulation or mediation of the social event. Photographs are sites of interpretation and expression, not merely reflections of some external social reality. In employing visual methods, sampling concerns may be relevant throughout the data collection process. Attending to the epistemological foundations of qualitative methods that we have discussed throughout this text is an important aspect of applying visual technologies to social science research.

*Chinatown in Sydney.*

## Internet Studies

The Internet is an excellent source of cultural representations for qualitative analysis. We are sure you have been warned many times not to believe everything that is found on the Internet, because often it is impossible to find out where something originates. However, if you treat Internet material as data for analysis, not as fact or reality, there is a vast network of topics available to you on the World Wide Web. Let us give you an example.

*Chinatown in London.*

One of Warren's areas of study is electroshock therapy, also known as electroconvulsive therapy or ECT (Kneeland and Warren 2002). In 1999 there were (at least) two Web sites on the Internet concerned with electroshock. One is an anti-electroshock site, the other a pro-electroshock site. The anti-shock site is luridly colored, featuring a drawing of a comic-book snarling animal (perhaps a fox) in purple and green. The site leads you, of course, to various horror stories about the effect of electroshock on people's brains, memories, emotions, and sense of self. The pro-shock site is completely different, looking much like a professional association conference program with its lists of learned MDs and journals. The site leads you, of course, to various scholarly articles about the success of shock in relieving depression and saving the lives of adults and children.

As a cultural analyst, you do not take either site as "the truth" about electroshock; rather, you take them both as cultural representations of the treatment. What are their similarities as well as their differences? Both use personal testimonials as a form of evidence; both, too, refer the browser to scientific and medical articles as another form of evidence. Both feature psychiatric experts: the anti-shock site Dr. Peter Breggin, the pro-shock site Dr. Max Fink. This tells you, the cultural analyst, about what our culture deems proper evidence. It tells you about the dimensions of both the anti-shock and pro-shock positions: erasure of self or restoration of self might be a more general way of putting it. So an outline of your analysis might look something like Box 8.3.

## E-mail and Qualitative Research

Other parts of the Internet, such as e-mail or chat rooms, can be used either as sources of data (the qualitative researcher simply collects material) or as forms of communication between researcher and respondents. Richard Hessler and his colleagues (2003) used e-mail diaries to study adolescents' views of risky behavior such as sex, drinking, drugs, and fast driving. They collected daily e-mail diary entries from 31 adolescents aged 14 to 18 for periods ranging from eight to 10 weeks. They discuss three issues in the use of e-mail as a research tool—technical difficulties, privacy issues, and the use of e-mail in the collection of qualitative data—and note:

> Security of data or confidentiality was the common theme running through most of the articles. . . . At the heart of the problem is the fact that these communication methods were not designed to have strong security features . . . transmitting confidential information was not part of the e-mail plan. (113)

Security problems were the main negative aspect of the study, according to these researchers. The use of e-mail data was cheap, rapid, and facilitated communication between different generations.

---

**Box 8.3**

### Electroshock Therapy on the Internet:
### A Comparison of Two Web Sites

1.  Similarities between the sites:
    A.  Types of evidence used:
        i.  personal testimonies from patients
        ii.  scientific and medical studies by physicians
    B.  Psychiatric experts as spokespeople
        i.  Dr. Peter Breggin (anti)
        ii.  Dr. Max Fink (pro)

2.  Differences between the sites:
    A.  Presentation:
        i.  anti: lurid
        ii.  pro: professional
    B.  Prognosis for the patient
        i.  anti: erasure of self by brain damage
            memory loss
            emotional flattening
        ii.  pro: restoration of self by relieving depression
            preventing suicide
            enjoyment of life

---

E-mailing was "anonymous enough to override the usual adolescent self-consciousness about sharing sensitive thoughts and actions with adults" (Hessler et al. 2003, 122). However, the researchers also warned that many adolescents are lonely and

> e-mail researchers have enormous potential influence over the thinking and behaviors of respondents. . . . The line between data gathering and the therapeutic interview is always thin and e-mail fieldwork makes it even easier to cross. Methodological work on controlling the power of this technique should proceed. (Hessler et al. 2003, 124)

The adolescents in the Hessler study were recruited by field coordinators, thus they were known to actually *be* adolescents. E-mail and other Internet research is most appropriate, in our view, when controls are in place ensure that someone is as she presents herself. On the Internet there is no validation of claimed identity: a "13-year-old girl" in a teenage girls' chat room may indeed be a 40-year-old man. Even photographs on the Internet can be misleading since the 40-year-old man can most certainly obtain photos of a 13-year-old girl and claim that he is she.

## Studying 'The Amplification of Deviance' on the Internet

The Internet, above all other data sources, can reveal to qualitative researchers the extremes of human behavior and selves (although without direct observation of either the behavior or the selves). Journalists in particular have tapped this source of data; sociologists can use and develop their findings and techniques to study various aspects of deviance, or norm violation, in society. As an example, twenty-first century Internet studies of anorexics ("anas") and of a psychiatric diagnosis "apotemnophilia" illustrate the potential of the Internet for the amplification of deviance.

Anorexia is a psychiatric diagnosis of self-starvation and/or excessive laxative use or exercise; most anorexia diagnoses are of young girls and women, although boys, men, and elderly people are also diagnosed as anorexic. Anorexia is an example of our cultural focus on thin bodies, especially for women, as purveyed by the media and the marketplace—but in this instance of thin bodies seen by family members and physicians as having "gone too far." The Internet was used during the late twentieth and early twenty-first centuries by anorexics and "wannabees" to fight the diagnostic label and imputation of deviance. "Anas," as the young women (mainly) on these Web sites referred to themselves, countered the medicalized definitions of anorexia, reframing them as "diets" or "choices." Self-starvation also appears on the Internet in another guise, that of longevity. Men and women, inspired by the calorie-restriction rat studies, post their calorie-restricted diets, recipes, problems, and suggestions on the Web.

The existence of this type of Web site amplifies the possibility of extreme deviance from social norms, as Elliott (2000) has discussed with reference to the psychiatric diagnosis of apotemnophilia, which refers to an attraction to the idea of being an amputee. Elliott, a journalist, writes,

> In 1977 the Johns Hopkins psychologist John Money published the first modern case history. . . . [distinguishing] apotemnophilia from "acrotomophilia"—a sexual attraction to amputees. (2000, 73)

Elliott used the Internet (one discussion listserv had 1,400 subscribers) for the accounts of apotemnophiliacs themselves. They described their feelings about their limbs and what they had done about them:

> "My left foot was not part of me," says one amputee, who had wished for amputation since the age of eight. "I didn't understand why, but I knew I didn't want my leg." (Elliott 2000, 20)

> In October of 1999 . . . a legal investigator . . . after being refused a hospital amputation, tied off her legs with tourniquets and began to pack them in ice, hoping that gangrene would set in, necessitating an amputation. She passed out and ultimately gave up. Now

she says she will probably have to lie under a train, or shoot her legs off with a shotgun. (Elliott 2000, 73)

Elliott also used newspaper accounts as data on a British physician who, most controversially, was willing to amputate the healthy limbs of apotemnophiliacs (2000, 73). Other apotemnophiliacs attempted to cut off their own limbs using crudely constructed instruments or by lying down in front of moving trains.

Both these studies suggest that publicizing ana, apotemnophilia, and other extreme conditions and disorders serves as a potential amplifier of them. Anas can chat on the Internet, justifying their self-starvation and possibly attracting web-surfing "wannabees" to their extreme diets. Not only can individual apotemnophiliacs describe their interests on the Internet, but they can also chat about amputation and perhaps locate ways of ridding themselves of arms and legs. This raises an ethical issue connected with both the Internet and with sociologists studying the far reaches of human experience via the Internet: are we now, and might we be even more in the future, contributing to what Elliott refers to as the expansion of deviance in society?

Magazines and newspapers, historical documents, photographs, and the Internet can all be rich sources of qualitative data in sociological research. Some of this research is quantitative, such as examining patterns of sales and circulation of magazines, but much of it is qualitative, focusing on culture. With the exception of photo-elicitation, we do not have to pass IRB muster, gain entrée to settings, or persuade respondents to be interviewed. Visual and textual research is pragmatically easier to set up than is research based on face-to-face context. And yet, with all their richness, these studies lack the interactional texture of interview and particular ethnographic studies—so we hope that during your stay in sociology, limited or extended as it might be, you try all three. In the next chapter, the analytic approaches common to all three methods of qualitative research are discussed and illustrated.

## Suggestions for Further Reading

Banks, Marcus. 2001. *Visual Methods in Social Research*. London: Sage Publications.

Goffman, Erving. 1979. *Gender Advertisements*. Boston: Harvard University Press.

Harper, Douglas. 2001. *Changing Works: Visions of a Lost Agriculture*. Chicago: University of Chicago Press.

Prosser, Jon. 1998. *Image-Based Research: A Sourcebook for Qualitative Researchers*. London: Falmer Press.

Rose, Gillian. 2001. *Visual Methodologies*. London: Sage Publications.

White, Shirley. 2003. *Participatory Video: Images That Transform and Empower*. Thousand Oaks, CA: Sage Publications. ❖

# Chapter Nine

# Analyzing Qualitative Data

*Fieldnotes, Interview Transcripts, Images, and Documents*

**Q**ualitative analysis requires a large quantity of thickly descriptive data, good organizational skills, and interpretive ability. When you look around you to see notebooks filled with thick descriptions, lengthy interview transcripts, stacks of images, or piles of document copies, you may feel a bit unsure as you face the task of analysis. This is not uncommon. As Mauthner and Doucet (2003, 414) comment, "Like other students coming to qualitative research for the first time, we were overwhelmed by the amounts of data we generated." As Denzin (1989b) notes, the analysis of qualitative materials is also an interpretive and creative endeavor. The researcher attempts "to filter through the myriad of relationships that make up our social worlds and show how they work together in ways that make sense to those who enact them" (Katz 2002, 72).

Unlike quantitative data that condense huge amounts of information into files that can be maintained, analyzed, and summarized numerically, qualitative data generate pages and pages of text. If you developed the kind of organizational system we discussed in Chapter 5, you will be ready to begin this next phase of analysis. However, at this point, we want to make clear that analysis is not something that begins after the data is completely collected. Rather, analysis begins as you add bracketed analytic notes while typing up your fieldnotes, as you transcribe your interviews, and as you work with your documents and images. This rereading or relooking process should occur throughout the data collection process; preliminary analysis and analytic ideas should be noted at all phases of the process. Some researchers keep ongoing research journals to record their thoughts and ideas as they conduct their study. Others routinely review their data on an ongoing basis between visits to the field or between interview appointments.

Analysis is a time-consuming, detail-oriented, and at times overwhelming task. Many novice researchers wrongly assume that collecting their data is the most challenging task they will face. However, once the data are collected and organized, it becomes necessary to focus on your interpretive analysis, conceptualizing, and theorizing. In some cases the analysis can take as much time as the data collection, and sometimes much more, depending on the complexity and wealth of data collected. For example, when Warren began her work with the 30,000 pages of data for the Bay Area study, the data had all been collected in the early 1950s and late 1960s. Warren's task, then, was to reanalyze the data sociologically. This analysis phase went through many stages as her conceptual understanding of the data evolved and the analytic themes became clearer. Warren estimates that she spent approximately five years engaged in the analysis and another two years in writing and rewriting the representation of her work *Madwives* (1987). In her later historical analysis of electroshock therapy, Warren estimates that she and her coauthor spent twice that amount of time in collecting, analyzing, and writing (Kneeland and Warren 2002). Timothy Diamond (1992) spent a number of years collecting data and then another decade or so analyzing and writing to produce his institutional ethnography of nursing homes. Richard Mitchell (2002) began his exemplary study of modern-day survivalists in 1983, analyzed his data, returned to the field, collected more data, reanalyzed, rethought, and rewrote his work for close to two decades before its recent publication.

We offer these examples not to scare the beginning researcher but rather to emphasize the need to allow adequate time for analytic "seasoning." The development of a strong and informed analysis requires many elements: an interesting topic or setting (if these are not interesting to the researcher, they are unlikely to be interesting to the reader); thickly descriptive data that have been gathered carefully over a meaningful space of time; a sound organizational strategy so data can be contextualized and retrieved; a deep and abiding familiarity with the data, setting, and topic; and most important, time to reflexively "play" with the data to interpret the story and to construct a faithful and ethical representation. Perhaps due to the exhilarating aspects of fieldwork and interacting with research subjects, some researchers find themselves physically and intellectually exhausted when they reach the point of intensive analysis. Lofland (1970, 35, 37) considers researchers who fail to follow through with the laborious detail work of analysis as suffering from "analytic interruptus" and producing "conceptually impoverished" work.

## Where to Begin

A useful first step in analysis is to have some idea where you want to end up. You have been conceptualizing and theorizing throughout the data collection process, so you are not arriving at this stage as completely unaware, but rather in the middle of a process that will now become a more focused endeavor. So, what should you hope to accomplish? What should your final analysis look like? By now you have probably read a number of qualitative studies to see how other researchers have approached similar topics or settings, and how they have structured their written summary of their analysis. Or perhaps you have had the opportunity to read sociological studies in your other classes that have relevance for your research. When you read these articles and books, you can identify some general patterns about how sociologists write up their studies (which we will talk more specifically about in the next chapter). More important, though, you can get a sense of the kinds of research questions that qualitative sociologists try to answer through their work. Gubrium and Holstein refer to these as the "leading questions" of qualitative research.

> Typically at the forefront are the *what* questions. The commanding focus of much of qualitative research is on questions such as *what* is happening, *what* are people doing, and *what* does it mean to them? The questions address the content of meaning, as articulated through social interaction and as mediated by culture. . . .
>
> At the same time, a sensitivity to the ways people participate in the construction of their lives and social worlds has led qualitative inquiry toward equally compelling *how* questions. While not ignoring *what* concerns, those pursuing how questions typically emphasize the production of meaning. Research orients to the everyday practices through which the meaningful realities of everyday life are constituted and sustained. The guiding question is *how* are the realities of everyday life accomplished?
>
> . . . There are, of course, other questions, most notably those dealing with *why* things are as they are, *why* people act in particular ways, and the like. Such questions, while not uncommon in qualitative research, are typically deferred until the *what* and *how* questions are dealt with.(Gubrium and Holstein 1997, 14–15; emphasis in the original)

As beginning qualitative researchers, we advise you to focus on *what* or perhaps *how* questions, and leave the *why* questions, for now, to more experienced researchers. Attempting to go beyond answering what is happening, what people in your setting are doing (or saying) or what it means to them, in the space of a college class is probably unrealistic even for the most talented students.

Now, you need to break these *what* and *how* questions into the tasks or steps that will take you from wading through your data to writing a thorough representation. First you will need to organize your data for analysis and second, chose your technology. We will take up these topics in turn, alternating between general processes and individual preferences. For now, you may want to just keep them in mind as we describe the systematic process of how analysis unfolds. Once you have an idea of the process you will be moving through, you will have a better idea of how to make organizational and technological choices that will best match your talents, skills, and way of approaching qualitative sociology. Because analysis is such an interpretive and creative process (Denzin 1989b), it is also individualized in terms of the logistics of how each phase of the process is approached. Whether you choose to use computers, colored pencils, or some technology in between to guard against Lofland's (1970) charge of "analytic interruptus," each aspect of conceptual development must be carefully and thoroughly addressed.

## The Process of Analysis

The first stage in your formal analysis is to become intimately familiar with your data. Reading, rereading, contemplating, thinking, and rereading is where you begin. The point of these processes is the generation of analytic descriptions from the thickly descriptive texts or images that constitute your data set. We use the phrase *analytic descriptions* to refer to the development of conceptual understandings of *what* (or *how* or *why*) research questions that your data answer. In earlier qualitative research methods texts, analytic descriptions were sometimes called typologies, classifications, or categories.

Analytic descriptions are one endpoint of qualitative analysis involving the identification of recurrent patterns or themes and attempting to construct a cohesive representation of the data. These recurrent themes are then linked to concerns or issues in the sociological literature—theoretical, conceptual, or applied—as you develop interpretations of what is happening in your setting (or interviews or documents or images) and what their words or images mean to the participants.

Some qualitative sociologists seek to go beyond analytic descriptions of what and how in their analysis, using qualitative data to propose causal relationships (why) at either the micro (individual or group behavior) or macro ("social facts") levels. We suggested in Chapter 1 that causal questions be left to more experienced researchers. However, some researchers suggest that qualitative methods, and perhaps even quantitative methods, in sociology may be inadequate to this task. Causal explanations are tricky at best, regardless of the method used to generate them. In some cases qualitative researchers may want to speculate about causation, but most often the careful researcher will limit qualitative analysis to "the empirical purview of the here-and-now or the there-and-then" (Gubrium and Holstein 1997, 195).

## Developing Analytic Patterns

As you are reading and rereading your data, you will undoubtedly begin to notice some similarities and consistencies throughout. You may also notice that you pay attention to different aspects of the data each time you examine them—this may be due to a recent conversation, class lecture, or journal article that has sensitized you to something in a new way, or you may have identified a key issue in one interview or set of fieldnotes that you now come to see appearing throughout your data. This kind of realization is why rereading is so important. We both have many stories, our own and our students', of how we missed fundamental themes or issues in our initial readings only to see them with seemingly blinding clarity on later readings.

The insights that come to you as you immerse yourself in your data are the initial steps in identifying analytic patterns and themes; the process is often referred to as "open coding." At this point, the researcher is open to whatever appears from within the data. This is a somewhat unstructured process of initially seeing what arises from the data. It is important to be "open" at this point so that you do not miss something important by precluding it from your attention too early in the process. Many researchers make margin notations with thematic labels and mark the referenced text throughout with underlining or highlighting. Boxes 9.1 and 9.2 demonstrate different strategies for open coding. In Box 9.1, Karner adds margin "comments" throughout a page of an interview transcription. For Karner, the first step in her analysis process is noting, in the margins, the ideas and interpretations that she identifies in her rereadings. Box 9.2 shows Warren's initial analysis of an ROTC Building on a University campus from the thickly descriptive fieldnotes shown in Chapter 5. Note that these approaches are the same in that they both represent analytic strategies, but they are also different because we are two different researchers. As we noted above, both organizational skills and individual creativity are part of qualitative analysis.

Before narrowing your focus, you need to have some sense of the "big picture" of your data. This is what you accomplish by open coding. When you feel sufficiently familiar with your data and the sociological answers they imply, it is time to begin to make choices about focus. As you begin to make notations or analytic reading notes, you may notice that you are paying attention to some things and not to others. Certain aspects of your data will seem more important or, perhaps, just more

---

**Box 9.1**

Mangum, 106, Interview #1b

Interviewer: you don't have anybody to talk to at home?

Mangum, 106.1 (p.23): ah well my wife, she hasn't been to VN, it's just like talking to that wall.

> Comment: Wife as unfamiliar
>
> Comment: Able to respond denotes good listener

Interviewer: I haven't been to VN.

Mangum, 106.1 (p.23): well I don't know how to explain it but, many men that's been to VN, man, I don't need that stuff,

> Comment: Contradiction between account and behavior of talking
>
> Comment: Cultural products for those who weren't there

Interviewer: they lived it they don't want to talk about it?

Mangum, 106.1 (p.23): yeah, and that's where you are and at time I got to, you know I was in such and such a unit and I was in such and such a unit, I went to such and such base, I went to such and such...I can deal with that, but when you start to get to close, I'm gone,

> Comment: Surface talk
>
> Comment: Meaningful talk
>
> Comment: Resistance to talk

Interviewer: so you...

Mangum, 106.1 (p. 23): I want to talk but really don't want to talk

> Comment: Desire for meaningful talk
>
> Comment: Resistance/fear of meaningful talk

Interviewer: when you think back about VN are there certain memories that come to the forefront?

Mangum, 106.1 (p.23): um hum, certain memories and certain days.

> Comment: Crystallizing memory

Interviewer: can you tell me about any of those...

Mangum, 106.1 (p.23): just like I was telling you about that Christmas eve and Christmas day when we beached into an ambush and they was blowing them back in as fast as they was coming off, guys running up side the bank, bloodied, lost their weapon, don't have no weapon, trying to get back on to the boat, but didn't make it, like I said the operation went on and brought 2 back of Charlie company. Lost 36 navy guys.

> Comment: Memory attached to holiday marker
>
> Comment: Combat as chaos
>
> Comment: Human cost of chaos

Interviewer: how do feel when you ...

Mangum, 106.1 (p.23): I don't feel responsible. But it just a, the screams and the hollering, and the blood and the flush, and only one I've, I don't know, I guess feel responsible for is, (but my hands were tied) took a B40 rifle through the gun turret, but we was in a fire fight, I'm on a gun, we hemmed down, and see we all wear headsets, radio, I can't get to him, and when we did get a chance to get to him, he'd bled to death, and that just was tough.

> Comment: Human cost of chaos
>
> Comment: Guilt over what did not happen—couldn't save friend
>
> Comment: Trapped in chaos
>
> Comment: Memory in present tense
>
> Comment: Summary gloss statement

Interviewer: were you close?

Mangum, 106.1 (p.23): yeah, we met up in San Diego, CA and went through training all together, and uh he lacked about two months from going home

> Comment: Military bond
>
> Comment: Time measured in closeness of end of tour—return to "world"

---

interesting to you. Or, as often happens with open coding, everything will seem important and you will be at a loss for how to make your data more manageable. Ask yourself: what is the most compelling aspect of your data? Is there something novel about your settings, interviewees, documents, or images? What is most surprising to you? However you make these decisions, it is important to begin to focus at this point. Once you feel comfortable that you are *very* familiar with your data and have completed a series of open coding sessions, you are ready to make some analytic decisions about the focus of your paper. It is important not to do this too soon, and although no hard-and-fast rule mandates when to begin tightening your focus, eventually you do have to do this!

Recall our example of a bus stop for a field site in Chapter 3. If you had chosen such a setting, you could focus on a variety of aspects of the social life of the bus stop (e.g., *what,* occurs there—*who* frequents the bus stop, *how* they use the bus stop, *what* kinds of communication strategies people use to engender conversations or avoid them, *how* space is negotiated) covers a myriad of sociologically interesting themes, and thickly descriptive fieldnotes would allow for in-depth analysis of any one of those. Many beginning researchers believe that everything is of equal import and must be included with the same level of emphasis in their papers. Each of these five examples of what may happen at a bus stop would be worthy of a sociological paper. However, *one* paper that tried to do justice (remember the loyal and comprehensive representation) to all five topics would be inadequate to the task! Even though there may be overlap among the possible themes, it is wise to focus on one main theme as the primary focal point of the analysis and analyze the "overlaps" in the context of the main point. You should be able to outline the subthemes of your main focus in the manner depicted in Box 9.2.

---

**Box 9.2**

### Analytic Characteristics of an ROTC Campus Building

- It is military (the Roman eagle, the uniforms).
- It is historically grounded or contextualized (the Roman eagle, the many years and decades of photographs of soldier-students and others on the wall).
- It is hierarchical (the arrangement of ranks in the photos from the highest to the lowest).
- It is rule-oriented (the many posted lists of rules of conduct, beginning with the outside of the glass entry door).
- It is organized (everything is organized, neat, symmetrically arranged).
- It is masculine (most of the photographs are of men).
- It is associated with sports as well as war; war and sports are connected (the sports trophies in the glass case).

---

Once you have identified your focus, you are ready to go back through your data, marking and labeling (sometimes called coding) each occurrence of your central theme and its subthemes. Then, you will want to gather each example of a selected theme or subtheme together.

Some people do this by cutting copies (not their original!) of their data into strips and sorting them into thematic piles. Others do this electronically, creating separate document files for each theme.

## The Logistics and Technologies of Analysis

Now we will take up the logistics and technologies of how we *do* the initial steps of analysis. The analysis process, as we noted above, can be individualized to match your skills and comfort level. Whatever technology you choose, you must begin by organizing your data in a manner that matches your technology. What you have to analyze at the end of your ethnographic interview or documentary research is texts: fieldnotes, interview transcripts, photographic images, or photocopied pages from magazines, newspapers, or old medical journals. For your ethnographic and interview research, your fieldnotes or interview transcripts can be found in three places (see Chapter 5): filed hard copies, a disk copy, and a copy on your hard drive. If you are doing documentary research, our advice is that you scan these materials (if possible) into your computer and have them in the same three formats.

Whether you want to work with hard or electronic copies, we offer a few pieces of advice. First, *maintain a main master copy* of everything that you *do not alter*, either in notebooks or on CD-ROM. This can save lots of heartache when the unexpected happens; so just trust us at this point; you will be glad that you have done this. Second, *organize your data by type and within type by chronological order*. For example, we separate our interview transcripts from our fieldnotes and then place each set in the order it was collected. In other cases, such as transcripts from a series of interviews with the same subject, you might want to separate your transcripts by interview subject and then place them in the order they were done. Third, complete a thorough *log or codebook* that includes a master list of your subjects, IRB forms, settings, dates of observations or interviews, and any other documents or materials you have collected. File a complete copy of this log with your master copy of your data for safekeeping. (Some scholars go so far as to keep full backup CD-ROM copies of their data in their safety deposit box or a fireproof home safe.) Fourth, decide on a means of backing up or *saving your work at each step* of the process. Yes, this may seem compulsive (it is!), but if anything problematic happens, such as the disappearance of a disk or the loss of a file, you will be overjoyed to have a backup copy.

Now that you have organized yourself and your data, you are ready to contemplate your technology choices. Contemporary analytic technologies range from the use of colored pencils to the use of specialized computer programs for analysis, one of the most recent of which is NVivo (a successor to the earlier NUD*IST program; see Gibbs 2002). Our preference, however—and that of most published qualitative researchers at the present time—is for the use of word processing, combined, in Warren's case, with colored pencils, and in Karner's case, with digital text editing tools (as illustrated in Box 9.1). For reasons of both individual and disciplinary preference, then, we will limit our discussion of technologies for analysis to those that facilitate the analyst's (re)reading and rearranging of materials rather than those that attempt to do the analysis.

The essential tool for everyone analyzing qualitative materials (fieldnotes, interview transcripts, and other documents) is, like the recording of those data, a computer with word processing capabilities. Warren's choice is an old program, WordPerfect 5.1; Karner's preference is MS Word XP. Yours can be any of the various programs available. However, it is wise to use what you are used to, since you do not want to spend the time available to you for analysis in trying to learn new software programs. For Warren, the other essential tool is a packet of different-colored pens or pencils, with at least ten colors in it (she believes that sometimes the most useful technologies are the simplest ones). The following examples of how to analyze assume that you have typed your fieldnotes or transcripts into your computer, or scanned documents or images into it, in the various kinds of marked files discussed in Chapter 5.

When the time comes in Warren's research to begin analysis, she prints out a hard copy of everything that has been typed or scanned into the computer. Warren then commences the task of reading and rereading these materials, a set of colored pencils by her side. As she identifies a theme, she selects a color to represent it. For example, as Warren read and reread the Bay Area interview transcripts and fieldnotes (all 30,000 pages of them) in her initial (open) coding, she noticed discussions of ECT or electroshock therapy, which she then marked in green in the margins, "ECT." Hydrotherapy, much less frequently mentioned, was blue "Hydro," psychopharmaceuticals purple "Pills," and psychoanalysis or other talk therapies red "Talk." Together, these four therapies clustered into a typology of treatments used at Napa, and the women's (and sometimes their husbands') interpretations of them. For ECT, as Warren continued to reread, she made subtheme notations (more focused coding) in other colors:

**Main Theme: Meanings of Electroshock (Green)**

Subthemes:
1. to the physicians: medical model (Yellow)
2. to the patients: memory Loss (Pink + Green)
3. to the husbands: marital social control (Orange)

As coding continues, the researcher may identify a third level of subthemes. For example:

2. Meanings of memory loss to the patients (Pink)

    a.   desire to forget their problems (Pink + Turquoise)
    b.   memory loss as identity loss (Pink + Magenta)
    c.   puzzling over why therapists urge her to remember but give her ECT to forget (Pink + Grey)

Using a word processing program, Warren then extracted and copied all these references to ECT from the main text, leaving the main text intact and pasting the excerpts into a new ECT document file. To do so she decided how much of the text surrounding the ECT to include in order to preserve the full, contextual meaning of the segment. Thus Warren could assemble the elements of an analytic (*the meanings*) description (*what was done*) of treatments at Napa in the late 1950s and early 1960s as interpreted by these women patients.

Karner uses the margins of her text for beginning to make notations, memos, and initial codes alongside, and within, the data. Instead of colored pencils, however, Karner works in the electronic files using the text editor and highlighting options in her word processing program. The "Reviewing" tool bar in MS Word allows her to add bracketed analytic memo notes in a different color within the text, highlight themes in the data in up to twelve different colors, and add "comments" on the themes she has identified in the margins. Thus, Karner follows a similar conceptual process as Warren, but limits the number of hard copies necessary. This also means that all her "marked" or coded data are stored electronically and can be saved to disks for safekeeping.

After identifying the conceptual themes in the data, Karner also cuts and pastes these data excerpts into a new document, again leaving the original data file intact. MS Word XP allows the user to have a seemingly limitless number of documents open at a time, so Karner is able to scroll through her primary data file and extract and paste into different thematic files at the same time (she has tested up to thirty open documents at once). Additionally, while copying the data, she makes use of macros to mark from where the data has been extracted. Macros are recorded keystrokes that are grouped together as a single command. The researcher can then use this "command" to execute the repetitive typing tasks. For example, Karner sets up macros to identify each of her main data files. One macro might contain the text "Ramsey, Interview 1, Page_." With this macro at the end of every extracted data excerpt from this file, Karner executes the command and "Ramsey, Interview 1, Page_" appears in the document and she then inserts the appropriate page number. This way, with each data extraction, Karner can locate the page in the original data file where the text appears in its entirety and in context (without retyping "Ramsey, Interview 1, Page_" over and over to identify each excerpt).

Now that we have discussed the initial analytic development of rich conceptual themes and some of the technologies used to assist in this task, we offer the following examples of what this process of analysis looks like. How does one move from "data collection [which] often produces a wealth of descriptions that have been created at great pain" to a "coherent narrative" (Katz 2002, 64). We illustrate this process through three examples of analyzing data: fieldnotes, interview transcripts, and documents or images. For the fieldnotes and interviews we use Warren's late 1950s and early 1960s *Madwives* (1987) research. Both the fieldnote and interview texts illustrate how, during this time period in America, psychiatric interpretations of mental illness were based not only on medical criteria, but also (as they are today; see, for example, Wirth-Cauchon 2000) on contemporary cultural ideas about the proper place of women and men in society, in the household, and in the workplace. The documentary analysis we discuss below is also related to gender roles, this time in the late nineteenth century, and is based on materials from Kneeland and Warren's (2002) study of the history of electroshock.

## Analyzing Fieldnotes

These fieldnote examples are from a Bay Area researcher's observation of Napa State Hospital discharge conferences, where a panel of physicians and others decide whether the patient should remain in the hospital, be discharged, or be given home leave. The comments that indicate marital, as well as medical, elements in the decision-making process have been italicized for illustration.

### Mrs. Peggy Sand's First Discharge Conference, 7/30/58

Dr. C: "Why are you here?"

P: *"My husband signed a petition to have me committed."*

Dr. C: *"Does he think you are crazy?"*

P: *"The hospital asked him before if he thought I was crazy and he said no. Then he said that the people at the hospital told him I was sick enough to be committed."*

Dr. C: *"Do you get along with him now or do you still fight?"*

P: *"I can get along with him after a fashion . . . for the time being I'll go home to him. I've been placed in a position where I'm dependent on him for everything I do."*

Dr. R: "What do you mean, 'go back home'?"

P: *"Oh, be a housewife, cook the meals, take care of the children."*

Dr. D: "How do you picture your future?"

P: "Very bleak" (She said this in a matter of fact way, but then her voice cracked and she appeared and sounded a little more depressed and almost on the verge of tears). "But I am tired of beating my head on a stone wall."

Dr. D: *"You say everything depends on him—how?"*

P: (she said something to the effect that, in the first place *she was married to him, and now she is in here and he has so much say over things that happen to her. . . .* Later, after Peggy had left the room, after a brief pause Dr. B asked Dr. D what she thought. She answered, "You mean, is she psychotic?—oh, I don't think so." Dr. C immediately chimed in "I don't think she is psychotic either." However Dr. McG said, "I think she is schizophrenic." He added that she probably has a lot of provocation for what has happened to her. He then concluded in a manner as though looking for some kind of out, "I don't think she's normal." [She was refused discharge or leave of absence. Later the researcher talked to her]

P: "If I was an accomplished liar it would help in cases like that." I asked her how that would have helped. She shrugged and then said, "Oh if I'd been able to say that I'm feeling fine, going out with my sister, get a job right away, file for divorce—then they would say she knows what she wants to do."

From this extract we learn that Mr. Sand, like other husbands in the late 1950s, had the power to sign a petition to have her committed. We also learn that the psychiatrist and the husband confer about her mental status, and make joint decisions about hospitalization that may not include her. The psychiatrist's questioning of Mrs. Sand includes not only psychiatric but also marital issues, about how she gets along with her husband. She is well aware of her legal dependence on her husband, and that the only possible escapes are either getting a job or filing for divorce.

### Mrs. Peggy Sand's Second Discharge Conference, 9/17/58

I asked her if she were expecting any particular things to be brought up at the conference. "Oh, I imagine there'll be *questions of how I'll be getting along with my husband*, something like that." (How will you answer that?) "That's a good question—*I get along with him all right, as long as I let him have his own way. I expect to go to work in two or three weeks, I think that will help—me anyway."* (How will that help?) "Well, when you are doing *clerk-typist work* you can't keep your mind on your job and something else at the same time. *Housework gives you too much time to think."* (What are you afraid that you might think about?) "Oh, *if I start on housework*—I usually think of something someone has done to me a long time back—and if I keep at it I work myself up into a boiling rage." At which she laughed. . . .

Dr H: [first question of the conference] *"Isn't it true that you had an argument with your husband* one day last week when you weren't there to meet him?"

P: "Yes."

Dr. H: "What do you think you have accomplished in the time you've been here?"

P: "I've learned to face things more realistically."

Dr. H: "What do you mean?"

P: *"Well, before, I was bound and determined to get a divorce—there was nothing else. Now, I'll go back to my husband, I'll get a job. Then, if I decide to get a divorce later, I'll be in a better position. I'll go to work to keep me occupied."*

Dr. H: *"How about the children?"*

P: *"I'll be home with them more than I am now—I'd be home every night."* (Indefinite leave of absence)

In a conversation with one of the Bay Area researchers prior to the second discharge conference we learn that Mrs. Sand has "learned the system"—that she must, in order to be discharged, convince the psychiatrists that she is getting along with her husband and is willing to go home and be a housewife. Dr. H's first question is, indeed, about an argument she had with her husband. She assures the psychiatrist that she has become more "realistic"—a contemporary analyst would say about her gendered place in society—and is given an indefinite leave of absence. However, she was subsequently returned to the hospital by her husband (on the grounds that she had had an affair with another man) and once again had to seek discharge at a conference.

### Mrs. Peggy Sand's Third Discharge Conference, 6/17/59

Dr. H agreed to "discharge her, and give a certificate of competence." He then went on, addressing his remarks to the rest of the staff, that there was considerable argument about whether she was psychoneurotic. He then went on, addressing his remarks to the rest of the staff, that there was considerable disagreement as to whether or not Mrs. Sand was psychotic, but it was felt that she could best be classified as schizophrenic reaction, chronic, undifferentiated. Dr. H then commented that this may have been a diagnosis of convenience. I asked her what the discharge will mean to her. . . . "I don't see how it will affect my life one way or another. If you can't lick them, join them." I asked her if she is referring to her marriage and she said, "I suppose so." I asked her what she thought the future of her marriage would be. "I can't say, for the next 12 years at least I expect to stay where I am." I asked why 12 years. "By that time the girls will be pretty well grown—and I'll be older and more set in my ways—too old to change, if I'm not too old already."

By the time of the third discharge conference Mrs. Sand had concluded that "if you can't lick them, join them," referring both to her mental patient and wife statuses in 1950s/early 1960s society. Follow-up research indicated that Peggy Sand was, indeed, still married to Floyd Sand 12 years after these hospitalization events. Dr. H's comment that her schizophrenic diagnosis "may have been a diagnosis of convenience" indicates that at least some of the psychiatrists at Napa may have been aware of the blending of gendered marital and psychiatric troubles, and gendered marital and psychiatric social control, that characterized mental hospitalization in America in the late 1950s and early 1960s.

## Analyzing Interview Transcripts

This ethnographic depiction of psychiatric decision making in the late 1950s is echoed by the interview material transcribed for the Bay Area study. Discussions of psychiatric symptomatology and diagnosis are mixed with questions and concerns about gender role—whether the woman patient is getting along with her husband, doing her housework, taking care of her children, getting a job (pink-collar), or thinking about divorce. One patient, Joyce Noon, when asked why she had been readmitted to Napa, said:

> Every time you ask me that you have to ask him [husband] because I don't know what he's doing . . . [he] doesn't feel secure unless I'm under some authority . . . as long *as I'm his wife he can do with me as he pleases.* . . . I cannot fight him . . . he will not let me work and he put me under these authorities.

These same themes were taken up by Shirley Arlen in one of the interviews done while she was hospitalized.

### Interview With Shirley Arlen

"I just don't see how *they could go ahead and stick me under his thumb like that*—for that's what it amounts to." I asked her if this was something she thought they deliberately tried to do. "I don't know—I wouldn't like to say that—at the same time, that's what it all amounts to." I asked her if she feels now that *she is pretty much under her husband's control.* "Yeah" (More so than when you went into the hospital?) "More so—yes." (In just what ways?) "Because whenever he takes a darn good notion—he can take me right back there—or call and have me picked up—although he may not be able to keep me there." (Do you think he would do this?) "I wouldn't be *surprised if he did." (What kind of circumstances might cause him to do that?) "I think the minute I went and filed for divorce, that's exactly what he'll do."* (Just what are you going to do with the situation?). She stared ahead reflectively and then answered, "I'll probably just go on like I did before. What else is there to do? *He doesn't want me to go to work."* (Why doesn't he?) *"He says he doesn't want me to have to work—besides which I belong here with the kids."*

Since the Bay Area study combined interview with ethnographic methods, many of the analyses written into the transcripts by the original researchers depended on both methods. In the following analysis by Warren of the original interviewer's notes, "indefinite leave" refers to the unconditional release from the hospital but with the indefinite possibility of the husband re-signing the ex-patient back into the hospital. After a few failed discharge conferences, the Napa patients were, like Peggy Sand, more prepared for what was to come: Kate White, who had earlier told the interviewer that she had finally "learned what to say," was successful in her attempts to be discharged once she declared that her marital relationship was improved and that hospitalization had helped her:

> Dr. B then asked, "Do you think your hospitalization has helped you any?"
>
> Mrs. White: *"It sure has."*
>
> "How do you and your husband get along now?"
>
> *"Wonderful." "Better." "We sure do."* (indefinite leave, 4/1/59) (Warren 1987, 106, italics added)

Note that both the fieldnotes and the interview transcripts illuminate the intersection of gendered marital and psychiatric social control in the late 1950s, but with different lenses. In the fieldnote extract, the observer recorded decision-making occasions during which the psychiatrists used marital as well as medical frameworks for questioning patients and discussing cases. In the interview transcripts, the respondents' own interpretative accounts of what happened to them during these decision-making events are illustrated. Joyce Noon, Kate White, and the other women were clearly aware that they were "under the thumb" of their husbands, who could take them back to the hospital at any time (as could wives whose husbands had earlier been committed). They knew that they were consigned by culture, hospital, and husband to the social place of women in the 1950s: dependent, responsible for housework and childcare, working in pink-collar jobs only if "allowed" to, and with divorce an unlikely future option (see Warren 1987).

The analysis of interview transcripts should be done keeping in mind that the respondent is not simply a vessel of answers to be poured out of them by the interviewer (Gubrium and Holstein 1995); rather, the knowledge gained from interview data is knowledge based on questioning and answering, talking and listening, between a sociologist (or more than one) with her own interests and agendas and a respondent (or more than one) with his own. Interview-based knowledge involves not only members' understandings of the social world he is being asked about, but also the time and place of the interview and the interaction and talk between the participants. The relative weight of respondents' meaning and social situation varies with the interview topic: the impact of hospitalization on the Bay Area was generally so great that they talked about it incessantly no matter what the situation—until discharge.

After discharge, the social situation of the interview often took on a different character. One of the adaptations made to ex-patienthood by some Bay Area women was trying to leave the past behind and forget the Napa experience. The research design of the study, however, called for repeated interviews not only during, but also after, hospitalization. Those women who sought to distance their discharged "new selves" from the mental patient "old selves" expressed reluctance, in several ways, to be interviewed about their mental hospital experiences after discharge, and some of the husbands were equally reluctant to "dwell on the past." The following original researcher's fieldnote and interview transcript segments demonstrate some of these ways, from the direct to the indirect:

> [in the interviewer's first telephone conversation after discharge] Eve Low said she should forget the past, continuing to see me would serve as a constant reminder of the past, and even if we did not talk about the past I would still remind her of it anyway, just by my presence.

> Rose Price: "I need people to stay out of my troubles for a while—get the house fixed up—do my own plans."

> Mary Yale: "It makes me uncomfortable . . . you write down everything I say."

> Ann Rand: "Anything is preferable to this . . . you keep asking a lot of questions. Things I want to forget about."

> June Mark tells me [the interviewer] that she cannot fully participate in the research simply because the research in itself signifies the stigma of deviance that she is struggling to avoid . . . "I don't like being a guinea pig . . . you keep asking a lot of questions . . . things I want to forget about . . . It's not normal, my talking to you. . . . It's just that I'm reminded I'm a patient. If you're a patient, you're always a patient."

Kate White's husband [a year after her release]: "I'm getting a little more reluctant to talk about it. I don't know if it's just that I'm more reluctant to talk about things, or that there's nothing to talk about."

Mr. Oren asked me if I wanted to join them for dinner, and was rather insistent about this despite my repeated declining. He later invited me to drop over to his place some afternoon, bring [along] a broad, and just let my hair down and enjoy myself. . . . I was emphasizing the fact that this was my job, probably in the hope of getting him to accept the situation as such and not redefine it.

This last quote, by a male interviewer, illustrates one strategy used by the interviewees to avoid reminders of the past: Warren (1987, 260–261) called this strategy redefining the interview situation as a social one. A second example of social redefinition comes from an interview with Ann Rand:

She repeated that she would only see the interviewer again if she would have her over to her house. While the interviewer was evasive, Ann said, "Then I suppose you still see me as a patient. To me you are either a friend or some kind of authority, now which is it? The way I see it, you either see me as a friend or a patient."

Another strategy, which Warren called *role reversal* (1987, 261), involved the wife or husband taking control of the interview situation by asking questions, introducing topics, or making psychoanalytic interpretations of the interviewer. The following examples of attempted role reversal (which the interviewers fought, as they did social redefinition) are from interview transcripts:

Ann Rand [at the beginning of the interview]

"What have you been doing?" (both laugh). As we sat down Ann said something to me like, "Well, what's been happening?"

Donna Urey [to interviewer] "You look slimmer and trimmer—you've let your fingernails grow out, haven't you?"

Jack Oren: "I think that you're a kid that missed happiness somewhere along the line." He then started speculating about my past life and thought that something had happened to me, maybe in high school, to make me feel like that. Mr. Oren first was critical about my interviewing technique, and then started to question me about my life, and so on.

Clearly, some of these classifications overlap; Donna Urey's comment about slimness, trimness, and fingernails could be interpreted both as role reversal and as an attempt to make the interview into a social visit. The post-hospital interview transcripts also indicate that the patients varied in their wish to distance themselves from the interviewer, and thus from their old selves. Some of the women who still felt quite troubled *cast the researcher into the role of therapist or adviser* in the later interviews (Warren 1987, 262). One interviewer recorded that "Irene James anticipated the next interview in one week, then corrected it to two weeks." Shirley Arlen said to the interviewer at their final meeting: "Goodbye, savior" (Warren 1987, 262).

In summary, interview transcripts provide accounts of individuals' interpretations of their social worlds in a particular context: a social and speech event in which questions are asked and answers provided, on topics which may or may not be welcome to the interviewee in the immediate situation. As indicated in Chapter 7, these social and speech events also take place between, and thus may be shaped by, people of a given gender, age, social class, ethnicity, appearance, and so on—all of which may influence what is said in the interview, and thus what appears to be analyzed in the transcript. The interpretive context of documents or images as sources of qualitative data is also significant, but may not be as readily available to the analyzer as the interview context (that is, providing the analyzer and the interviewer are one and the same person!).

## Analyzing Documents and Images

In Chapter 8, we provided examples of the use of textual and visual data in qualitative research, including contemporary magazine advertising, the Internet, and historical documents. In this section, we use two one-page historical documents, with both texts and images, as an example of how to analyze all these types of texts (see Figures 9.1 and 9.2). We use historical documents rather than contemporary advertisements for our example of textual analysis for two reasons: it is interesting to listen to voices from the past as well as the present, and our publisher does not have to pay money to reproduce materials that are more than a 100 years old.

The two documents are exactly as Warren found them at the Bakken Museum and Library of Electricity in Life in Minneapolis, Minnesota—two separate loose pages and not very easy to read. Although you, the reader, are less familiar than she with the interpretive context of these documents—after all, Warren does research on nineteenth-century psychiatry and gender—we do not think you will have much difficulty doing a basic analysis of their similarities and differences. We have listed a few in Box 9.3; what else do you find?

What is most interesting sociologically about these advertisements, however, is their gender differences. The Sanden's advertisement is clearly pitched to male readers: "MEN! WHY ARE YOU WEAK?" since it is women who were supposed to be, in the late nineteenth century, the "weaker sex." In addition, among the many cures promised by the electric belt are specifically sexual ones: " . . . seminal weaknesses, losses, drains, impotency or lost manhood. . . ." The Owen advertise-

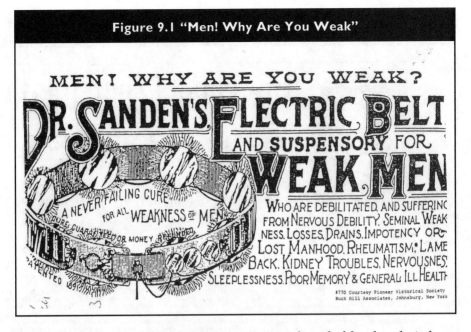

**Figure 9.1 "Men! Why Are You Weak"**

ment is just as clearly pitched to women, and probably also their husbands (who would probably control the purse strings and determine whether or not the belt would be purchased). This advertisement does not mention sex, but rather, domesticity. The belt promises a restoration of the woman using it to her social place:

> I was a young wife of six months and had *kept house* only four months. . . . [After the treatment] we commenced to keep house on Thanksgiving and *I have done our work with my husband's help ever since.* (italics added)

We can conclude from analyzing these two historical documents that electrical devices were sold directly to consumers via advertisements during the late nineteenth century, and that they were supposed to cure many kinds of ailments. Physician authority and personal testimonials were used to sell these products, as they are today. These two advertisements were highly gendered, selling sexual potency to men, and a return to domestic duties to women and their husbands. They tell us something about medicine, advertising, and gender roles in late-nineteenth-century America.

The images displayed in these documents reveal, to the viewer, both the technologies and the visual conventions common in late-nineteenth-century print advertising. The images in both illustrations are black-and-white and are drawings rather than photographs. Dr. Sanden's print is elaborate and curly, while the Owen Electric Belt uses a plainer font. Dr. Sanden's advertisement shows the device being sold, while Dr. Owen's shows the people involved in medical treatment. Both advertisements use visually larger and smaller, bolder and nonbolded

## Figure 9.2 "Snatched From Death and the Grave"

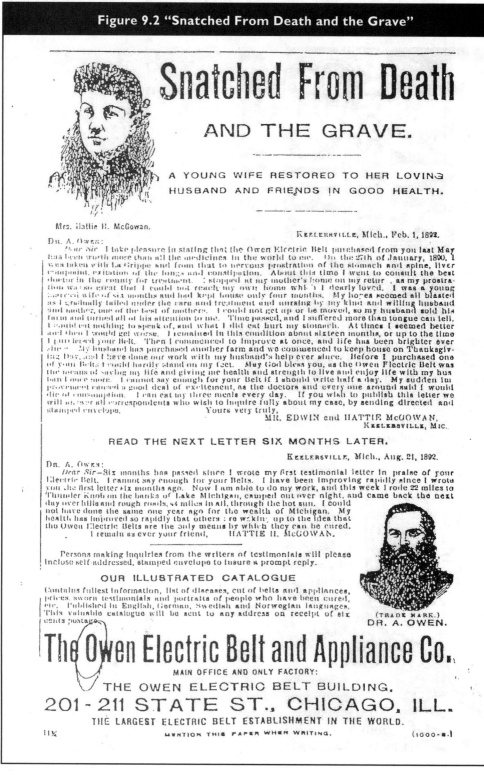

---

**Box 9.3**

## Analyzing Two
## Nineteenth-Century Electrical Advertisements

**SIMILARITIES:**

- They are both advertisements.
- They both advertise electrical belts used medicinally.
- A medical doctor is mentioned in both advertisements.
- Both the advertisements claim the cure of many conditions if you use the device.

Anything else?

**GENERAL DIFFERENCES:**

- The Owen advertisement has a picture of Dr. Owen while the Sanden's does not depict Dr. Sanden.
- The Owen advertisement depicts a patient while the Sanden's does not.
- The Owen advertisement features personal testimonials (common in contemporary advertising) while the Sanden's does not.
- The Owen advertisement mentions that the catalog may be acquired in Norwegian, Swedish, and German as well as English (can you guess why?).

Anything else?

---

text to highlight and emphasize aspects of these treatment devices. In Dr. Owen's advertisement, for example, by bolding and setting off the words "Read the next letter six months later," attention is drawn to the claims of the long-term efficacy of his belt.

Dr. Sanden's advertisement displays the technological device it is marketing. The electric belt is full of power and gadgetry, with metal disks shooting out electric rays. The text contrasts the device visually with the large, bold printed words "Weak Men." This contrast tells the reader that if he is a weak man, this powerful belt can make him a strong man. And he will be strong in all areas of the body, from his kidneys to his testicles. In contrast, Dr. Owen's advertisement looks, visually, more scientific and sober than Dr. Sanden's. The place of publication may be quite different, although there was no information on where either of these advertisements had been published in the archives where Warren found them. Dr. A. Owen himself is shown with a full beard and a severe countenance, neither of which—at least in our view—would be effective representations of medical competence in today's advertisements. The patient is shown as a normal-looking woman of the late nineteenth century with a modest high collar and upswept hair, someone who could be, and has been with Dr.

Owen's belt, restored from emotional and physical "prostration" to mental health and domestic functioning.

If you were to write a paper about the gendered advertising of electrical medical devices in the nineteenth century, you would do some background research into the area as you do for any paper topic in qualitative—or for that matter quantitative—social research, as well as develop your analytic points into a fully developed analytic description. You would do the same kind of background research if you wrote a paper on contemporary gendered advertising. If, for example, you were to write a paper on the images of girls and women in *Seventeen* magazine advertisements in the early 2000s, you would want to find out how advertisements and copy were related to one another during that time period: did the editors, for example, sell advertising space first and then fit the copy to what was being advertised, or the reverse? (See if you can find this out.) Part of the interpretive background of documents is what has gone into their construction; the other part is the reflection of the cultural context of these documents.

Another approach to the use and analysis of documents and images is seen in the work of Jerry Krase. As a visual sociologist, Krase documented the symbolic transformation of a Brooklyn neighborhood following the destruction of the World Trade Center Towers (*http://www. brooklynsoc.org/WTC/KraseWTC/index.shtml*). A year and a half later, Krase again photographed the same locations to record both the passage of time and the reincorporation of the symbolic spaces into the neighborhood. We include two comparison images (of his over 300) here.

And that is what the analysis of documents, interview transcripts, and fieldnotes and images is all about: listening to and interpreting the voices and representations of others, from past or present, culturally. The analysis of fieldnotes is both similar and different: in them we may listen to and interpret the voices of others in the present, but we can also observe action and interaction. Our analysis of these is through the lens of our own interpretations—not idiosyncratic lenses, but lenses shaped through learning sociological and other (perhaps feminist, or activist) perspectives. In the next section, we will address how to bring these disparate themes (and perhaps voices) together into a fully conceptualized analysis.

## Linking Themes Into Analytic Descriptions

Up until now, we have been discussing and showing how researchers identify themes, codes, or patterns in their data. This is commonly where some scholars fall prey to Lofland's charge of "analytic interruptus," because they stop at this point. At this point, you have lists or compilations of examples of themes, and now you need to make sense of what you have, conceptually or theoretically. Some qualitative researchers link their analysis to concepts derived from the literature

*Park Slope Brooklyn: In the Aftermath of the Destruction of the World Trade Center, Fall 2001 (Photoessay). http://www.brooklynsoc.org/WTC/KraseWTC/index.shtml*

(e.g., Goffman and Foucault in Warren and Kivett's [2002] study), while others, such as Jack Katz (2001, 2002) and Michael Burawoy (1991), seek to move from analytic description to a more elaborated theoretical model. Either way,

> In essence, the ethnographer's task is to filter through the myriad of relationships that make up our social worlds and show how they work together in ways that make sense to those who enact them. We accomplish this goal by using our specialized ethnographic skills to help our readers experience the unfamiliar in terms that make it familiar and vice versa. In essence, we try to impose a little order on what could quite easily seem like chaos. (Vail 2001, 720)

In order to move from lists of data excerpts to creating order out of chaos, much remains to be done to develop a fully conceptualized analytic description, including the following:

• Making Connections: How do the themes relate or interrelate with each other?

• Interpreting: What sociological questions do the data answer?

• Validating: How do you know what you say you know?

We will take up each of these steps in turn.

*Park Slope Brooklyn: In the Aftermath of the Destruction of the World Trade Center, Spring 2002 (Photoessay). http://www.brooklynsoc.org/WTC/KraseWTC/index.shtml*

## Making Connections

At this point, you have identified your themes and subthemes and collected examples of each into separate piles or documents. Now you need to decide how each of the themes connects the others. This is the time to begin making connections and mapping how your various data elements fit together into a whole and comprehensive representation of your research. Some sociologists use visual diagrams, process flow charts, or organizational structure charts. Others have drawn maps of their settings to identify where various types of interactions occur—how they are spatially clustered. Most often, we find ourselves using the tried-and-true format of an outline. Recall the discussion of colored pencil coding of the Bay Area study that we discussed earlier. Using an outline format, the ECT part of the analytic description of treatment is below.

### Perspectives on Electroshock

1. The medical model of ECT (from interviews with and observations of physicians)
2. The everyday social control uses of ECT (from interviews with and observations of nurses)
3. The meaning of ECT to the woman patient (from interviews with hospitalized women in the 1950s and 1960s)
   a. as punishment

      b. as treatment
          i. the purpose of which is memory loss
          ii. confusion over whether to remember (psychoanalysis) or forget (ECT)
      c. the context of forgetting
          i. forgetting troubles
          ii. forgetting domestic tasks
          iii. forgetting husbands or children
  4. ECT in the family context
      a. as a threat by the husband after discharge
      b. memory loss and marital strategies
          i. reminding the expatient of things she has forgotten
          ii. not reminding her
          iii. "reminding" her of things that never happened

This outline could be used for the development of a chapter or article on psychiatric treatments at Napa in the 1950s and 1960s, although it would probably change throughout the process of writing and rewriting drafts. As you write and rewrite outlines, think about how your themes and subthemes are ordered. There are three basic principles of ordering:

1. Random, like a shopping list (I need oranges, cat food, and toilet paper)

2. Temporal, ordered by time as in narrative history

3. Analytic, makes connections based on logic (and is actually quite tricky)

If your study is based on fieldnotes or interview transcripts, you will be using analytic ordering.

Analytic ordering requires that you make the connections between your themes or categories by some logical progression. One analytic strategy is to progress from the most general to the most specific points. In the discussion of electroshock from *Madwives,* you might begin with the most general theme (the gender and marital roles of the 1950s and 1960s), then link this discussion to the subtheme of psychiatric uses of electroshock to reinforce gender roles in that era. Armed with your linked analysis of women and electroshock, you would proceed to analyze the more specific or microlevel ethnographic and interview data on the meaning of treatment to these women and their husbands. These microlevel data, too, should be ordered analytically rather than randomly. Try this exercise: Identify whether the above outline for "perspectives on electroshock" is random, analytic, or some combination. Then try reordering it to become more analytic.

As you begin to make your connections among the data themes and patterns, the relationship between analysis and interpretation is at this point reflexive, with the quotes leading to the analytic themes or categories, and the analytic categories used to illustrate the analysis. For you to have identified an analytic theme as important, you should have multiple examples of data to use illustratively. Since you have grouped each example together in your separate documents or piles, as we discussed above, you can easily choose which quote or quotes appears most appropriate. Examples of quotes that led to the development of the category, and that would also be used to illustrate the category, could also be identified as this point. For example:

### ECT for women as forgetting troubles (outline 3ci)

Shirley Arlen (interview transcript): "I think the shock treatments are supposed to make you forget—when you do break down or whatever it is you do to get in here—I mean you're pretty sick and I think shock treatment is to make you forget a lot of things that got you sick and the way you felt and everything like that—I mean it succeeded with me—I can't remember a lot of things—and a lot of people try—try to remember—but I'd rather not. There's some things I'd like to but I think it was for the best that I can't remember a lot of things."

### ECT for women as forgetting husbands or children (outline 3ciii)

### and as a marital strategy of not reminding (outline 4bii)

Rita Vick (interview transcript): "I forgot all my children [she names the six of which she had lost custody]. Well, Sunday I was going through my album and I seen these children, and I asked my husband, 'who are these children? They look so familiar. They ring a bell but I don't know who they are.' So he lied to me and told me they were the children of some friends of ours. So I accepted it and I believed it. I said, 'oh.' So I looked at some more pictures and he left the room and went to his mother who was in the other room. And he told her that he lied to me so I wouldn't worry. . . . And I was relaxed. I wasn't thinking about those children or missing them. I understand why he did it but it made me angry when I found out. I kept looking at pictures and then I found a piece of paper, which explained all my children. I got very angry . . . I started yelling . . . after he explained I accepted it and forgave him. But now I remember those children all these worries are back."

Once you have developed your initial understanding—your own big picture—of the story your data have to tell, you will be able to create your diagram or outline or other visual display of the links between various elements of the story. This chart or outline should illustrate your understanding of the data and is unlikely to ever be used in your final manuscript. Rather, it can assist you as a road map or a tool for the next stage of your analysis—developing your interpretation of the data.

## Developing Interpretations

After you have made the initial connections between your analytic themes, you need to develop these themes and connections further and begin to illustrate them with data examples. In the excerpt below from their paper on loss of the remembered self in individuals with Alzheimer's disease, Karner and Bobbit-Zeher develop and illustrate their analytic description of Alzheimer's caregiving by relatives.

> Through representing a self that existed in the distant past temporally, caregivers invoke memories of who their relative was previously before providing examples of their current Alzheimered state. A daughter explains:
>
> "My mother has been, up to age 92, very independent. A person that had good judgment, was very alert, was always bright . . . and now to see this, that she is deteriorating, it hurts me. Then she turns on me . . . with verbal things, then, oh my, it does hurt."
>
> The desire to maintain the memory of the old self of the enselfed individual is important to the caregiver. In order to counteract the sting of the abusive symptoms that can occur with Alzheimer's disease, this daughter paints the picture of the mother she knew before Alzheimer's disease as well as the pain it causes her to watch her mother now act in this unfamiliar way.
>
> As Alzheimer's disease progresses, this transformation of the afflicted person becomes more pronounced. "She would take things," a daughter-in-law remembered, "Then she didn't know whose they were and she would claim sometimes that they were after her husband, and her husband had been dead for years." This changed self is often manifested in behaviors that the previous, known self would not have engaged in. "It got progressively worse to the point where she might mess in the middle of the floor and then wrap it up like a present," said another daughter-in-law. These illness behaviors are often embarrassing to the caregivers. "She flirts with men specifically sometimes and that is kind of embarrassing," offers one daughter of an example of how her mother has changed. One wife told the interviewer in whispered tones, ". . . it isn't very nice to talk about, [but] he did spit on the floor and I tried to get him to quit that . . . that would bother me." (Karner and Bobbit-Zeher 2003)

This excerpt exemplifies the fact that data do not speak for themselves but are represented within a researcher-organized framework—here the quotes are organized around the interpretation of loss of a remembered self. Though the quotes are illustrative of this loss of the known self, Karner and Bobbit-Zeher (2003) do not merely label or name it as such but rather rely on symbolic interactionist theories of self for their interpretation. Second, it also shows the exploration of both *emic* and *etic* (Emerson 2001a) meanings. Emic interpretations are understood and communicated by the respondent. In the Karner and Bobbit-Zeher example, caregiver comments about behavior changes ("she would take things") and their emotional responses ("it does hurt" and "that is kind of embarrassing") illustrate emic meanings. Etic interpretations are the researchers' understandings, combining the emic meanings with concepts and concerns in the discipline. Karner and Bobbit-Zeher interpret these caregiver comments etically, in the context of symbolic interactionist theories of the self and its transformation.

Some qualitative methodologists refer to the initial articulation of etic interpretations as "memoing." *Memos* are conceptual notes that tie together various data excerpts into a coherent and cohesive assemblage. They are "one of the most useful and powerful sense-making tools" available to the social analyst (Miles and Huberman 1994, 72). Whether you write your interpretations as separate memos or weave them throughout your thematic quotes, your analysis is not complete without these linkages and connections made as apparent as possible. Writing these clear descriptions of how you, the researcher, are thinking about the data is a final component of analysis that can then be useful in constructing the final document. Memoing is also a process by which you will become more aware of how you are thinking about your data. It is an insightful, interpretive exercise that allows you to make your assumptions and understandings obvious to yourself as well as to your future readers. However, before you begin drafting your manuscript, there is still the step of deciding whether your interpretation and analytic description is a valid one supported by the data.

## Validating Your Analysis

Positivist, quantitative sociologists seek to establish generalizable knowledge, which is knowledge that can be generalized from the people studied to the entire population of similar people. This is done in experimental social psychology by randomizing subjects into experimental and control groups, and it is done in survey research by randomly sampling people from populations. As a very rough example, if you want to know how rural black Mississippi males will vote in the next election, you select a random sample of such males and then generalize your results to the entire population of black rural Mississippi males. While positivist sociologists are on firmer ground with generalizability than they are with causation, qualitative sociologists do not seek to establish generalizable knowledge. We, who do ethnographic or interview research, know that our conclusions—our analytic descriptions—are specific only to the population that we studied, and perhaps even to the time and process of our involvement.

Where qualitative sociologists have the edge is with *validity:*—in its simplest definition—the closeness of the relationship between the people studied and the conclusions arrived at by the sociologist about the people studied. There are many more technical definitions of validity in general methods texts, but this one will suffice for our purposes here. Clearly, studying settings, interactions, and individuals firsthand (the empirical world) provides the researcher with at least the possibility of coming to valid conclusions about those settings, interactions, and individuals. The more remote methods such as large-scale surveys are at a far greater distance from this empirical world than are qualitative methods. Although such methods are ideal for studying, say, voting behavior, they are less than ideal for studying the meaning of that voting behavior to the people doing the voting.

You know that your data have been gathered in an experience-near fashion, and that you are quite familiar with your setting, respondents, or other data, but how do you know that your interpretation is valid? How do you know that you haven't "discovered" in your data only what you wanted to see? What can you do to verify or confirm your analytic description? How can you be sure that your interpretation is actually supported by your data? This is the final task of your analysis.

In order to verify your analysis, we offer three specific processes for assessing your interpretations:

- Evaluating your data in the contexts of your methodological and analytic choices

- Reframing your analysis—testing its "goodness of fit" with the data

- Seeking external verification from respondents, from other sociologists, or by triangulation.

Your first test of qualitative validity is to *evaluate your data* as to their appropriateness to the analytic interpretation you proposed. It is important to have the appropriate data: If your analysis is about employers' assessments of subordinates' morale, it should be composed of interviews with employers rather than employee perceptions of management. Or might a study of morale be better accomplished by field research than by interview? Is morale a matter of accounts, or behavior and interaction, or both? Think about these questions, and perhaps discuss your responses in class. What do you think?

Your data need to be conceptually and logically appropriate to your research questions, your choice of methods, and your analysis. Your data also need to be comprehensive. For example, if you noticed a specific hand gesture being used frequently in your setting during your last observation, but hadn't really paid attention to hand gestures prior to that, then your data would be incomplete for an interpretation of the use of hand gestures in that community, and you might want to go back into the field for a while. So, this is the first check of your analysis: do you have the right kind of data, in sufficient quantity and quality, to make the claims you are suggesting?

Second, you should consider the *goodness of fit* of your analysis. This can be done by proposing other, alternative interpretations, then researching the data to support or refute this new interpretation. One common way to do this is by *negative case testing* (Denzin 1989b). You have already compiled lists of the examples of specific themes in your data. Now go back and see if there are examples of countering themes or patterns. If a negative case is found, you need to rework your analysis to account for this occurance as well. By searching the data to disprove your analysis, you can reframe your interpretation, making it all the more robust. Another, similar test is called the *null hypothesis trick* (Becker 1998). In this process, you assume that no relationships or patterns exist in your data; in quantitative terms the null hypothesis refers to the proposition that the two variables of interest are not related. You, the qualitative researcher, using this "trick," then return to your data looking for evidence of such a relationship and connection. Always remember, however, that qualitative is not quantitative research, and more than one interpretation of the data may fit.

A third way to validate qualitative interpretation is to seek *external validation* from the research subjects, colleagues, instructors, or other data (triangulation). One approach is to offer your interpretation back to the research subjects for confirmation. Liebow (1993) had the homeless women and shelter staff where he had been a participant observer read and make comments on his analysis. He included their alternative interpretations as footnotes in his final manuscript. Stacey (1998) also used this approach in her study of two extended Silicon Valley families and included their comments in her appendixes. If your goal, as we've mentioned before, is to understand the meaning of the life world of your subjects, then asking them if you have it correct is one way to verify your approach. However, for many reasons and in many cases, external validation is not always appropriate. Bloor (2001, 394) reminds us "all validating techniques are social products, constituted through particular and variable methodological processes." Indeed drawing from his own research, Bloor offers examples of member validation experiences where respondents were uninterested in providing feedback (they only read the fieldnote excerpts that they were featured in), anxious about others' perceptions (they provided interpretive feedback based on their funding agency's criteria), and unconvinced by analyses that went well beyond their own understanding (that is, it did not contain the psychodynamic concepts that were the basis of their daily practices).

Another source of external validation is to have other sociologists read your materials to evaluate the strength of your analysis. Professional sociologists working alone rarely use this strategy, but it is commonplace in classrooms and in team research. Karner and Warren both read their students' fieldnotes and interview transcripts to advise them on the "fit" of their analyses. Karner has also worked in applied team research where fieldnotes and interview transcripts were discussed and reviewed by fellow team members during the development of the analytic interpretations. In an interview study of community service providers, Lisa Cox Hall conducted the interviews and Karner developed the initial analysis (Karner and Hall 2002). Karner and Hall then discussed the data and analysis with other team members who were involved with different aspects of the same funded project. Similarly, when Karner and Dobbs interviewed nursing home staff persons, they both reviewed the data and worked with other team members to further refine the analysis (Karner et al. 1998). In this study, however, they also compared the qualitative findings to quantitative data collected in the same nursing homes as part of another study. Thus, in this example, Karner and her colleagues both validated their analysis externally with their team members and through triangulation with survey data.

"Triangulation" of data may also be used, by itself, to establish external validity. In triangulation, fieldnote data may be used to corroborate interview data, or other data sources can be used along with fieldnotes or interview transcripts to corroborate events or accounts. Among these other data sources are, for example, newspaper accounts of events claimed by respondents, or the contents of garbage cans in relation to claims of not drinking alcohol. Lembcke (2000) sought out any mass media documentation to support the "myth of the spit upon Vietnam veteran." Though there were many informal accounts of such events occurring, Lembcke could not find a single image or media report of the claimed "spitting" and thus concluded that the myth could not be substantiated as historical fact and more likely had been politically motivated propaganda.

Quantitative sociologists are concerned not only with various kinds of validity but also with various kinds of reliability. In qualitative sociology, the key reliability question is: would any qualitative sociologist examining the texts or images that constitute the data develop (roughly) the same analytic description? From a quantitative standpoint, the answer would be no, because qualitative analysis is interpretive, with members' meanings examined through a particular analytic lens and located in a specific interaction bounded by time and space. However, if you are a qualitative sociologist, the answer might be yes, or it might be no. Warren, for example, studies gender and social control, so that quite often her graduate students learn, like her, to analyze a variety of data from the standpoint of gender and social control (as you may have noticed in many of the examples earlier in this chapter).

However, a researcher interested in race and ethnicity, analyzing the same *Madwives* data might have focused on the numerous accounts of white women psychiatric patients in the 1950s interacting with African-American male staff persons. Warren (1987) made the conscious decision to focus on gender, and to exclude race, in her analysis.

Analysis is a multistep and multilayered process occurring in a particular time and place, done by an individual or team with various applied or theoretical interests, and subject to the readers' assessment of its validity. Developing a thorough and compelling analysis proceeds by working back and forth between what has been typed or scanned into the computer and what has been printed out for reading, rereading, and classification, whether with colored pencils or some more elaborate technology. We have demonstrated in this chapter how to develop bits and pieces of analysis from qualitative materials, as well as how to develop an analytic description from elements of qualitative text. In the next chapter, we follow the analytic process with that of writing class papers, articles, or books.

### Suggestions for Further Reading

Becker, Howard. 1998. *Tricks of the Trade: How to Think About Your Research While You're Doing It*. Chicago: University of Chicago Press.

Gubrium, Jaber, and James Holstein. 1997. *The New Language of Qualitative Method*. New York: Oxford University Press.

Miles, Matthew, and A. Michael Huberman. 1994. *Qualitative Data Analysis: An Expanded Sourcebook*. Thousand Oaks, CA: Sage Publications. ❖

# Chapter Ten

# Writing Well

After you have completed the fieldwork or other data collection and worked through your analysis, it is time to begin writing your paper, article, or book. Qualitative researchers often view the writing phase as a separate and final step in completing a research project. However, for qualitative researchers, the process of writing is an integral part of understanding the "story" of the data rather than just the final phase. Crafting a qualitative manuscript is a process through which the writer clarifies how his data and concepts fit together. This process is much like putting together a puzzle. You may try ordering the "puzzle pieces" in an initial pattern, but through additional writing, organizing, and contemplating, you may find several ways of placing the "pieces" together. For a paper or article you need only one primary thematic focus with subthemes. You can often write several papers from one set of qualitative data, so you do not have to try to use everything in one manuscript! In this chapter, we discuss writing qualitative sociology research well. We focus initially on the general process and practice of writing before turning our attention to the specifics of crafting a qualitative research paper for a sociology audience.

The written product of your research, whether a book, journal article, or research report, should have a *clear purpose:* as a researcher you have an ethical responsibility to represent your subjects and your fieldwork experience in a thorough and accurate manner. This does not mean that your writing has to be sympathetic to your subjects, but rather that you will present to the best of your ability an account of their life worlds that reflects the complexity of their lived experience. A trite or simplistic overview does not do justice to the individuals whose lives you have shared and observed. Laurel Richardson reminds us that how we write has both ethical and political implications. As sociologists, our most important task is to construct a representation of our research that is "faithful to the lived experience of people" (Richardson 1990, 64–65). A desire to construct a thorough and compelling representation of the individuals and community that you have studied should guide your writing. As an author, you engage in what Denzin calls "the art of interpretation" as you fashion your representation: "Confronted with a mountain of impressions, documents and field notes, the qualitative researcher faces the difficult and challenging task of making sense of what has been learned" (Denzin 1994, 500).

As sociologists, how we write and what we write—the writing decisions we make—are influenced by our own experience and disciplinary perspectives, and these choices are also embedded within broader truth claims and power relations. How we write shapes "the forms of knowledge we are able to construct, including the kinds of theories and understandings we have the potential to develop" (Rhoads 2003, 241). Moreover, the manner of our description can have political implications for those we study. Accounts of the lives of marginalized, powerless, or deviant peoples can be used to support or refute various political interventions (Emerson 2001c, 314–315). Writing qualitative research well means being attentive to how our representations (and their attendant knowledge claims) reflect on those we study and the broader social and political contexts within which they may be read.

## The Practice of Writing

Writing qualitative sociology well has two aspects: general English requirements for correct grammar, spelling, punctuation, paragraphing, and organization, and disciplinary requirements particular to the genre or type of writing. Writing well, for sociology as well as other venues, is both a practice and a craft. Even though in this chapter we focus on the general practice of writing and the disciplinary requirements for writing qualitative sociology well, you should still keep in mind that the general writing principles you have learned in English and composition classes should not be forgotten as you write in other areas of the college curriculum.

Anyone who has attempted to write something for an audience beyond themselves knows that writing well is much more than just putting words on a page. Writing is, indeed, the physical act of typing into the computer or working with pen and paper, but it is also the cognitive process by which the writer decides what ideas to convey and how best to communicate them. It is those decisions about *what* and *how* to write that make the craft of writing a complex, creative practice. As we discussed earlier, these decisions should be guided by your desire to construct a faithful representation of the individuals you have studied. In this section, we will focus on the physicality of writing—*when* and *where* to write—before turning our attention, in the second part of this chapter, to a discussion of *how to write* for a sociology audience and the various decisions that good writers must make.

*The first aspect of the practice of writing is to set aside enough time to do it* (see Box 10.1). Many students have experiences of sitting down and writing a paper in one all-night session. This is rarely a successful approach to writing well regardless of the topic or subject matter; in writing qualitative sociology, this approach almost guarantees an inadequate final product. Allowing a significant amount of time for the writing process is crucial for contemplating, refining, and rethinking the representation you are crafting. Many scholars find that writing up their research takes as long as the data collection or analysis phases. Novice sociology writers often underestimate how much time must be spent on the writing phase. Although time spent writing is loosely correlated to the amount of data one is working with, more data also equals the need for more writing time!

---

### Box 10.1

### Preparing to Write

**Step One: Allow a reasonable amount of time.**

Qualitative research papers cannot be written in one all-night session. Time is required to craft an appropriate representation of your subjects' life worlds and your efforts in the field. Your first responsibility in writing up your research is to do justice to the individuals you are seeking to understand and represent. This cannot be accomplished without adequate time.

**Step Two: Identify your writing process.**

Once you understand the factors that facilitate productive writing sessions for you—time of day, creature comforts, organizational strategies—you can consciously identify when, where, and how the time you spend writing can be most productive. Some people write best in the morning; others at night. Some people need quiet; others like music or background noise. Learning about your process—what works best for you—will help you make the most of the time you have. (Identifying your personal writing process does not, however, negate the need for step one—a reasonable amount of time—and step five—begin!)

**Step Three: Organize your materials.**

Before getting ready to write you will have coded and analyzed your fieldnotes, transcripts, and other data. Organizing your materials to begin the writing phase is yet another opportunity to reframe and refine your perspective of the data. You have to decide what data to report first, which components of the story follow your introduction, and how to integrate your analysis within the representation. You will be paying attention to logic and clarity as well as accuracy. At this point you should make an outline of your paper. Additionally, you will need to have the literature and citations you plan to refer to close by. The more organized you are as you begin to write, the less time will be spent in interruptions to find quotes, books, or other seemingly productive distractions from the task at hand.

## Box 10.1 (Cont)

### Step Four: Plan your logistics.

Be reasonable here and plan on a process that is not too cumbersome but that will save you from common mishaps. We assume that you will be using a personal computer for your paper. So, first plan a backup procedure for your computer work. Save your writing in more than one place (hard drive and floppy disk) and consider printing out what you write at each session—this is a further backup procedure that also can help with your editing phase.

Second, think about compiling your reference section as you write. You might type the citations in a separate document as you cite a source. This can save you lots of time and aggravation in trying to identify your references after the fact.

Third, plan your writing schedule. For example, you may plan to work with the methods section this week and subsections of your findings over the next four weeks. Work backwards from your deadline and plan enough time for each component of your research paper.

### Step Five: Begin.

The twin traps that hinder writers the most are the perceived need for inspiration and perfectionism. Waiting for inspiration to strike may sound like a reasonable excuse for procrastinating, but it seldom strikes without beginning the process of writing. You will already have your materials organized and a writing schedule thought out. This will allow you to begin with some of the instrumental aspects of writing: the literature overview or the methods section. By beginning to work with your data and thoughts, you are more likely to become inspired. Insight most often comes through familiarity with the material and practicing the craft of writing. The old adage of 10 percent inspiration and 90 percent perspiration is very appropriate here.

Perfectionism can leave a writer rewriting the same sentence or paragraph over and over. After an inordinate amount of time, the writer may have a nearly perfect sentence and little else. Remember that editing is essential for good writing, and that editing what you have written is much easier than beginning with the blank page. In this early phase, your goal should be to "put it on paper" knowing that you will continue to refine and craft your writing after you have a draft with which to work.

Writing well takes time. There are no shortcuts. Writing, as we have come to understand the process, is really another way of knowing (Rhoads 2003; Richardson 1994). It is an extension of the analysis as you continue to "work with" your data to code and identify themes, prioritize concepts or processes, and determine how concepts are connected. Attempting to write in an immersed and logical manner necessitates a clear understanding of the data. Likewise, confusing and convoluted writing often comes from a (mis)understanding of the data and their context. Most sociologists who practice qualitative writing stress the need for adequate time to be allowed for the maturation of the writer's understanding.

> Fieldworkers can neither make sense of nor understand what has
> been learned until they sit down and write the interpretive text,
> telling the story first to themselves and then to their significant
> others, and then to the public. (Denzin 1994, 502)

You might think of this as similar to the adage that you don't really
know something until you try to teach it—in this case, you may not really understand your data until you try to communicate (write) a faithful representation.

*The second lesson about writing well that we have learned is the
importance of identifying your own process for writing productively.* In
the now classic *Writing for Social Scientists* (1986), Howard Becker
describes the various preparatory rituals that writers may engage in.
All those behaviors that one does seemingly to avoid writing, Becker
says, may in some cases be part of the process of getting ready to write.
Like the story of Ernest Hemingway ritually sharpening twenty pencils
before beginning his writing sessions, many people have practices, like
cleaning their office or collecting and ordering reference materials in a
specific manner, that enable them to begin writing. Becker advises
social scientists to acknowledge these practices as part of identifying
their own preparation processes, and to plan time for them rather than
viewing them as ways of avoiding the task of writing.

Also, most of us are more productive at some times of the day than
at others (see Boxes 10.2 and 10.3). Some people like to write in the
evenings when it is quiet and they are less likely to be interrupted.
Other people carve out times during the day to work. If you can identify when you are most productive, scheduling your writing time
accordingly will allow you to make the most of the time you do have.
Generally, you can identify your productive time through trial and
error—and sometimes your productive time will vary with other com-
mitments in your life. When Karner was in graduate school, she found
her best time to think and write occurred when she arose at three in the
morning. This gave her approximately three solid hours of work time
before her children woke up and the responsibilities of the day envel-
oped her. Now that her children are grown, Karner still prefers to work
in the mornings, though she no longer rises quite so early to do so.

In addition to the time of day that may work well for you, think also
about the creature comforts that will help you stay on task. Just as with
interviewing, physical comfort allows individuals to continue what
they are doing longer. If you are hungry, tired, or uncomfortable at a
desk that is too high or a chair that is too hard, you are not likely to
continue writing. Part of planning your productivity is providing for as
much of your comfort as possible. Will you need snacks close by? Are
you able to be more focused at your home computer—or will you have
multiple distractions? Are you more likely to work well at a table in the
library? As you will see in the examples of our work processes that we

---

**Box 10.2**

### For Example: Warren's Writing Process

I have written qualitative sociological articles and books for more than 30 years, first at the University of Southern California and subsequently at the University of Kansas. I learned to write directly onto the computer during the 1980s at USC, replacing my earlier yellow-lined pad and typewriter technology. I still like to work in WordPerfect 5.1 for DOS on my PC. I have always preferred to work in my Sociology Department office rather than at home; even when there is no one else in the house, there is always the cat, or the laundry, or reading a novel.

In my University of Kansas office I set up a very large table with about 15 plastic trays, each of which contained written materials (copies of articles, bibliographies, primary historical data, hard copies of fieldnotes, and research: an article on Eyes: Seeing and the Social Order; the Smokers' Steps ethnography; Genital Surgeries and Stimulation in Nineteenth-Century Psychiatry; Qualitative Interviewing; and several for this book). I also have disks and hard-drive copies of data, outlines, chapters, and drafts of these papers to work on.

I prefer to work for a couple of hours on my writing, either first thing in the morning or late in the afternoon, about 3:30. Such blocks of time are rarely uninterrupted, however, so I have learned over the years to be a "10-minute person" and do a bit of writing for whatever 10-minute or half-hour period I can find for it. I no longer use outlines as much as I should, but I do start with writing and rewriting the introduction so that I have some idea where I am going. But I also find that writing the conclusion to an article often leads me to rewriting the introduction. (So this is where this piece was really going!)

For an article or chapter I generally start with a short first draft of about 20 to 25 pages. Then I rewrite at least twice and usually more, adding and refining concepts, reordering, and selecting quotes from fieldnotes, interviews, cultural artifacts, or historical documents. Next, I impose on several colleagues to read my draft (I do the same for them) before I take the step of submitting the article to a journal. I rewrite according to their comments with a triage strategy: yes, I agree I should change that; no, I do not think I should do that (and why I should not) and the most difficult category, the middle one—maybe, maybe not. Then . . . off to the journal or book publisher!

---

offer in Boxes 10.2 and 10.3, we have different approaches to the craft of writing—yet we each have identified our own process. We offer our examples to help you think about the various aspects of identifying your own process to enable you to be as productive and insightful as possible.

After you have identified a good time and place for your writing, you might give some thought to your approach to writing in general. Writing approaches can, for the most part, be divided into three patterns: the all-night adrenalin writer, the consistent everyday writer, and the sporadic secluded writer. We have already discussed the inadequacies of the all-night adrenalin approach for writing faithful and ethical representations of qualitative research well. If that has been your pattern in the past, we urge you to consider either of the other two approaches at least for your qualitative work.

---

**Box 10.3**

### For Example: Karner's Writing Process

I have written in many different environments and with a variety of coauthors over the years. I have found what works for me through trial and error and mostly from needing to be productive in places and at times that were a real challenge to my personal style. Mostly, I've found that I enjoy writing in my office at home. In my home office, I have long worktables to organize my materials on and an extremely comfy desk chair. I learned long ago that if I was not physically comfortable, it was harder to stay on task.

My worktables are antique yellow pine doors that I have covered with glass tops and put legs under. These tables suit my need for a pleasant aesthetic environment as well as my visual organizing style. I organize my data and literature, visually, on my tables (and in larger projects I sometimes spread it out on the floor as well). I stack hard copies of the materials together for each section of my writing and then physically organize the literature and data, within each section, in the order I plan to write about it.

Mornings are the most productive writing time for me. I usually review what I wrote the day before over my morning coffee and then move to the computer to tackle the current day's project. I write in two- to three-hour blocks interspersed with short breaks to eat or walk my dogs or visit the gym. When I am writing, I like to clear my calendar (as much as possible) so that the writing process is my central task and focus for that time period. Though in the real world this is seldom possible, it is my preference.

When I am beginning a new project, I start with the instrumental writing tasks first. I usually write the methods section first, then the findings and results. I usually have a rough outline of my literature overview before I write my findings, but I do not begin to draft the literature section until after I have "written through" my data and analysis. After drafting these three sections, I work on the introduction and conclusion somewhat concurrently. When I have a draft of all the components, I begin editing and refining the work. The abstract is the very last thing I write. Throughout the writing process, I maintain a separate file so I can compile my references as I use them. I also make backup copies rather compulsively; I save to hard disk and floppy disk as well as print a hard copy at the end of each day's writing for larger projects.

---

The consistent, everyday approach is perhaps the most disciplined pattern for writing. Scholars who use this process carve out time to write on a regular basis and proceed to write a small section or subsection of their project each day. This is often the most fruitful pattern of writing, as those who write regularly are always moving forward on their projects no matter what other obligations they may have. Professional writers often recommend this steady, ongoing approach. As you experiment with various processes and come to understand your own better, this is an approach to strive to emulate for both its discipline and steady rate of productivity.

The sporadic secluded approach is perhaps the more common pattern among academic writers, who often attempt to accomplish their writing between semesters and over summer breaks. These writers generally put a lot of thought into conceptualizing and organizing their data and literature prior to beginning to write. When they write, they set aside specific amounts of time to focus on their writing to the exclusion of other tasks. They may isolate themselves from colleagues and family during these writing periods and emerge only after completion of their initial draft.

As students, your time and thus your approach will be somewhat constrained by both your instructor's requirements and the semester (or quarter) system of your school. The consistent, everyday approach may be your only real option to writing well for your course. If so, you can be assured that you are engaging in a productive and successful approach that is used by many, and aspired to by many others, not only in sociology but in other disciplines as well.

## Preparing to Write

Prior to beginning to write your research paper or report, you need to *organize your materials for the writing process*. Again, this is something that you should do in a way that works for you. Our organizational strategies work for us but may not work for you. Think about how you understand materials and organize other aspects of your life. Are you a visual organizer like Karner (see Box 10.3)? Or do you like a neat desktop with materials filed electronically (ready for cutting and pasting into your document) or in nicely labeled file folders or in tabbed notebooks for quick reference? Think about what kind of system is likely to work well with the way you think and work.

In organizing your materials to write, keep two things in mind: One, you need a system by which you can *find and retrieve* images and text from the data to illustrate your analysis, and two, you need something *manageable* so that you don't waste all your writing time chasing down details. How you choose to organize should address both concerns. One approach is to construct a thorough outline of the document you plan to write, including notations of where the quotes and materials you wish to put in the various sections are located. This outline can then be used as the guide for writing the various sections and fitting them together. One caution about this process is that it assumes the analysis is complete prior to the writing, which may not be an accurate assumption given the reflexive quality of qualitative research.

Another approach (favored by Karner) is to physically organize the materials. You can identify the quotes and illustrations from the data that you plan on incorporating into your writing and excerpt them into a separate document—you might create a separate document for each subtheme for manageability (as we suggested in Chapter 9). Be sure to include notation labels with each excerpt as to where it came from (e.g., *Gary: Interview one, page 6* or *Park observation, 12-03-03, page 5*). At this point, a working outline for the paper can be developed. We see this as a flexible road map for the process of writing. A working outline gives you an overview of how all your data and conceptual components relate to each other.

Over the years, we have heard many interesting stories of how our colleagues have fashioned their outlines with movable parts, allowing for a flexible writing process interspersed with further refinement and contemplation. Karner's favorite story is the graduate student who taped section notes to the sliding glass doors in her apartment. She organized them conceptually and began to work on a specific section. At the end of each session, she would draw the curtains closed. At the beginning of her next working session, she would open the curtains and view her conceptual organization with fresh eyes. In light (literally!) of what she had written the previous day, she would then rearrange her section notes and continue her writing. Others have used dry-erase boards or poster boards with Post-it notes to allow them to organize their thoughts both visually and physically in a very flexible manner.

This is also a good time to *plan your logistics* of writing. By this, we are referring to the process by which you back up your writing and compile your reference section. These are instrumental details of writing that can cause anguish if not addressed initially. We recommend that you back up everything in a regular and systematic manner. As we discussed earlier in terms of your data, you should back up what you write everyday. Many a deadline has been missed due to computer crashes and files lost in cyberspace. Since these events seem to happen only when you have not backed up your work, it is wise to do so often. Equally aggravating and time-consuming is trying to construct your reference section after you have completed the manuscript. We recommend that you initiate a process to record the works you cite and use while you are writing. You can open a separate document and enter citations as they are used, as we do. Or you may enter all the works you have used at the end of your writing session. Either way, it will alleviate the need to identify works long after you have returned the book or journal to the library. Make sure you also record the page numbers of any quotations you include from the literature.

The other aspect of writing to decide on at this point is what style guide you are going to use. Style guides provide the format for headings and subheadings, capitalization, citations (in text or in footnotes or endnotes), and references. As students, you should follow your instructor's directions as to the style guide required. If you are writing something for submission to a journal or for inclusion as a book chapter, you should check the style requirements of the journal or publisher. If you are unsure where you might be submitting your work, it is generally safe to use the American Sociological Association Style Guide (*http://www.asanet.org/apap/quickstyle.html*) when writing for a sociology audience. This would also be very appropriate for a paper you plan to submit for presentation at a professional meeting.

*Beginning to write* that first sentence signifies that you have begun the process of representing your subjects' life worlds and communicating your research experience. This is a daunting task to be sure, but it is also something that you have been doing all along if you have followed our advice. You have been writing conceptual notes to yourself, you may have been keeping an analytic journal, and you have written organization notes as you have developed your writing outline (whether thorough or flexible and movable). These notes can serve as the beginning of the writing process—the fitting of the puzzle pieces together. You have already organized the relevant literature and the illustrative excerpts from your data; now your task is to join all the pieces together in one well-written and -crafted document.

At this point, we offer you two cautions from experience: Do not wait for inspiration and do not expect perfection in your first draft. Waiting for inspiration before beginning to write is a common excuse for procrastination. Inspiration and insight most often occur when you are actively engaged in writing; seldom do they occur out of the blue. We recommend beginning with the methods section, as this should be a relatively straightforward and temporally ordered (see Chapter 9) account of the work you have done and how and why you did it. You might begin as though you were telling a friend or a colleague about your project. What did you set out to do? What challenges did you face and how did you overcome them? How did you approach the various methodological and analytical decisions that you had to make? What impact did these decisions have on the research? Beginning your writing with the methods section is a good reminder of all the work that you have done, and it will give you an instrumental place to begin your representation.

The key to perfectionism is later editing! Many writers get caught up in constructing perfect sentences or paragraphs; rather than continuing to write, they proceed to rewrite small sections, hoping to achieve perfection. Perhaps some people can do this, but we have yet to write the perfect sentence—especially not in our first drafts! Remember that everything you write can be edited later. Initially, you just need to put the words on paper that convey your ideas. Only when you have written a full draft and know what the document in its entirety will look like can you effectively edit and seek to refine and perfect your words and phrases. Remember that qualitative work is emergent and that the writing process is iterative. Seeking perfection too early in the writing process can inhibit much of the insight that comes only through reflection and working with the materials.

## Crafting the Qualitative Research Paper

The end point of qualitative research is often a paper written for a class, a journal article, or a chapter in an edited book, and sometimes a book-length scholarly monograph, thesis, or dissertation. Applied qualitative researchers may complete program or other evaluation reports for the government or for granting agencies. And the researcher may also have to present his work orally as well as (or instead of) in writing. Whichever format you are working toward, the basic, guiding principles are similar: pay attention to the audience for your work, and make sure your presentation follows a coherent and complete outline.

If you write a paper for a class, the audience for your work is your instructor, who will provide you with requirements for your paper in terms of length, reference format, and other elements. For example, in sociology classes using qualitative methods, we both require papers of approximately 18 to 20 pages for undergraduates and 30 to 35 pages for graduate students. We expect all students to use a consistent and recognized format, such as the American Sociological Association Style Guide, *http://www.asanet.org/apap/quickstyle.html*, or the Chicago style of referencing used in this textbook.

The audiences for published qualitative sociologists' work are likely to be fellow sociologists, or perhaps interdisciplinary scholars working on the editorial boards of scholarly journals or putting together edited books. The content of journals and edited books varies according to the theoretical and methodological principles espoused by the editors, from positivist, quantitative applied journals and readers to social constructionist qualitative ones. Obviously, for the purposes of this chapter, our examples come from audiences attuned to qualitative, social constructionist work. Within this general framework, as we saw in Chapter 1, there are a variety of perspectives including symbolic interactionism and the work of Goffman on everyday life. If you want to present or publish your work among those who have these qualitative and conceptual interests, you will not only use qualitative methods in your research but also various conceptual frameworks from the social constructionist literature.

The paper you write using your qualitative data will not only cite and use conceptual frameworks from the social constructionist literature but will also include anything substantive that has been written on the topic by sociologists and perhaps others. It will also follow certain conventions, such as a balance of (say) 60 percent analytic text and 40 percent illustrative description. Although your instructor may or may not require this, sociologists who write articles and books as part of their professional work generally write a number of drafts prior to the finished draft to be submitted for publication.

You should be aware of the process a paper goes through to be published in a journal. The first step is submission of the paper to the journal's editor, following the guidelines stated at the beginning of each issue of the journal. The editor typically requires the submission of three to five hard copies and perhaps an electronic version on a diskette, and some journals also ask for the payment of a fee of $10 or more for processing the submission (other journals ask for a processing fee after the article is accepted for publication). The editor then asks three to five experts to read the paper and judge its suitability for publication. These reviewers may be members of the journal's editorial board (listed toward the front of the journal), or other scholars known to the editor for their expertise in the topic, theory, or methods of the paper.

The reviewers make recommendations to the editor as to whether the paper should be rejected, accepted with major or minor changes, or returned to the author for revision and possible resubmission. They provide detailed suggestions for the author, including recommendations for changes in writing style, methods, or conceptualization, and the inclusion of prior scholarly work on the topic that might have been overlooked. The journal editor then writes a letter to the author indicating whether or not the article has been accepted for publication and summarizing the most important suggested revisions. The comments of the reviewers are generally included, anonymously, in the materials sent to the author. The author then revises and resubmits the paper for publication, at which point the editor may accept the paper or send it back to the reviewers for another look. This process may take several months, and the entire process from submission to publication may take more than a year.

## Elements of the Qualitative Research Paper

Qualitative research papers generally include the following components: title, author's name and affiliation, abstract, introduction, literature review, methods, findings and results, conclusions, and references (see Box 10.4). We discuss each of these sections in the order it would appear in a published work, though that is seldom the order in which the sections are written. We also discuss the issue of representation—the ways in which findings and results are framed by the author.

The general guide to writing order that we offer is to begin with your flexible outline or overview. Then draft the methods section—a straightforward account of what you have done. Follow this with a draft introduction so that you know, roughly, where you are going, and perhaps the literature section. Write your analysis, including your illustrative data excerpts. Then write the conclusion and return to polish the introduction and literature review to make sure that the conclusion addresses the issues raised in these sections. At this point you will want to edit the entire manuscript for coherence, accuracy, and consistency. Again, we recommend that you compile your reference section as you refer to others' works so the references will be complete when you have finished writing. The last thing you will work on will be the abstract. Finally, the manuscript title may be tentatively held throughout the writing process and adopted or changed at its conclusion.

---

**Box 10.4**

### Qualitative Research Paper Components

**What to write first?**
> Begin with the **Methods** section
> Outline or draft the **Literature Review**
> Write the **Findings and Results**
> Craft the **Conclusions** and **Introduction** concurrently
> Polish the Literature Review to lead to Findings and Results
> Compile the **References,** endnotes, or footnotes
> Write the **Abstract**
> Select a vivid and informative **Title**

**How is the paper organized?**
> **Title**
> **Abstract**
> **Introduction**
> **Literature Review**
> **Methods**
> **Findings and Results**
> **Conclusions**
> **References**

---

## Title

There are two main approaches to title selection in qualitative research. In titling their work, some researchers begin with a compelling or vivid phrase followed by a more descriptive subtitle. Warren's 1996 paper demonstrates this two-part approach: "Older Women, Younger Men: Self and Stigma in Age-Discrepant Relationships." The first phrase, "Older Women, Younger Men," is meant to capture the potential readers' interest so they will take the time to read the paper. The subtitle "Self and Stigma in Age-Discrepant Relationships" locates the paper within the sociological concepts of interest (self, stigma) and the study sample (age-discrepant relationships). You can see this same pattern in the following selection of sociology titles:

• *Tell Them Who I Am: The Lives of Homeless Women*

- *Dancing at Armageddon: Survivalism and Chaos in Modern Times*
- *Making Grey Gold: Narratives of Nursing Home Care*
- *Slim's Table: Race, Respectability, and Masculinity*
- *Kitchens: The Culture of Restaurant Work*
- *Gendered Transitions: Mexican Experience of Immigration*
- *Hard Hats: The Work World of Construction Workers*
- *Medicalizing Masculinity: Post Traumatic Stress Disorder in Vietnam Veterans*

Other researchers select a single descriptive title that signals only the conceptual focus of the manuscript to the reader. For example, Karner and Hall's 2002 paper is titled "Successful Strategies for Serving Diverse Populations." The reader can tell that the paper is about strategies of providing services to multicultural communities. In making decisions about how to title your work, it is important to keep in mind the disciplinary conventions and expectations of your audience. Warren's "Older Women, Younger Men" title was intended for a qualitative sociology audience and was published in *Clinical Sociology Review*. The Karner and Hall manuscript, in contrast, was published as a book chapter intended for an audience of community service practitioners and researchers.

## Author's Name and Affiliation

Both Tracy X. Karner and Carol A. B. Warren use middle initials in their publications. The use of middle initials in published work seems to be less popular than it was a decade or so ago in this country; in England, however, social science researchers often use only initials to identify themselves, as in "A. E. Smith." Additionally, women researchers have to decide, if they marry (or for that matter divorce and remarry), whether they want to keep and use their "maiden" name or change it for publication purposes. There has been some speculation that articles submitted for publication using only initials or male-sounding first names are more likely to be accepted than clearly female names. No matter which form of name the author chooses to use, this section also commonly includes academic level and affiliation, for example, "Associate Professor, Department of Sociology, Arizona State University," together with an address and an e-mail or phone method of contact.

## Abstract

Although the abstract is printed at the beginning of the article, after the title and author, it is generally written after the article has been completed. Abstracts enable the editor of the journal (and potential readers) to determine what the article is about, substantively, conceptually, and methodologically. The number of words allowed for the abstract, generally between 150 and 250, is determined by the editor. It is a challenge to compress the essence of a study into these few lines, but it is also a useful exercise; if an abstract can be written only with great difficulty, it is probably because the paper is unclear and unfocused, its point or points lost somewhere in the text. The abstract serves as a concise overview of what will be found in the manuscript that follows. It should include the central conceptual focus of the work, the theoretical approach used, the methods employed (sample, data collection, and analysis), and the key findings. If applicable, and space permitting, the author may include any implications for practice or policy that the research findings offer.

In the following example, Karas and Karner (in 161 words) outline their topic and its relevance (diabetes as the sixth leading cause of death in the United States), their theoretical approach (Arthur Frank's ideal body types), the method of data collection (interviews) with their sample (two practitioners and eight individuals with diabetes), the key finding (persons with diabetes tended to be most closely associated with the "disciplined body type" and pursued high levels of bodily control and predictability), and the practice implications (more effective treatment and better practitioner-patient relationships).

> Diabetes is the sixth leading cause of death from disease, shortens the average lifespan by up to 15 years, and is the main cause of new blindness, kidney failure and amputations in the United States. In this study, interviews were conducted with two practitioners and eight individuals with diabetes to discover which embodiment choices and ideal body types were most frequently expressed. Developed by Arthur Frank (1995), the ideal body-type provides a framework for better understanding the behavior and needs of ill persons. Interviewed persons with diabetes tended to be most closely associated with the "disciplined body-type" and pursued high levels of bodily control and predictability. Frank offers a prescriptive, idealized type, the communicative body, as an ethical ideal for bodies living with illness. This framework is evaluated for its heuristic value in providing insight into the behaviors, needs, and struggles of persons with diabetes, as well as providing a means to promote more effective treatment options and better practitioner-patient relationships. (Karas and Karner 2004, 1)

## Introduction

The first sentence and the first paragraph of a qualitative research paper are extremely important, because it is there that the reader should be able to discern the analytic descriptive topic of the paper and how it will be developed. In the first paragraph from our paper "The

Dangerous Listener: Unforeseen Perils in Intensive Interviewing," for example, we let the reader know that our focus is the potential dangers of social science research to participants. Since our intended audience is other sociologists and social scientists, we hoped this beginning would hold their attention.

> Human subjects legislation over the past ten years has framed so-cial science research, like the biomedical, as potentially danger-ous. What such legislation frames as dangerous is the interview or questionnaire topic, or the way questions are posed, particularly for vulnerable respondents. What we propose is that in the inten-sive interview, the act of listening, thus the listener her- or himself, may become perceived as dangerous. The conditions under which this danger arises are those in which a past, suppressed or forgot-ten self emerges in the interview, and becomes associated with the listener. We suggest that mental patienthood, and the events and relationships that preceded and led to it, may be one such set of circumstances. (Karner and Warren 1995, 80)

Following the first sentence, we go on to distinguish our analysis of po-tential danger from those other dangers that human subjects regula-tions are meant to address. The remainder of the first paragraph develops our analysis of the ways in which being interviewed invokes past (damaged or spoiled) selves—like mental patienthood—that rep-resent a threat to the interviewee's current presentation of self.

The author should also reaffirm, in the introductory paragraphs, why this work is important and relevant to other researchers. Clinton Sanders accomplishes this in the first paragraph of his paper "Actions Speak Louder Than Words: Close Relationships Between Humans and Nonhuman Animals":

> Relationships, which are composed of routine and patterned in-teractions, are central to the symbolic interactionist view of social life. Relationships range from those that are instrumental, emo-tionally uninvolving, and typically of short duration to those that are intrinsically rewarding and long-term and in which partici-pants have considerable emotional stake. Conventionally, interactionists and other analysts of social life have seen the inter-dependence, commitment, and emotionality of close relationships as existing within, and sustained by, the symbolic exchanges of hu-mans. I maintain that this characterization of close relationships is overly restrictive. It excludes from consideration a class of affili-ations that are commonplace, imbued with emotion, and central to the shaping of the identities and selves of those involved. Tradi-tionally, conventional sociologists (e.g. Perrow 2000, 473) have ig-nored or denigrated relationships between people and their companion animals. However, the intense, involving, and routine interactions forming these relations are worthy of serious atten-

tion and have the potential of adding significantly to the sociology of intimate exchanges. (Sanders 2003, 405–406)

Sanders tells his readers that even though relationships are a central research focus of sociologists and especially interactionists, these scholars have excluded a significant and commonplace relationship (between humans and animals) from serious investigation. In his last sentence, Sanders assures his readers that their time will be well spent by considering his work and the insights it brings to bear on the sociology of intimate exchanges. In addition to his analytic themes, Sanders has revealed who will (or should) be interested—sociologists and interactionists—in reading the manuscript.

The introductory section of a paper sets the tone of the work and gives readers a good idea of what awaits them in the rest of the paper. A common mistake that novice writers make is in not leading the reader through the work. It is fundamental to tell the reader what you are going to say, why it is important, and to whom the information will be most useful (the expected audience). It is also useful to offer a summary at the end of each paper section, with a transition to the next section. The introductory section of a paper may vary in length from a couple of paragraphs to a couple of pages. However, it should conclude with a strong statement of the value of the research and its broader relevance. See how Sanders returns to the key points of his opening paragraph in a more direct and vivid manner in the final paragraph of his introduction:

> Identity, personhood, empathy, love, mindedness, culture, and other key issues are of considerable interest to interactionists and are of central relevance for the sociology of close relationships. The central point of this article is that these key issues may be fruitfully explored if we turn serious and appreciative attention to the human-animal bond and the social exchanges that both define and result from this unique form of sociation. The task requires that we move beyond the analytic restraints imposed by the presumption that shared symbols are the sole foundation for "real" intimate relationships and "authentic" interactions. (Sanders 2003, 407)

Providing readers with these summary sections continually reminds them of your purpose in writing this representation and helps guide them through your work.

## Literature Review

After the introductory paragraphs, the literature review situates the study in the substantive literature on the topic and the conceptual literature that will be used to frame the topic. Like the introduction, this section may be drafted early on or just outlined and then written after the findings and results portion has been completed. The literature review is a key part of the manuscript because it sets your analysis in the context of the relevant and up-to-date published work. The purpose of discussing the literature is to present your work as the next step for research in this area.

The review of the literature should be ordered analytically (see Chapter 9) rather than author by author. A listing such as "Jones says . . . ; then Smith found . . . ; later Johnson elaborated" is not only boring to read; it does not give the reader any clues as to why the materials are even being presented or what their relevance is to the current project. The literature review should discuss any debates or controversies related to the topic, and any limitations of previous research that the author's project will be addressing. The literature review section then concludes with a strong restatement of the central research questions (or goals) of the current project. Box 10.5 presents the literature for Warren's "Older Women, Younger Men" paper. A reverse outline of this literature review—a handy device for assessing the ordering of written work—indicates that she arranges the substantive literature in the following way:

1. Age discrepancy in relationships
   a. contemporary demographic patterns of marriage, divorce, and age discrepancy.
   b. historical inequality between the genders in marriage, in general and in relation to age-discrepant marriage.
   c. contemporary media discussions of older women and younger men.
   d. attitude studies demonstrating unfavorable views of age-discrepant relationships, especially those involving older women and younger men.

Warren then uses the attitude studies to make the transition into the conceptual frame:

2. stigma
   a. stigma and its impact on the self (using Goffman 1961).
   b. techniques of neutralization (citing the sociological literature on this topic) used to counteract the stigma of age discrepancy and its impact on the self.
   c. the relationship of the general cultural themes of stigma to clinical practice.

Note that Warren concludes with the issue of clinical practice that she had previously introduced in the last paragraph of her literature review. Warren did this not only because she published the paper in a clinical sociology journal but also because it is at the point of separation that one or both members of the couples stop seeking to neutralize the stigma and reveal the ways in which they share it. In her final two sentences, Warren offers the reader an idea of what she proposes to demonstrate in the pages that follow:

> I propose that people in age-discrepant marriages neutralize stigma through the denial and refocusing techniques described below, protecting their relationship from the implications of stigma. By contrast, I expect that people who seek counseling for what they perceive as marital trouble redefine cultural stigma as legitimate, and seek to change themselves. (Warren 1996, 65)

---

### Box 10.5

## Literature Review Section From

### "Older Women, Younger Men: Self and Stigma in Age-Discrepant Relationships"

Studies of contemporary demographic patterns indicate that marital age discrepancy is related to gender, divorce, remarriage and lifespan. A study of marriage in England and Wales showed that the tendency to marry a younger person peaks for both sexes at 30 to 34 years old, and falls to its lowest point at 50 to 54. Unmarried people in their 50s are more likely to marry someone younger (Bytheway 1981), although there are many more unmarried women than men at this age and upward. Remarriages are more likely than first marriages to involve an age discrepancy (Veevers 1984); women who were married previously are more likely to marry younger men who are marrying for the first time, and vice versa (Presser 1975).

Age-discrepant intimate relationships are part of Western history, and have had different historical meanings over time (Banner 1992). What has remained fairly constant is the institutionalized power relation between the genders which fosters resource inequalities between men and women, and which, at its worst, frames women as men's resources. Throughout Western history, women have been traded in marriage by fathers and brothers, to cement aristocratic alliances, to end wars, or settle disputes (Banner 1992). A woman's dowry or bride-price, lineage, virginity, appearance and age were all bargaining chips in the marriage market; older women (even widows) were sometimes "married off" to younger men who could not obtain better bargains.

The development in the eighteenth century of notions of choice in marriage based on romantic love (an idea that was superimposed on, rather than a replacement for, earlier patterns), precipitated some changes in older women's romantic options. Since romantic love was, and is, viewed as the property of youth, older women were seen as even more undesirable than when they only had to bring a higher bride-price. With the twentieth century development of competitive dating, a process which located all the power of choice normatively with men rather than women, older women faced an interesting situation. Rhetorically, they were free to love a man of any age. Realistically, women's choices were made within a structural context that virtually mandated men's choice of a younger woman.

**Box 10.5 (Cont)**

Contemporary media discussions of older women and younger men insist that romance and marriage between older women and younger men are on the increase, both statistically and normatively (Houston 1989). These discussions focus neither on psychodynamic nor cultural areas of possible difficulty, but, rather, seek to justify and celebrate these relationships. A letter to Dear Abby, and Dear Abby's response, exemplify media treatments:

> Q: I am a 43-year-old woman, divorced, no children, have an excellent job, and am secure in my position. Fourteen months ago, a bright 31-year-old man came to work here in another department. The last thing I had in mind was a serious relationship with this kid, but you guessed it. It happened. I fell in love with him. He didn't pursue me. I invited him out first. We discovered we had so much in common we couldn't wait to see each other again. We're still "in the closet" about our relationship, but we can't keep it under wraps much longer. . . . I'm embarrassed—almost ashamed—and terribly concerned about what people will think about "us." He's more in charge and mature about this than I am. . . . Am I crazy? Can this work? Meanwhile we are sneaking about like a couple of thieves. Help me! . . .
>
> A: Quit sneaking around and don't worry about what people will think. Can it work? Yes, if you both want it. Please read the new book *Loving a Younger Man* by Victoria Houston. . . . It's written by a woman who once walked in your shoes. She resolutely reaffirms my advice: "Forget the numbers, and follow your heart." (*Los Angeles Times* Nov. 7, 1987, p. 3)

Although statistics on changes in rates of younger women/older men marriage over time are not easily obtainable (at least in published form), there is no doubt that the mass media have publicized the idea of increasing, and increasingly legitimate intimacy between older women and younger men. And it is also possible that the increasing ability of women to earn high salaries and develop their own resources enable some women to operate in the dating and marriage market much as men once did. However, while cultural and normative changes may indeed be occurring, intimate relationships between older women and younger men remain stigmatized.

In attitude studies (Derenski and Landsburg 1981; Cowen 1984; Hartnett, Rosen, and Shumate 1981) both adults and adolescents viewed age-discrepant relationships unfavorably, especially where the discrepancy was large, and saw the older woman/younger man type as more suspect and less promising than the older man/younger woman type. There were almost no gender or age differences between male and female respondents in their stigmatization of age-discrepant relationships.

Much has been written, following Goffman (1961), on stigma and its impact on the self. Goffman (1961) defines stigma as an elusive intersection of culturally disvalued attributes and identities with particular audiences and with the generalized other. He identifies three types of stigma: moral stigma, based on engagement in disapproved behaviors; "tribal" stigma, or racial difference; and physical stigma, based on anomalies of the phys-

**Box 10.5 (Cont)**

ical self. The knowledge that one is stigmatized leads to an attempt to change the self in the culturally desirable direction, or to techniques that neutralize the stigma.

Techniques of neutralization are those ways in which the stigmatized seek to bridge, verbally, the gap between cultural expectations and their violation. While accounts are features of everyday disjunctures of conduct (Mills 1959; Lyman and Scott 1970), techniques of neutralization are directed toward the justification of stigmatizing behaviors or statuses such as juvenile delinquency (Sykes and Matza 1959) or mental patienthood (Goffman 1961; Warren and Messinger 1988).

A theory of stigma in age-discrepant relationships can illuminate the clinical interpretation of those relationships. Problems that are brought to marriage counselors not only have psychodynamic elements (Singer-Magdoff 1988) but also reflect general themes in the culture. These themes are neutralized during the idealizing phase of the marriage; once marital trouble is experienced and defined, they emerge as clinical problems. I propose that people in age-discrepant marriages neutralize stigma through the denial and refocusing techniques described below, protecting their relationship from the implications of stigma. By contrast, I expect that people who seek counseling for what they perceive as marital trouble redefine cultural stigma as legitimate, and seek to change themselves.

(Warren 1996, 63–65)

## Methods

The first thing to be said about this section is that it should be called "Methods"; do not use "Methodology," as this word means the study of methods. Often this is the first section that is written. This section should give a complete accounting of the research process—what was done and how and why. The methods section of a qualitative research paper typically discusses the research design or research questions, the method(s) used, data collection, data analysis, and any special problems or issues raised by the methods. Positivist, quantitative researchers generally include a section on topics such as the validity and generalizability of the research in this section, but this is not usually done with qualitative research papers.

In general, the methods section should contain enough detailed information for a reader to be able to evaluate the analysis and conclusions. For example, stating that the data consisted of twenty intensive interviews is not enough. Rather, a reader will need to know if you interviewed respondents once in a casual setting or multiple times over the course of the research. Additionally, readers want to know how the data were recorded—did you write your fieldnotes in the field or immediately after or was there some delay? Were your interviews tape- or video-recorded and thoroughly transcribed? In order to evaluate and understand the data you will be presenting in your analysis, the reader needs to have a pretty detailed idea about how your research has been accomplished.

The methods section should include a discussion of the following: description of the setting, interview sample, and images or documents and how they were selected; data collection procedures, including any challenges that had to be overcome and decisions that had to be made; and how the analysis was accomplished. For example, Karner's (1995) "Medicalizing Masculinity: Post Traumatic Stress Disorder in Vietnam Veterans" detailed her methods and procedures:

> Using the techniques of naturalistic inquiry—specifically participant observation and intensive interviewing of veterans on a Vietnam unit of a VA Medical Center in a large midwestern city—I was able to find men steeped in a therapeutic process of retelling. Tracing their childhood recollections of family, religion, and community through basic training, their military experience in Vietnam, and the years that followed, I analyzed the veterans' stories with attention to how their strategies may have shifted and evolved over the years. Since the social context of meaning was an integral aspect of the study, it was important to find a single consistent environment within which to interact with the veterans. An initial intensive participant observation phase served as interpretive backdrop for the rest of the study by allowing me to familiarize myself with the therapeutic milieu. Subsequently, I continued my unit participation and observation throughout my entire time in the field, although my primary focus shifted toward the interviews.
>
> After the initial immersion process, I began lengthy intensive interviews with the newly admitted veterans. These interviews provided a conceptual interplay with the observations of the social context. The webs of significance from the observations and interviews were approached from several different viewpoints. The veteran interviews allowed me to make comparisons between the men as well as to consider the discourse of the environment. At the end of my time in the field, I also interviewed staff members for approximately an hour each, which illuminated the differences between the intention and the reception of program goals. Veteran autobiographies afforded representational documents written early in treatment permitting another life story for contrast to the narratives expressed publicly on the unit and privately in the interviews. Thus I sought interpretations of the process of reconstructing Vietnam in the setting as well as by the individual.
>
> The data that form the basis of this study are drawn from these intensive interviews (see Karner 1994). In the Midwest during the Spring of 1991, one half of the inpatient population—15 veterans—were interviewed one to four times each, and were observed in a variety of hospital settings. In addition, I interviewed hospital staff, sat in on staff meetings, and had access to autobiographies written by the veterans as they entered the hospital. During the

study, all the patients were Vietnam veterans and one was also a Gulf War veteran. All but one of the men interviewed were white, one was African American. The veterans ranged in age from 38 to 47 years and all were from the midwestern states. (Karner 1995, 33–34)

Following this overview, Karner provides a table of her interview sample demographics and a narrative description of the site of her research, the PTSD unit of a Veterans Administration hospital. A reader is able to discern the variety of data sources Karner was able to access (participant observation, interviews with veterans, veteran autobiographies, interviews with staff members), why this site was selected (unique opportunity to study therapeutic retelling in a gendered—all male—setting), how the interviewees were chosen (new admissions), who was interviewed (all staff members and half the inpatient population), and the time frame of the data collection (Spring 1991). In referencing her previous work (Karner 1994), she also lets the reader know that this paper is part of a larger project where the research design has been more thoroughly described and discussed.

Although the principles we have outlined suggest a fairly lengthy methods section, the extensiveness of methodological discussion varies by the journal editor's policies and the type of article. *The Journal of Clinical Sociology* prefers relatively short methodological discussion, so that in our "Dangerous Listener" article, the methods section was very brief:

> Our data are two sets of intensive interviews, one with female mental patients-to-expatients in the 1950s in California (see Warren 1987), and one with ex-Vietnam veterans on a trauma ward at a Veterans' administration hospital (see Karner 1994). In the first study, referred to as the "Bay Area" study, seventeen women were interviewed at intervals ranging from one week to three months for a period of 36 months between 1958 and 1961 (see Sampson, Messinger, and Towne 1964). In the second, in the Midwest in the 1990s, 15 men were interviewed one to four times each, and were observed in a variety of hospital settings by Karner. In addition, Karner interviewed hospital staff, and had access to autobiographies written by the veterans as they entered the hospital. (Karner and Warren 1995, 81)

In addition, Karner's 1995 paper is substantive and conceptual (post-traumatic stress disorder as medicalized masculinity), while Karner and Warren's 1995 paper is methodological and conceptual (interviewers as dangerous listeners). Methodological articles such as "The Dangerous Listener" often emerge from doing a series of substantive studies and thinking about methodological issues that are common to, or differ between, these studies. Methodological articles may be written about aspects of interview, ethnographic, or other qualitative research. In "The Social Relations of Intensive Interviewing," Harkess and Warren (1993) wrote about interviews as social encounters, and the variations that occur depending on the kind of prior association between interviewer and respondent, from stranger to intimate. In another methodological article, "Writing the Other, Inscribing the Self" several student coauthors and Warren (2000) used fieldnotes from a variety of settings, including a gay bar, a Hispanic health care association, and a group home for delinquent boys, to explore ethnographic writing. They analyzed the ways in which fieldnotes are designed to communicate the interactions and meanings of the other in the setting, and the ways in which they also communicate (if read by another) aspects of the self of the writer. Because the focus of such papers as "The Dangerous Listener," "The Social Relations of Intensive Interviewing," and "Writing the Other" is methodological, the formal methods section is often abbreviated.

## Analysis: Findings and Results

The analysis is the conceptual "heart" of the paper. This section should not, however, be given a first-level subheading such as "Analysis" or, as in quantitative research, "Findings" and "Results." Your analysis section subhead may be a reiteration of part of the title of the paper, for example, "The Dangerous Listener." In this longest section of the paper, the writer develops her main theme and subthemes.

In writing qualitative sociology well, the author is presented with a number of decisions that must be made about how to best present the data. The actual details and complexities of representing qualitative research are "handled only upon putting ideas into words on paper" (Emerson 2001c, 311). The decisions we make as writers influence both the understanding and the representation of the data. "By writing in different ways, we discover new aspects of our topic and our relation to it" (Richardson 1994, 516). Denzin identifies four central problems or decisions that a writer faces in moving from the "field to text to reader" of "interpretation or sense-making, representation, legitimation, and desiring" (1994, 503–504).

Interpretive or sense-making decisions are contemplated by the author throughout the research process. Interpretation guides what Emerson (2001c) refers to as the overarching framework for organizing the text. Whatever broad-based understanding of the data the researcher arrives at—how the "puzzle pieces are put together"—constitutes the frame of interpretation within which other decisions about how to "write the data" will be made. Which aspects are considered important to the story or understanding and will be included? Which elements will not be told? Maines (1998, 388) reminds us that writing is also "a way of not knowing" the components that remain absent from our interpretation. The goal of writing qualitative research well, from our perspective, is to provide a compelling interpretation of the data that provides a faithful representation of the lives of those studied.

## Representation

Although not a section of the paper, the representation of the data (see Chapter 1) is a key component of "telling the story." Whose voice or narrative will be at the center of your account?

> Deciding how to present voices and lives is a continuous problem for qualitative writers. Because we use their voices and experiences of the people we study, both for their own sake and as evidence of our credibility, we are constantly making writerly decisions about who gets to say what and how often in the text, and who the narrator talks about, how and how often. (Richardson 1990, 39)

How will you represent the individuals that you have studied? Will you tell the research story through your experience? These questions about representations have been asked and answered in various ways for the past three decades in sociology (e.g., see Gusfield 1976; Clifford and Marcus 1986; Van Maanen 1988; Rhoads 2003).

Diamond (1992) and Mitchell (2002) both employ the strategy of narrative unfolding. They locate themselves at the center of the narrative and invite the reader to share their experience by describing their understandings, and interactions in the field, and by telling a story that has a beginning, middle, and end. Geertz (1988, 78) calls this first-person, biographical form of writing "I-witnessing." I-witnessing highlights the "ethnographer's inner life and social experiences in the field as a personal story" (Emerson 2001c, 307). In another variation of I-witnessing, Krieger (1991) borrows the term "quest form" from Heilbrun's *Writing a Woman's Life*. In the quest form, writers "chronicle a problem of inquiry using their personal dilemmas and research experiences as the central interest of their account" (Krieger 1991, 51). Much like in autoethnography (e.g., see Ellis and Bochner 1996, discussed in Chapter 1), the writer is on a quest to understand some aspect of his or her own biography by studying others with similar experiences.

Another approach to representation is to place the individuals studied at the center of the account. Richardson (1990) discusses two options for this: individual sociobiographies and the collective story. In individual sociobiographies, each person's story is presented and analyzed separately, a format generally associated more with literature than sociology, but used by some qualitative sociologists (Richardson 1990, 35–36, and see Chapter 1). The collective story, which seeks to understand the individual's experiences within a coherent social context, is more commonly used in sociology. The collective story uses an analytical chronology, that is, the common elements to each individual's story are used to frame the collaborative, joint accounting. The weaving of individual voices together to tell a collective story can be a powerful mode of representation (e.g., see Richardson 1985).

Perhaps you will opt to represent your data from the perspective of a sociological narrative of conceptual themes. With this approach, the main theme and its subthemes are developed from ethnographic, interview, visual, or documentary data; these same data are then used, reflexively, to illustrate the analysis descriptively. One of two rhetorical devices is used in the analytic-descriptive approach to representing the data: the typology or the continuum (Richardson 1990). A *typology* classifies the data into categories and offers a discussion of each. There are examples of typologies throughout this book, including the discussion of references under "Endnotes and References" below. A *continuum*, on the other hand, arrays the data along some kind of imaginary line, for example Goffman's (1961) discussion of the "moral career of the mental patient" as pre-patient, patient, and ex-patient.

One outcome of these representational choices is legitimation: To which readers will your work appear legitimate, and to which illegitimate? Legitimation of representations involves questions such as how do you know what you say you know? What support can you offer for your analysis? Emerson, Fretz, and Shaw (1995, 179–180) offer two strategies of legitimation: excerpt and integrative. Using an excerpt strategy, sections of data (quotes from fieldnotes, interviews, or documents; selected visual images) are presented as indented quotations and set off from other text. With an integrative strategy, briefer sections of data are inserted within the surrounding text and identified with quotation marks. Often, both approaches are used within a single paper, and it is up to the writer to decide how to best make use of the data as evidence.

As a writer, you will also have to decide how many examples to include and how much support is needed for your analysis. There is wide variation on what constitutes enough. Esterberg (2002, 213) says there are "no magic numbers" and that support should meet the "believability" test. That is, you should include enough examples for your analysis to be believable, but not so much that your reader will be bored. On the other hand, Berg (2004, 284) offers a rule of three as a guide and states that every assertion in the analysis should be backed up by a minimum of three examples. We recommend using the goal of "faithfulness" of your account as the criterion for making decisions about how much documentation to include.

## Conclusion

The Conclusion or Discussion—or both!—is the final narrative section of a sociology paper, and its length can vary from a few paragraphs to a few pages. In this section, it is important to return to the major conceptual, theoretical, or applied issues discussed at the beginning of the paper and restate what has been learned or can be concluded. The conclusion should include an overview of any new insights the research has offered and how it contributes to (or advances) sociological knowledge. Any limitations of the current research should be addressed, as well as suggestions for future research (if relevant). If any practice or policy implications can be derived from the research, they should be specified in this section as well, especially in applied work.

As our example of a conclusion (see Box 10.6), we return to Warren's 1996 paper. Notice how she returns to the themes discussed in the introduction: the mother/son psychodynamics of these age-discrepant relationships; the embodiment of social stigma, with the wife worrying about her appearance, and whether she looks like or is acting like her husband's mother; the husband privately lamenting the loss of children and the loss of his own age cohort. Warren notes that these themes tend to be verbalized only after separation or divorce, because during the marriage the focus is on techniques of neutralization that attempt to deny the stigma and shore up the sense of belonging together. As Warren's example illustrates, there should be some symmetry between the introduction and conclusions—as one frames the upcoming discussion and the other concludes it.

---

### Box 10.6

### Conclusion Section From

#### "Older Women, Younger Men: Self and Stigma in Age-Discrepant Relationships"

The uneven psychodynamic, cultural, structural, and gendered set of relations between older men and younger women arises from the context of contemporary Western marriage, and from stigma—the public and private distrust of intimacy between older women and younger men. When older women and younger men are embarking on what they perceive as viable marriages, they protect the sense of self and other in the relationship by neutralization techniques. When older women and younger men enter the clinical setting, or contemplate divorce, the stigma of age discrepancy may be affirmed rather than denied or neutralized.

The central feature of stigma for the women in these marriages is the visual: the appearance of an older woman with a younger man. For the men, it is the cohort: exile from one's proper age group and place in history. But the lurking fear, for both, is the relation between child and parent: the playing out in the marriage of a mother and a son, and the absence of a mutual child within the marriage.

What, given a theory of stigma, can clinicians expect from older women and younger men? Once couples decide that they are experiencing troubles and seek help, the mutual and individual neutralization of stigma

## Box 10.6 (Cont)

may give way to a redefinition of stigma as legitimate rather than illegitimate. The husband may reconnect with cultural themes related to fathering children, and to the definition of involvement with older women as related to being mothered. He may take up the woman's theme of visual differentiation, and begin to find his wife's appearance problematic. He will re-connect with his cohort.

The wife may, in turn, take up the theme of the cohort self, re-finding her own place in an age cohort with its more sedate musical expression. She will approach the youth-reviving techniques of our culture with renewed tenacity, blaming her own aging for the breakdown of the marriage. Perhaps she will come to define herself as having sought to mother this younger man. The psychodynamic principles of suppression, repression, and the Oedipal-parental origins of current problems will be pressed into service by spouses as well as clinicians to replace techniques of neutralization.

This is the prediction of stigma theory to a clinical setting; it is borne out by our interview with Keith, the divorced man, and contact with him and his ex-wife throughout their marriage and divorce. His post-divorce comments indicate a marital history of neutralization followed by a separation-linked reinterpretation:

> she was seeking a bearded entity to father more children. I didn't know that was her agenda, so I was kind of agenda-ized by her without my knowing it clearly. . . . the negative thing for me was the rush to have children. . . . Another negative thing was just the complications inherent, she was married twice before, she had a stepdaughter, a son and a daughter, none of which I particularly wanted, then she had two daughters from the second marriage that I was very close to. . . .

> I: Was this sort of an attraction for you that she had some of the things you didn't have?

> K: Oh yes. In part some of the difficulty now is that since we've been separated I'm sort of growing up all over again . . . I think consciously and to a larger extent unconsciously, I had an instant family to walk into. I didn't have to make those decisions. I had to catch up real quickly. It was illusory in some ways, but I kind of caught up real quickly SES wise . . . I was an overnight success. . . . But it was in a pretty illusionary sense.

Thus, in the waning or aftermath of an age-discrepant marriage, the real becomes illusory, and the illusory real. What seemed, during the days of idealization, to be the cultural illusion of stigma now becomes the suppressed reality. What seemed to be the reality of a good relationship now becomes illusory. This process, of course, occurs in the wake of any relational breakdown. It is the content, not the structure of the redefinitions, which will vary with age discrepancy and other marital patterns. And it is this content that is shaped by the interaction of psychodynamic with the cultural images of ideal marriages, and of stigmatized ones.

(Warren 1996, 83–85)

## Endnotes and References

The first endnote (or perhaps footnote, depending on what the journal or book publisher requires) is often used to thank organizations and people who were helpful in carrying out the research presented in the paper. If the research is published in a book format, the acknowledgments generally go in a separate section at the beginning of the book (as you will note in this text), following the preface. The remaining endnotes consist of comments, asides, or addenda to the main points made in the text. Scholarly articles or books almost always have footnotes or endnotes, although a few do not (Kneeland and Warren 2002).

References in qualitative sociology publications are generally of three types, the first two of which correspond to the sections of the review of the literature discussed above: (1) substantive references dealing with the topic of the article; (2) theoretical, conceptual, or applied references situating the article in a particular qualitative sociology tradition; and (3) methodological references linking the study to others in the same tradition. In general, all works quoted, paraphrased, or referred to should be properly cited and included in the reference section. Most universities and colleges have a statement of academic honesty that outlines what constitutes plagiarism and should be avoided. We recommend that you get a copy of your school's statement and familiarize yourself with the issues.

## Editing and Rewriting

After completing a first draft of your text, it is time to begin editing and rewriting. Editing and rewriting, as we have mentioned before, are fundamental to writing well. In the process of writing, you are crafting communication—attempting to share your insights and perspectives in a way that others will understand. As you reread what you have written, ask yourself, is the writing clear and does it make sense? Does your argument seem logical? Does each sentence follow logically and easily from the sentence before and lead naturally to the sentence that follows? Then read through each sentence again, and delete any non-essential words. Each word and sentence that remains in your final version should be necessary to communicate your ideas. Continue to reread, refine, and reflect. Remember, writing well takes time, patience, perseverance, and practice.

For classroom purposes, your instructor may require only one finished draft of a paper, or perhaps two drafts. But if you, as an undergraduate or graduate student, want to publish your work, you will generally have to write one, two, three, or even more versions. Sociologists commonly circulate their work to other sociologists prior to publication submission; this is a good way to get informal feedback and editing assistance. The paper you submit to a journal should be polished and free of typographical or other errors, and it should already have been read and edited by at least two or three other people working in the field. Polishing is especially important if you have to pay an up-front submission fee that many journals now charge to offset publishing and reviewing costs. If you are serious about publication, your instructor will often be willing to help you even after the semester is over—both Karner and Warren have, over the years, helped students to publish class materials successfully. A successful publication is, of course, more likely if you are a graduate student, but it is certainly possible for undergraduates to at least present a finished paper at a regional professional meeting such as the Pacific Sociological Association or the Midwest Sociological Society (for example, see the Epilogue for a discussion of the "LA at Play" project at UCLA and student presentations, *http://www.sscnet.ucla.edu/nsfreu/*).

Throughout this arduous editing and rewriting process, it is important not to lose your desire (Denzin 1994). Denzin describes desire as the interest that keeps both the writer *writing* and the reader *reading*. Though not often discussed in the context of academic writing, the pleasure of the text (to borrow Barthes' phrase) is a key aspect of whether research gets finished (as many papers, theses, and dissertations do not) and whether sociological writing is read or gathers dust on library shelves. Part of writing qualitative sociology well is crafting an engaging, compelling account that is vital as well as carefully edited and rewritten. Vital texts (Richardson 1994; Denzin 1994) engage readers intellectually; they are not boring to write, or to read.

Whether the article you write is substantive or methodological, or you venture to write a monograph or book, the important thing is to write well, and to write well for your specific audiences. As we indicated at the beginning of this chapter, the organization, grammar, spelling, and even appearance of your paper is important. Equally important is your analytic description, using both your qualitative analysis of your data, and illustratively, parts of the data themselves. This analytic description should be at least somewhat original and novel, not just reflecting analyses that have been published elsewhere. And it should be set within both a thorough, up-to-date substantive literature review and a relevant social constructionist conceptual framework. Then you will have a good, publishable work of qualitative sociology—and, always remember, an ethical one. As we mentioned at the beginning of this chapter, written and published sociological work also has ethical and political implications for a variety of individuals and groups—those who are written about as well as those who do the reading. In the Epilogue, we address the question of the future of qualitative sociology in the millennium of the global and the postmodern.

## Suggestions for Further Reading

Becker, Howard S. 1986. *Writing for Social Scientists.* Chicago: University of Chicago Press.

Rhoads, Richard A. 2003. "Traversing the Great Divide: Writing the Self Into Qualitative Research and Narrative." In *Studies in Symbolic Interaction,* Vol. 26, ed. N. K. Denzin, 235–259. Oxford: JAI Press.

Richardson, Laurel. 1990. *Writing Strategies: Reaching Diverse Audiences.* Newbury Park, CA: Sage Publications. ❖

# Epilogue

# The Future of Qualitative Sociology

$\mathbf{A}$s we look forward, it seems clear that sociologists will continue to discuss the merits of qualitative and quantitative approaches for social research. Quantitative methods, such as survey research, are still of central importance in the social sciences of the 2000s, particularly when the measurement of different social problems and conditions over time is at issue. The media turn to quantitative studies when they want to give their readers or viewers a sense of the changing nature of social problems. Qualitative methods are, however, no longer on the fringes of disciplines such as sociology, education, or social welfare but are approaching the mainstream (Emerson 2001b). Some sociologists have begun—and some continue—to talk about qualitative and quantitative methods as complementary rather than opposing approaches.

The movement of qualitative methods toward the mainstream is related to the increasing sensitivity to cultural diversity that flourished during the last decades of the twentieth century. In place of the early-twentieth-century social focus on assimilation, the late twentieth century saw the development of social movements founded on diversity—of race, ethnicity, gender, age, sexuality, and language. While quantitative methods may be appropriate for the discovery of relationships between variables—say, gender and income—they are less suitable for uncovering the meanings diverse groups of people attach to identity and culture. Governmental agencies responsible for financing social science research, such as the National Science Foundation and the National Institute of Mental Health, have come to recognize that meanings, as well as numbers, are important components of knowledge.

Qualitative sociologists Robert Emerson and Jack Katz received a grant from the National Science Foundation to teach ethnography to undergraduate students from California and elsewhere for eight weeks each summer. Students work with Professors Emerson and Katz as part of a research team with their student colleagues to study "LA at Play"—how people use public spaces (see Box E.1). The focus of this ethnographic training experience is on theorizing leisure behavior through ethnographic observation and analysis and on preparing future teachers of qualitative methods in sociology. The students receive intensive training and are paid stipends. This internship is described on the Web in both text and images at *http://www.sscnet.ucla.edu/nsfreu/*. Successful students from the program also presented research papers from their work at the Pacific Sociological Association in 2003.

---

**Box E.1**

## LA at Play

Become an
### URBAN ETHNOGRAPHER
*at UCLA this summer!*

"LA at PLAY" draws together ongoing faculty research projects looking at contemporary urban life in Los Angeles. This summer we will examine public place conflicts and their resolution, how people organize visits to beaches, museums, malls, parks, clubs, and other entertainment venues as collective "outings," and other dimensions of public place interaction in these and similar settings.

Through course work and field experience, students will be trained in ethnographic research, including observational methods and interviewing techniques. Additional career advising will also be offered.

(http://www.sscnet.ucla.edu/nsfreu/flyer2004.doc)

---

The use and teaching of qualitative methods to graduate students was commonplace in Chicago School sociology (see Chapter 1), but waned after World War II with the expansion of large-scale survey methods. Interest in qualitative methods later revived during the late 1960s and early 1970s with the study of "deviant communities." Graduate seminars in qualitative methods were taught during the 1970s and 1980s, but the teaching of qualitative methods to undergraduate students has been less common—a gap that Emerson and Katz have begun to rectify with their summer program as well as the courses they routinely teach at UCLA. But if you are a student reading this book, you may be studying qualitative methods as part of a general methods course or for a qualitative methods course. Undergraduate qualitative methods courses are now being taught in a number of colleges and universities across the United States, including the University of Houston, University of Illinois at Urbana–Champaign, University of Georgia,

Grand Valley State University, University of Connecticut–Storrs, and Loyola University, among others. In Canada, institutions such as Simon Fraser University and the University of Waterloo also have undergraduate classes in qualitative methods.

The appreciation of qualitative methods, however, is not confined just to the discipline of sociology. At the beginning of the twenty-first century, qualitative research is also flourishing in two interdisciplinary venues: in applied research and in cultural studies. Applied research seeks to use knowledge gained through empirical methods to ameliorate some kind of individual, organizational, or social problem. In cultural studies, sociologists work with the media, the Internet, and other cultural materials such as historical documents or images to explore some aspect of social life. Despite the growth of qualitative research in the late twentieth and early twenty-first centuries, there have also been challenges to the methods on several fronts. Postmodern and global theorists have questioned the epistemological status of ethnography and interviewing from various philosophical and political standpoints. Feminist debates over the gender, class, and ethnic politics of ethnographic and interviewing methods continue into the new millennium.

## Interdisciplinary Directions

Sociological and other social research can be disciplinary or interdisciplinary. Disciplinary sociological research uses the methods and theories of the discipline and is published in sociological journals such as *The American Sociological Review, The American Journal of Sociology*, and *Sociological Inquiry*. Qualitative studies are specifically sought for such journals as the *Journal of Contemporary Sociology, Qualitative Sociology*, and *Symbolic Interaction*. Interdisciplinary work may be published in interdisciplinary fields such as education, communication, and gerontology. In gerontology, for example, there are a number of interdisciplinary journals including *The Journal of Gerontology, The Gerontologist*, and *Journal of Aging Studies*. These journals bring articles together on issues related to aging from various perspectives, including but not limited to anthropology, nursing, linguistics, and history.

Interdisciplinary research in gerontology is often applied, while cultural studies research tends toward the theoretical. In cultural studies research, cultural products (the media, the Internet, images, or documents) are researched and analyzed critically from theoretical perspectives ranging from Marxist to feminist to postmodernist. Cultural studies scholars may use the methods of their own discipline (literary criticism, history, or sociology), or they may use the tools of another discipline. Both applied interdisciplinary work and cultural studies work have, of late, embraced qualitative methods, and we expect this trend to continue.

## Applied Qualitative Research

Both Karner and Warren have, at times, done applied qualitative research. Applied research, in sociology and in other fields, is often team-based, and may also be funded. Prior to the late 1980s, great interest and a considerable amount of government funding was devoted to social problems research, though most of this was quantitative in nature, using either survey or scale-based research. By the 1990s, far fewer government funds were flowing into the social sciences. Although applied social research received less funding, those studies that were funded were more likely than 20 years earlier to use qualitative methods—in particular, ethnography or interviewing—or at least to have a qualitative component. One example is Charles Lidz's large-scale ethnographic and interview study of electroshock therapy (Lidz et al. 1984).

Social problems research funding tends to follow both demographic shifts and changes in political or media focus on particular problems. In the late 1970s and the early 1980s, for example, there was a focus on delinquency and on mental illness, and a good deal of funding in those areas came from government agencies that still exist—for example, the National Institute of Mental Health—and those that do not, such as the Law Enforcement Assistance Administration. In the mid to late 1980s, research on homelessness received a significant share of those funds available for sociological research. By the late 1990s, social research into the causes of delinquency had given way to more biological approaches, and rehabilitation to punishment.

Today, an enormous range of applied research uses qualitative methods (and still many more studies use quantitative methods). Three areas in particular stand out: research in education, research in gerontology, and program evaluation. Sociologists may be involved in these research teams, but so are scholars from other disciplines: educators, anthropologists, nurses, practitioners, and others. Applied social research always involves some attempt to change something, such as the level of literacy, the philosophy of care used by retirement home administrators, or the illegal use of drugs. Such changes may be aimed at social policies or institutions, organizations, or individual behavior.

Ethnographic methods have become especially common in educational research (Spindler 1988). Applied, funded research in education is focused on improving learning and classroom environments and empowering those who teach and learn in classrooms (e.g., see LeCompte and Dworkin 1991). Penn (1997) conducted a cross-cultural comparison of day care facilities in three countries to evaluate which aspects of the environment and which philosophy of care are most likely to promote learning and social development for young children. Others use an applied approach to enhancing the learning experience (Marullo 1998). Carson (2001) and Wright (2001) both advocate *"service learning"* whereby graduate and undergraduate students use ethnographic methods to better understand the life worlds of disadvantaged populations.

Eric Margolis employed visual documentary methods to explore the "hidden curriculum" in education from a historical point of view.

> While the education literature refers to socialization curricula as "hidden" they are actually quite visible and have readily been photographed. From a critical perspective, class pictures can be viewed as an historical record of certain elements of the hidden curriculum. The photographs show bodies with certain race, gender, age, and ability characteristics spatially arranged in an environmental setting. As social scientists, historians, and educators we interpret these visible relationships as representations of social relations learned about elsewhere: segregation, integration and hierarchy, gender socialization, social class structures. Moreover, we infer that the images were not randomly produced but were carefully fashioned using agreed upon conventions of representation to be symbolic representations of such social qualities and others including: order, discipline, purity, equality, patriotism, and community pride and stability. In these photographs we can see attempts to denote social processes such as socialization, assimilation and acculturation which cannot be directly photographed. (Margolis 2000, *http://epaa.asu.edu/epaa/v8n31*)

Margolis has also explored similar socialization processes in the contemporary "hidden curriculum" of higher education. Presented in an online, multimedia format as well as a companion traditional text, Margolis (2001) uses visual methods in a series of videotaped interviews with scholars of higher education produced by former students Marina Gair and Guy Mullins. The hidden curriculum, he argues, "cannot be directly measured or easily quantified because it is an experiential rather than physical phenomenon; therefore, it is the contemplative observations of those scholars at the forefront of educational theory that are essential to its understanding" (*http://ether.asu.edu/peekaboo*). Margolis blends the qualitative methods of visual, interview, and historical analysis to bring sociological insight to education research.

In educational settings, qualitative research has gradually gained appeal as a way to incorporate the original "voices" of the actors in everyday life toward a broader understanding of the social reality of educational contexts (Eisner and Peshkin 1990; Schratz 1993). Besides reflecting a growing disenchantment with the inability of statistical

*What does this photograph say about the hidden curriculum in this school? (Flag allegiance pledge at Raphael Weill Public School, San Francisco, CA, March 20, 1942. Department of the Interior. War Relocation Authority. Still Picture Branch (NWDNS), National Archives, included in Margolis 2000).*

Photo credit: The flag salute to War Relocation Authority, National Archives and Record Service. Dorothea Lange, photographer.

data, mathematical relations, and other abstract parameters to fully account for the diversity of human life, the qualitative paradigm in educational research has also incorporated criticisms of traditional educational practices. From this tradition has come a reexamination of the role of researchers in Native American and other minority communities and the development of "culturally responsive" approaches to teaching, evaluation, and research.

Peter (2003), in her naturalistic study of the Cherokee Nation's first attempt to revitalize the Cherokee language through a language immersion preschool called *Tsa-la-gi A-ge-yu-i*, makes a strong case for addressing the complexity of reversing Cherokee language shift through an approach that accounts for the perspectives of a diverse group of stakeholders. As an adviser to the immersion preschool project funded by Cherokee National Enterprise (CNE), Peter's goal was to describe the program to the fullest extent possible while remaining responsive to Cherokee traditions and values. The method of choice for her research involved a fusion of naturalistic inquiry principles developed by Lincoln and Guba (1985) with Fetterman's (2001) empower-

ment evaluation techniques. Her design involved a holistic and participatory approach in which extensive classroom observations and
interviews with parents, teachers, tribal council members, and community members were coupled with a more quantitative survey of
community members' attitudes toward language revitalization and an
assessment of the preschool children's acquisition of Cherokee. What
emerged was a means for evaluating the success of *Tsa-la-gi A-ge-yu-i*
that incorporated the Cherokee stakeholders as both collaborators in
the study's design and as key participants in shaping the direction of
the study through the issues and themes that they raised during interviews, surveys, and community meetings. Indeed, the group charged
with the task of planning and implementing the preschool even gave
the evaluation process a Cherokee name, *i-di-go-li-ya-he
ni-da-duh-na-hu-i*, which translates as "Let's take a look at what we are
doing," a concept found in Cherokee tradition as a means to step back
and observe, or, as the deputy chief remarked, to "let your ears be big-
ger than your mouth."

Among Peter's findings was that, while the preschool children did
indeed learn Cherokee, there were also indications of a growing awareness among community members of the declining status of their language, the role the language plays in Cherokee culture and heritage,
and a need to do something to reverse Cherokee language shift. Deter-
mining the extent of this awareness was an important component of
the overall evaluation because the long-term support of children's language development depends largely on the dedication of parents and
other members of the community to the overall goals of the program.

In an era of aging populations, gerontology is an important area of
research and policy. "Geriatrics" refers to the physical and medical
care of the aged, whereas gerontology focuses on the social and behavioral aspects of aging. Similar to qualitative research in education,
gerontological research is often focused on improvement of the quality
of life of old people, nursing homes and other environments for the
aged, and the social situation of the person with Alzheimer's disease.
For example, Karner (1999) explored how organizational cultures of
aging service programs shifted and changed as they began to interact
with new ethnic communities and families. This research was part of a
federal demonstration grant that provided flexible funds to develop
community dementia services for underserved minority populations.
Karner and her colleagues identified how successful organizations
became aware that their service approaches needed to be adapted to
cultures and beliefs of their "target" families and delivered in new,
more acceptable manners (Karner and Hall 2002; Montgomery,
Karner, and Kosloski 2003; Montgomery et al. 2002).

The insight of qualitative research within gerontology has perhaps
been most important for going beyond the stereotypes of aging and
older adults as inhabiting a distinctly different stage of life. Early bio-

medical approaches to the study of aging focused on illness, increasing dependency, and detachment from social life. By investigating the life worlds of older adults, the social processes of aging, and the emergent meanings of aging, qualitative researchers have disputed the "stereotypes of aging [that] make it seem that growing old is a uniform occurrence—a singular way of life" (Gubrium and Holstein 2003, 3). For example, Karp (2001) examined the meaning of careers and how success in work might influence one's approach to aging by interviewing professionals in their fifties. Similarly, Globerman (2001) interviewed family caregivers of aging relatives with dementia, and found differences in the meanings of responsibility for care among family members. Black and Rubinstein (2004, S17) sought to understand the "personal meaning of suffering" by interviewing a group of individuals over the age of 70. Experiences of suffering, they found, were particular to each individual's personal history and his or her perceptions and understanding of the cause of the suffering.

Other qualitative work in gerontology is concerned with issues of selfhood and autonomy. Morganroth (2003, 101) suggests that Americans share "master narratives about aging" that focus on decline, difference, and change, whereas "age autobiographies" are narratives about "being aged by culture" (Morganroth 2003, 101). This notion is further explored by Waid and Frazier (2003). Through interviews with Spanish-speaking and non-Hispanic English-speaking older adults, Waid and Frazier examine the reflection of cultural themes in the possible selves expressed in their respondents. Debora Paterniti also looked at self within the bounded institution of a nursing home.

> It wasn't long before I realized that residents told stories that significantly contrasted with those that staff might tell about who and what the residents were. These were accounts and claims that differed in meaning and intention from how staff members often framed their intentions and their lives. (2003, 61)

These various qualitative understandings of social processes and of negotiated or contested meanings has led to a broader awareness of aging individuals as actively engaged in development and growth (Gergen and Gergen 2003). A qualitatively informed conceptualization of aging has policy and service implications as well, since policies and services are more useful if they are informed by cultural understandings (Karner 2001).

Because of our American society's focus on and belief in behavior changing—including behavior modification—programs for all kinds of problems ranging from illegal drug use to delinquency, program evaluation is also an important arena for qualitative research in the early twenty-first century. In part, program evaluation seeks to measure how well a program has achieved its goals—how many participants stopped using drugs, for how long, and the effects of gender, class, and race, as well as many other social variables, on use. Process evaluation, however, is also a significant part of evaluation research since it is the process—presumably—that produces the desired change in behavior.

The qualitative methods of ethnographic and interview research are ideally suited to the work of process program evaluation, and indeed were used in some 1970s evaluation research. However, today's focus is on how evaluation research takes into account the political and social context of the programs or processes being studied, and on empowering the subjects of such research—thus perhaps changing organizations and society rather than just the behavior of individuals. Indeed, Greene sees qualitative program evaluation as offering the promise for enhancing social justice:

> In this vision, evaluation is viewed primarily as a process for promoting empowerment and requisite structural change [and] . . . offer[s] an explicit political agenda for program evaluation, thereby not only recognizing the presence of values in inquiry, but specifically promoting one particular normative frame. (1994, 540)

Peter's (2003) research on Native American language immersion programs described above is a case in point. Despite an increase in indigenous groups creating language immersion programs as a means to revitalize their increasingly endangered languages, an overview of 34 programs in the United States provided by the Indigenous Language Institute Field Research Project (ILI 2001) indicates that little has been done to evaluate the effectiveness of these programs in relation to the goals from which they were initiated. In some cases, when evaluation is conducted, education specialists are brought in from outside the community on a consulting basis to evaluate the program. These evaluations often rely on conventional education indicators such as test scores and classroom observations, not necessarily taking into account the complex process required to reverse language shift, including community values, perspectives, and interpretations. And so, whether or not fluent speakers are emerging or are likely to emerge from these programs is not fully known—unless more evaluation research using qualitative methods can be done.

Indeed, social programs, by their very nature, are the result of political and economic decisions—whether funding is targeted toward minority groups, delinquents, homeless people, elderly people, or classroom teaching. These decisions will continue to be either supported or disputed in political arenas; these arenas, in turn, influence how program "effectiveness" will be seen and understood. Qualitative process research into behavior-changing programs illuminates the cultural and individual meaning of "effectiveness" or "ineffectiveness" in local, political contexts.

## Cultural Studies Research

Cultural studies research today is highly interdisciplinary. Many of the authors we introduced you to in Chapter 8, such as Susan Bordo and Joan Brumberg, are not sociologists. Bordo is a philosopher; Brumberg a professor of history and women's studies. But the work they do and the methods they use are similar to those used by cultural sociologists such as Erving Goffman (1976) or at times, your coauthors Karner (1991, 1998b) and Warren (2002).

Karner (1991) traced the role of cultural objects in ethnic identity formation and mobilization of nationalist movements. Using a secondary analysis of historical accounts, she analyzed how the *Kalevala*, a book of "Finnish" folk poems, was constructed and used as an accessible symbol of authentic Finnish culture by nationalist activists, reified as pure national heritage—unspoiled by ruling occupiers, and used as a cultural reference point to promote mobilization of the Finnish independence movement. In a later study, Karner (1998a) again focused on the use of cultural products. Her intention in this research was to examine how Vietnam veterans used films and television programs to explain themselves and their combat experiences to non-veterans. Karner's work illuminated the ways in which individuals use mass culture in highly personal ways to both make sense of their own experiences (in relation to others) and create a frame for the shared communication of a nonshared event (combat).

To study the uses of electricity in psychiatric treatment from ancient times to the present (Kneeland and Warren 2002), Warren not only teamed up with a historian, Timothy Kneeland, but also adopted many of the methods and strategies used by historians. She learned about the various archives relevant to her work, such as the Museum and Library of Electricity, also known as the Bakken Institute, in Minneapolis. She discovered both the systematic approaches and serendipities of historical research—both the necessity to mine everything available and the joy of unexpected findings. She learned about such indexes to nineteenth- and early-twentieth-century medicine as the *Index Medicus*, and the usefulness of browsing through the tables of contents of medical journals as well as the indexes. She discovered that assortments of papers were often bound together in eighteenth-century volumes, and all kinds of things could be uncovered by just paging through them.

But qualitative approaches in sociology no longer depend entirely on the textual. The exploration of visual material in sociology is facilitated, increasingly, by the lessening cost and increasing availability of visual technologies. Just about anyone can afford an inexpensive camera and film. Some sociology programs provide students with the tools of visual approaches, such as video cameras, while most students have access to computer-based programs. The expansion of visual sociology of all kinds is limited only by the imagination of the discipline and its practitioners.

In this postmodern interdisciplinary era, some sociologists are experimenting with methods derived from the humanities rather than the social and physical sciences. In addition to using photography (Becker 1986, 1995), sociologist Howard Becker and his students and colleagues have experimented with the use of the theatrical format to communicate sociological concepts (Becker and McCall 1990; Becker, McCall, and Morris 1989). Other sociologists, such as Norman Denzin (2003) and Patricia Ticineto Clough (1996, 2000) believe that "performance ethnography" is a means to "contribute to radical social change, to economic justice, to a cultural politics" (Denzin 2003, 187). Practitioners assert that performance ethnography extends critical theory and can promote radical democracy.

> The performance event, as in good ethno-drama, provides a forum for the search for moral truths about the self and the other. This forum explores the unpresentable in the culture, the discontents of daily life. The performer stirs up the world, objectivity is a fiction, and the writer-performer's story (mystory) is part of the tale that is told. The writer has a theory about how the world works, and this theory is never far from the surface of the text. Self-reflexive readers-viewers are presumed, citizens who seek honest but reflexive works that draw them into the many structures of verisimilitude that shape the story in question. (Denzin 2003, 252)

Not only are sociologists using other disciplinary approaches, but scholars from other disciplines are also using sociological approaches. Kneeland, Warren's historian colleague, learned to look at the gender of electroshock patients in medical journal reports as well as claims for positive or negative outcomes. And journalists and freelancers use a combination of historical, sociological, and other approaches to write cultural histories of a wide range of phenomena, from the X ray (Michette and Pfauntsch 1996) to the breast (Yalom 1997). For example, in *A Mind of Its Own*, Friedman (2001) offers a cultural examination of the penis, from ancient Sumer to the present, suggesting that social attitudes toward the penis have been influential in mapping the course of world history.

## The Internet

Perhaps the most important challenge to cultural studies, sociological, and other qualitative research today is the Internet. The Internet is the first new site, in time and space, for data collection, analysis, writing, and representation, to have appeared since the invention of moving pictures. Sociologists and others are wasting no time in the exploration of the Internet and e-mail, not only to interview respondents but to seek out (in the manner of Star Trek's Enterprise) new social worlds such as the Anas and apotemnophiliacs discussed in Chapter 8—and an entire globe of potential respondents, collaborators, and information sources. Indeed, some scholars, Silver among them, go so far as to identify "Internet studies" as a new "meta-field" that constitutes "an important and interesting site of intellectual, academic, and political work" (2004, 55). There are sociologists and others working literally on the cutting edge of Internet studies, mapping what some of them regard as new forms of social interaction and relationship based on a simultaneous visibility and opacity (is my correspondent really the 13-year-old girl shown in the photo or is it a 40-year-old man?), and democracy and autocracy (I can enter the chat room but I may be censored or removed). Danah Boyd (*www.danah.org*) studies digital identity management and articulated social networks, or YASNS (Yet Another Social Network Service), as she refers to them. In her work, Boyd focuses on "the role of design in affecting an individual's ability to maintain control of personal representation and identity information" (Boyd 2002, 2). Qualitative sociology is . . . having a field day with this new feast (see Mann and Stewart 2002).

The Internet—like the computer before it—has transformed the conduct of social research, including qualitative research. The development and spread of computer technology enabled us to write fieldnotes, drafts, and bibliographies with an ease unknown to prior generations of ethnographers. The advent of the Internet has taken us to new heights not only with respect to information and data sources, but also for bibliographic searches, "googling," and all the other possibilities of the Web. In writing this book, we have been able to send drafts to one another in different states (California and Texas) without visiting the post office, and communicate via e-mail a dozen times a day without playing telephone tag. Your task as student ethnographers is incredibly easier than ours was "back in the day" in its technical dimensions of computers and the Internet, but it is just as challenging as ours in the actual doing of social research.

## Postmodern Challenges to Qualitative Research

The Internet might be seen as a postmodern form of culture, which represents one facet of postmodernism's impact on contemporary qualitative sociology. Another force is a set of postmodern critiques of qualitative method. Ironically, the most trenchant challenges to our methods during the past decade have come from inside, rather than outside, the discipline, in the form of the postmodern critique, as well as from anthropology. This critique has focused on ethnography and interviewing rather than textual analysis. Indeed, the study of texts is proposed by some postmodernists as the answer to those problems of representation inherent in studying interaction.

The social context of the postmodern critique of ethnography is political colonialism and cultural globalization. Early anthropological ethnography took place among a variety of colonial regimes, which came to an end in the decades after World War II (Pratt 1986). During the 1980s and the 1990s, however, many areas of the world that had been politically decolonized were culturally recolonized by the globalization of American material goods and social values (Clifford 1986). Pratt contends that in contemporary times anthropology, and thus ethnographic sociology,

> no longer speaks with automatic authority for others defined as unable to speak for themselves ("primitive," "pre-literate," "without history"). . . . The critique of colonialism in the postwar period—an undermining of "The West's" ability to represent other societies—has been reinforced by an important process of theorizing about the limits of representation itself. (1986, 10)

Postmodernism, as a critique of the cultural authority of Western knowledge systems, challenges the right of ethnographers to speak for those they study—their social other.

Postmodernism is perhaps the most discussed intellectual movement in the contemporary social sciences and humanities. While many versions of postmodernism can be found in everything from architecture to philosophy to social science, certain themes are common to most of them: the deconstruction of modernism, the deprivileging of the voices of scholars, and the polyvocality of texts. Modernism is the world of realism, reason, science, order, empiricism, and structure derived from the Enlightenment; it is what postmodernism challenges, from bureaucracies to ethnographies. As Emerson notes, during the past decade

> ethnographic concerns with interpretation, reflexivity and representation coalesced with postmodernist sensitivities and approaches to produce a fundamental reorientation within fieldwork: Whereas in the 1960s and 1970s fieldwork defined itself by contrast with the positivist assumptions of survey and quantitative research, by the 1990s its primary dialogue engaged radically anti-positive postmodern theories that challenged many of [ethnography's] core notions, including "description," "theory," and even "the field." (2001b, viii)

Such challenges are referred to by postmodernists as deconstruction. The deconstruction of modernism, for postmodernists, involves breaking down what they see as the illusions of structure, order, and even reality, revealing the shifting nature of moment-by-moment experience. Ethnographies from the Chicago School onward are critiqued for their "naïve realism," or the presumption that there is a reality "out there" knowable and reproducible by ethnographic methods. For the radical postmodernist, ethnography is just as positivist and deductive as quantitative survey research because it purports to describe an observed "reality."

Postmodern ethnographies also attempt to deprivilege the voices of the writers themselves, as persons with special or true knowledge of the setting. All written documents of the setting are equally valid or valuable—or neither; the ethnography written by the scholar is not more valid or valuable than the poem written by the asylum inmate (e.g., see Rhodes 1995). In response to this aspect of the postmodern critique, postmodernists have advocated for texts that represent multiple voices.

There have been various attempts since the 1980s to represent multiple voices in the ethnographic text, not just the voice of the author reflecting the voices of important people—often male political and economic leaders—in the field. In anthropology, the work of Vincent Crapanzano (1980, 1985) is a 1980s exemplar of textual multivocality. In his book *Tuhami* (1980), Crapanzano arranges, in dialectic fashion, the descriptive voice of the protagonist, a lower-class Moroccan tile maker, with the analytic voice of the ethnographer. In *Waiting* (1985), Crapanzano "uses the dialogic capturing of multiple voices to expose the condition of entrapment among the whites of contemporary South Africa" (Marcus 1986, 192). And as we noted above, attempts at postmodern ethnography among sociologists from the 1980s to the present have included "personal narratives . . . poems . . . plays . . . playful dialogues . . . and fictional stories" (Emerson 2001c, 309).

## Critiquing the Postmodern Critique of Ethnography

The response among some ethnographers has been to critique, and even reject, the postmodernist critique itself. Postmodernism has been criticized for returning anthropologists and sociologists to the armchair that they had occupied before the Chicago School's admonition to researchers to "get out of your armchair and into the field" (see Chapter 1). Another critique of the postmodern critique is that it is too self-focused. A joke associated with this second critique goes something like this: the anthropologist has been talking at length with an informant. The informant finally says, in desperation, "Now can we talk about me?"

Other debates over postmodernism criticize its claims of egalitarianism; some of these critiques can be found in the postmodern texts themselves. Although Crapanzano does not seek to privilege his own interpretation over Tuhami's own words, he adds that

> I am not suggesting here that the Westerner's scientific explanations and Tuhami's symbolic interpretive explanations are equally

satisfying. That is for the reader to decide on the basis of criteria
he finds acceptable. (1980, 23)

Crapanzano also recognizes the inevitability of privileging the author's voice of any text through the processes of writing and publishing that text:

> His text . . . however accurately I can present it, is in a sense my text.
> I have assumed it and afforded myself, as narrator, a privilege he
> has not been granted . . . the privilege of (re)encounter. (1980, 23)

Another ethnographically informed response to postmodernism is
to accept the insights it offers into interpretation, reflexivity, and representation, but reject the most radical of its proposals: the erasure of
any concern with reality. This middle-ground approach has been
referred to as "subtle realism" or "analytic realism" (Emerson 2001a,
52). Hammersley, in arguing for subtle realism, says that it

> retains from naive realism the idea that research investigates inde-
> pendent, knowable phenomena. But it breaks with it in denying
> that we have direct access to these phenomena, in accepting that
> we must always rely on cultural assumptions. (2001, 108–109)

Kotarba (1991) also argues that our work can benefit from
postmodernism's sensitivity to certain features of everyday life often
overlooked or misconceptualized by traditional ethnographers. Symbolic interactionist-informed ethnography, for example, has tended to
treat culture as taken-for-granted meanings embedded in a group's
standard practices. Postmodern thinking, in contrast, brings cultural
aspects of social life to the forefront of our observational attention.
Furthermore, traditional ethnography has tended to frame unusual
behavior, activity, and meanings in terms of *deviance*, invoking moral-
istic analytical criteria. Postmodern thinking introduces the possibility
of incorporating *aesthetic* criteria in our analyses, so that we can also
see unusual aspects of everyday life as exotic, stylistic, beautiful, signi-
fying, or even elegant.

These middle-ground responses to postmodernism are what
we—Karner and Warren—teach our students: be aware of the interpretive, reflexive, and representational in qualitative research, but do not
lose sight of the experiential and emergent realities of human interaction and behavior.

## Critiquing the Interview Society

The intellectual context of the postmodern critique of the interview
can be traced to the work of French poststructuralist philosopher
Michel Foucault, especially his *Discipline and Punish* (1977). Foucault
pointed out that from the Enlightenment onward in Western culture

there has been an expansion of "the gaze" of the expert. Experts measure and quantify all aspects of the body, the mind, and behavior, establish norms and deviations for populations, examine everyone systematically, detect and punish or treat violations, and keep extensive records so that the results of all this gazing are preserved over time. Sociologists—as well as physicians, psychologists, and others are among the gazers within what has become an "interview society" (Gubrium and Holstein 2002, 9).

Using Foucault's framework, Gubrium and Holstein (2002) point out that in pre-Enlightenment society only royalty and the upper classes were the object of the gaze. Only the lives of the elite were thought important enough to be chronicled. Since the time of the Enlightenment, and accelerating during the nineteenth and twentieth centuries, everyone has gradually become subjects of the gaze in the context of what has been referred to as "the modern temper" (Gubrium and Holstein 2002, 5). They note that the modern temper

> denotes a shared understanding that the individual has the wherewithal to offer a meaningful description of, or set of opinions about, his or her life. Individuals, in their own right, are accepted as significant commentators on their own experience; it is not just the "chief" community commentator who speaks for one and all, in other words, or the local representative of the commonwealth whose opinions are taken to express the thoughts and feelings of every mind and heart in the vicinity. (Gubrium and Holstein 2002, 5)

The Foucaultian argument is that experts of all types contribute to discourses of expertise in which the normal is defined and distinguished from the abnormal. Everything from the weight and height, intake and output of bodies to the psychological realm of the mind is observed, recorded, and normalized. Sociologists contribute to the development of this knowledge/power nexus through their expertise at survey, and even qualitative interviewing. In premodern times the bodies and opinions—the subjectivities—only of elites mattered, but in modernity we monitor the subjectivities of everyone, and everyone becomes a subject.

Just as postmodern anthropologists critique ethnography for imposing the authority of Western interpretation on non-Western society, postmodern sociologists critique the interview for its intensification of the gaze. In contemporary America, and indeed around the world, everyone's everyday life is deemed the proper subject of media and social science investigation:

> Interviewing of all kinds mediates contemporary life. . . . the experiential conduit par excellence of the electronic age . . . questions and answers fly back and forth on the Internet. (Gubrium and Holstein 2002, 9)

The subjectification of everyone—now like premodern royalty in the significance of their opinions—is not in itself problematic; as Gubrium and Holstein argue, both the large-scale survey and the individual interview are "democratizing agents" (2002, 8). What is problematic, to critics of the interview society, is its embeddedness in a global capitalist system and its use in upholding such a system. Interviews played a key role in building modern Western society after World War II, with the enumeration and tracking of the citizenry (Gubrium and Holstein 2002; Briggs 2002). Today interviews play a key role, in the view of postmodern critics, in the "technologies and social relations of a globalized world" (Briggs 2002, 920).

Briggs further refers to interviews as "a key discursive machinery . . . used in extending and naturalizing social inequality" (2002, 920), although media interviews in particular foster the "illusion" of equality:

> The cable television news network's broadcasts take the voices and images of East Timorese refugees or victims of Venezuelan floods and project them to audiences worldwide, creating the sense of a global conversation. (Briggs 2002, 918)

The transnational corporations that own these global media foster an "illusion of social interaction and self-expression that fuels both scholarly and popular senses of interviews," which "positions them even more crucially within the technologies and social relations of a globalized world" (Briggs 2002, 920). According to Briggs, media interviewing provides "a key discursive machinery to be used in extending and naturalizing social inequality" (2002, 920).

There may be some truth to Briggs' critique of media interviewing, but most sociologists would stop short of extending it to research interviewing. Social scientists who use, or write about, qualitative interviewing do not act as, or consider themselves part of, a system of global inequality; but rather as acting within it and subject to the same restraints as other social actors. Indeed, as we indicated in Chapter 1, a number of qualitative approaches are designed specifically to illuminate and challenge systems of inequality, or to effect social change. Among these are various feminist approaches that use ethnographic, interviewing, and textual approaches to understand gender inequality.

## Feminist Reframings

Feminist reframings of the interview began with an exploration of its emancipatory power. As Reinharz and Chase note,

> Throughout the 19th century and for much of the 20th century, most male researchers did not consider women worthy of study. One of the most blatant examples of the disregard of women as in-

terview subjects is found in the work of Alexis de Tocqueville who traveled through the United States in the early 1830s, without interviewing women at all. (2002, 222)

During the nineteenth and twentieth centuries the interview was seen by some women scholars as a way to give voice to those people and topics, particularly women and their domestic lives, that had not found a place in the sociologies and histories of America and Europe. Mirra Komarovsky, writing in the 1950s, did a study of working-class women and men, and noted their different spheres of interest: "The husbands talked easily about their jobs, but when the discussion changed to the marriage relationship, many became noticeably uncomfortable" (quoted in Reinharz and Chase 2002, 224).

In addition, interview studies of women from the nineteenth and early twentieth centuries, often done by women, were "recovered" by feminist sociologists during later decades. Harriet Martineau, as Reinharz and Chase (2002, 223) point out, was "one of the many under-recognized women sociologists of the nineteenth century who also traveled throughout the U.S. in the 1830s." The difference in de Tocqueville's and Martineau's methods led them to different conclusions:

> Martineau's contact with women led her to draw an analogy between the status of women and slaves, and to predict that women would eventually win the right to vote. By contrast, Tocqueville . . . believed that women were satisfied with their domestic lot. (Reinharz and Chase 2002, 222)

Beginning in 1981 with Ann Oakley's question "Is interviewing women a contradiction in terms?" feminist scholars sought to reframe the interview, through the development of "sisterly bonds," as a form of egalitarian interaction between women (Reinharz and Chase 2002, 229, and see Chapter 6). Such bonds entail changing the power dynamics of one-way questioning-and-answering into a more mutual disclosure, and assume the obligation of an ongoing rather than time-limited relationship with respondents. Feminist ethnographers question the power relations inherent in the method, and experiment with various ways of ensuring that the voices of the women they study are heard through the text (e.g., see Shostak 1981). Particularly in anthropology, feminist ethnographers also question the male-dominated paradigms of the field:

> Why has mainstream anthropology been so recalcitrant in acknowledging that gender makes a difference to ethnography? Why have the practitioners clung so tenaciously to a gender-neutral positivist paradigm or jumped on the postmodern bandwagon? . . . The tendency to associate engagement with the feminine, and the feminine with the emotional, has locked women out of mainstream anthropology and removed them from accounts in the postmodern schema. (Bell 1993, 3)

The 1970s and early 1980s literature on feminist ethnography sometimes assumed that being a woman—respondent and researcher—would ensure the development of sisterly bonds. Later feminist scholarship identified differences in the political stances, social class, nationality, ethnicity, and other social attributes besides gender that could affect the feminist interview or ethnography, and in effect deromanticized feminist methodology (Warren 2002; Reinharz and Chase 2002; Luff 1999). In discussing her interviews with mothers in the late 1990s, for example, lesbian and nonmother Ellen Lewin commented:

> How their narratives would have been shaped had I also been a mother I cannot know, but I feel sure that they would have been different, if not in substance, then in emphasis. (quoted in Reinharz and Chase 2002, 231)

Recent discussions of interviews have also emphasized their role in constructing modernity and its particular knowledge/power relations. These discussions often take their cue from Michel Foucault's analysis of the role of the expert in constructing the social order. As Briggs notes,

> The power invested in interviews to construct discourses that are then legitimated as the words of others points to their effectiveness as technologies that can be used in naturalizing the role of specialists in creating systems of difference. (2002, 913)

As interviewers focus on the "fetishism of words" (Miczo 2003, 469), they treat "words as real entities that stand for the experiences they represent." Moving beyond this "fetishism," by acknowledging the impossibility of objective accounts and the promise of qualitative approaches to give voice to disadvantaged populations, will free researchers from the more "enlightened" forms of despotism that may inadvertently reinforce inequalities.

## Reinvigorating the Promise of Qualitative Research

Disciplinary debates will inevitably continue as we move into the twenty-first century. What constitutes knowledge and how we come to know what we know will continue to interest social scientists. As we reflect self-consciously about what we do as ethnographers and interviewers or as analysts of social documents and images, Emerson reminds us that the distinctive value of the qualitative method is

> its insistence that the researcher quit academic settings, moving out to make direct, close contact with people and the circumstances within which they live their lives. (2001b, ix)

If our work remains "experience-near" (Geertz 1976), and our knowledge claims well grounded in "what the fieldworker has seen, heard, and experienced" (Emerson 2001b, ix), we can address the postmodern challenge without getting lost in the possible nihilism. Recently Ruth Behar (2003) offered the following advice:

> I say that more than ever, if ethnography [and qualitative methods in general] is to realize its emancipatory promise, what we are going to need are strong, personal, heartfelt voices, the voices of love, trust, faith and the gift. One thing remains constant about our humanity—that we must never stop trying to tell stories of who we think we are. Equally, we must never stop wanting to listen to each other's stories. If we ever stopped, it would all be over. Everything we are as human beings would be reduced to a lost book floating in the universe, with no one to remember us, no one to know we once existed. (2003, 37)

In this text, we have provided an overview of qualitative approaches for the beginning researcher. One of our goals in writing this text has been to raise the ethical questions that every researcher will face at each stage of a project. We take the standpoint that a respect for those we study and their local knowledge, a desire to "do no harm," a strong and committed loyalty to thick description, and accurate, comprehensive representation leads to ethically informed research. Though this foray into qualitative methods may have been a one-time experience for some of you, it may also have been the exciting beginning of a career path for others. Whichever the case might be, we have enjoyed sharing our passion for the work we do with you. We hope that, whatever research, reading, and writing you do within the field of qualitative sociology, you will play your part in reinvigorating the promise of qualitative research. ❖

# References

Adams, Laura L. 1999. "The Mascot Researcher: Identity, Power and Knowledge in Fieldwork." *Journal of Contemporary Ethnography* 28:331–363.

Adler, Patricia A. 1985. *Wheeling and Dealing: An Ethnography of an Upper-Level Drug Dealing and Smuggling Community.* New York: Columbia University Press.

Adler, Patricia A., and Peter Adler. 1987. *Membership Roles in Field Research.* Newbury Park, CA: Sage Publications.

———. 2002. "The Reluctant Respondent." In *Handbook of Research Interviewing: Context and Method,* ed. Jaber F. Gubrium and James A. Holstein, 515–535. Thousand Oaks, CA: Sage Publications.

Altheide, David L., and John M. Johnson. 1994. "Criteria for Assessing Interpretive Validity in Qualitative Research." In *Handbook of Qualitative Research,* ed. Norman K. Denzin and Yvonna S. Lincoln, 485–499. Thousand Oaks, CA: Sage Publications.

Ammerman, Nancy T. 1987. *Bible Believers: Fundamentalists in the Modern World.* Rutgers, NJ: Rutgers University Press.

Anderson, Elijah. 1990. *Streetwise: Race, Class and Change in an Urban Community.* Chicago: University of Chicago Press.

———. 1999. *Code of the Street.* New York: W. W. Norton.

Arendell, Terry. 1997. "Reflections on the Researcher-Researched Relationship: A Woman Interviewing Men." *Qualitative Sociology* 20:341–368.

Arksey, Hilary, and Peter Knight. 1999. *Interviewing for Social Scientists: An Introductory Resource With Examples.* Thousand Oaks, CA: Sage Publications.

Atkinson, Robert. 2002. "The Life Story Interview." In *Handbook of Research Interviewing: Context and Method,* ed. Jaber F. Gubrium and James A. Holstein, 121–140. Thousand Oaks, CA: Sage Publications.

Bailey, Beth. 1989. *From Front Porch to Back Seat: Courtship in Twentieth-Century America.* Baltimore, MD: Johns Hopkins University Press.

Bailey, Carol. 1995. *A Guide to Field Research.* Thousand Oaks, CA: Pine Forge Press.

Banks, Marcus. 2001. *Visual Methods in Social Research.* London: Sage Publications.

Barber, Bernard. 1976. "The Ethics of Experimentation With Human Subjects." *Scientific American* 243 (2): 25–31.

Bateson, Gregory, and Margaret Mead. 1942. *Balinese Character: A Photographic Analysis.* New York: New York Academy of Sciences.

Becker, Howard S. 1986. *Writing for Social Scientists.* Chicago: University of Chicago Press.

———. 1995. "Visual Sociology, Documentary Photography, and Photojournalism: It's (Almost) All a Matter of Context." *Visual Sociology* 10 (1–2): 5–14.

———. 1998. *Tricks of the Trade: How to Think About Your Research While You're Doing It.* Chicago: University of Chicago Press.

———. 2002. "Studying the New Media." *Qualitative Sociology* 25 (Fall): 337–343.

Becker, Howard S., and Michal McCall. 1990. "Performance Science." In *Social Problems*, 37:117–132.

Becker, Howard S., Michal McCall, and Lori Morris. 1989. "Theaters and Communities: Three Scenes." *Social Problems* 36:93–112.

Behar, Ruth. 2003. "Ethnography and the Book That Was Lost." *Ethnography* 4 (1): 15–39.

Bell, Diane. 1993. "Introduction 1: The Context." In *Gendered Fields: Women, Men, and Ethnography,* ed. Diane Bell, Pat Caplan, and Waxir Jahan Karim, 1–18. London: Routledge.

Berg, Bruce L. 2004. *Qualitative Research Methods For the Social Sciences.* Boston: Allyn & Bacon.

Bloor, Michael. 2001. "Techniques of Validation in Qualitative Research: A Critical Commentary." In *Contemporary Field Research,* 2nd ed., ed. Robert M. Emerson, 383–395. Prospect Heights, IL: Waveland Press.

Black, Helen K., and Robert L. Rubenstein. 2004. "Themes of Suffering in Later Life." *Journal of Gerontology* 59:S17–S24.

Blumer, Herbert. 1969. *Symbolic Interaction: Perspective and Method.* Berkeley: University of California Press.

Boelen, W. A. Marianne. 1992. "Street Corner Society: Cornerville Revisited." *Journal of Contemporary Ethnography* 21:11–51.

Bordo, Susan. 1999. *The Male Body: A New Look at Men in Public and in Private.* New York: Farrar, Straus, and Giroux.

———. 2003. *Unbearable Weight: Feminism, Western Culture, and the Body.* Berkeley: University of California Press.

Boyd, Danah M. 2002. "Faceted Id/entity: Managing Representation in a Digital World." Masters Thesis, School of Architecture and Planning, Massachusetts Instite of Technology.

Brajuha, Mario, and Lyle Hallowell. 1986. "Legal Intrusions and the Politics of Fieldwork." *Urban Life* 14:454–478.

Briggs, Charles L. 2002. "Interviewing, Power/Knowledge, and Social Inequality." In *Handbook of Interview Research* ed. Jaber F. Gubrium and James A. Holstein, 911–922. Thousand Oaks, CA: Sage Publications.

Browne, Joy. 1976. "Fieldwork for Fun and Profit." In *The Research Experience,* ed. M. P. Gordon, 77–84. Itasca, IL: F. E. Peacock.

Brumberg, Joan J. 1997. *The Body Project: An Intimate History of American Girls.* New York: Random House.

Bryant, Clifton. 1999. "Gratuitous Sex in Field Research: 'Carnal Lagniappe,' or 'Inappropriate Behavior.'" *Deviant Behavior* 20 (4): 325–329.

Bulmer, Martin. 1984. *The Chicago School of Sociology: Institutionalization, Diversity, and the Rise of Sociological Research.* Chicago: University of Chicago Press.

Burawoy, Michael. 1991. *Ethnography Unbound: Power and Resistance in the Modern Metropolis.* Berkeley and Los Angeles: University of California Press.

Carson, Barbara A. 2001. "Creating Grassroots Change Through Service Learning." In *Applying Sociology: Making a Better World,* ed. William Du Bois and R. Dean Wright, 193–200. Needham Heights, MA: Allyn & Bacon.

Cavan, Sherri. 1966. *Liquor License: An Ethnography of Bar Behavior.* Chicago: Aldine.

Chalfen, Richard. 1974. "Akeret's Photoanalysis." *Studies in the Anthropology of Visual Communication* 1 (1): 57–60.

Clifford, James. 1986. "On Ethnography Allegory." In *Writing Culture: The Poetics and Politics of Ethnography,* ed. James Clifford and George E. Marcus, 98–121. Berkeley: University of California Press.

Clifford, James, and George E. Marcus, eds. 1986. *Writing Culture: The Poetics and Politics of Ethnography.* Berkeley: University of California Press.

Clough, Patricia Ticineto. 1996. "Autotelecommunication and Autoethnography: A Reading of Carolyn Ellis's Final Negotiations." *Sociological Quarterly* 38 (1): 95–110.

———. 2000. *Autoaffection: Unconscious Thought in the Age of Technology.* Minneapolis: University of Minnesota Press.

Collier, John. 1967. *Visual Anthropology: Photography as a Research Method.* New York: Holt, Rinehart, & Winston.

Cooley, Charles H. 1922. *Human Nature and the Social Order.* New York: Scribner.

Crapanzano, Vincent. 1980. *Tuhami: Portrait of a Moroccan.* Chicago: University of Chicago Press.

———. 1985. *Waiting: The Whites of South Africa.* New York: Random House.

Damico, Sandra B. 1985. "Two Worlds of a School: Differences in the Photographs of Black and White Adolescents." *The Urban Review* 17:210–222.

Daniels, Arlene K. 1967. "The Low-Caste Stranger in Social Research." In *Ethics, Politics, and Social Research,* ed. Gideon Sjoberg, 267–296. Cambridge, MA: Schenkman.

De Andrade, Lelia Lomba. 2000. "Negotiating From the Inside: Constructing Racial and Ethnic Identity in Qualitative Research." *Journal of Contemporary Ethnography* 29 (3): 268–290.

Denzin, Norman K. 1989a. *Interpretive Biography.* Newbury Park, CA: Sage Publications.

———. 1989b. *The Research Act.* Englewood Cliffs, NJ: Prentice Hall.

———. 1994. "The Art and Politics of Interpretation." In *Handbook of Qualitative Research,* ed. Norman K. Denzin and Yvonna S. Lincoln, 500–515. Thousand Oaks, CA: Sage Publications.

———. 2003. *Performance Ethnography: Critical Pedagogy and the Politics of Culture.* Thousand Oaks, CA: Sage Publications.

———. 2003. "The Call to Perfomance." *Symbolic Interaction* 26 (1): 187–207.

———. 2003. "Reading and Writing Performance." *Qualitative Research.* 3 (2): 243–268.

DeSantis, Grace. 1980. "Interviewing as Social Interaction." *Qualitative Sociology* 2:72–98.

DeVault, Marjorie L. 1995. "Ethnicity and Expertise: Racial-Ethnic Knowledge in Sociological Research." *Gender and Society* 9 (5): 612–631.

DeVault, Marjorie L., and Liza McCoy. 2002. "Institutional Ethnography: Using Interviews to Investigate Ruling Relations." In *Handbook of Interview Research,* ed. Jaber F. Gubrium and James A. Holstein, 751–775. Thousand Oaks, CA: Sage Publications.

Diamond, Timothy. 1992. *Making Grey Gold: Narratives of Nursing Home Care.* Chicago: University of Chicago Press.

Douglas, Jack D. 1985. *Creative Interviewing.* Beverly Hills, CA: Sage Publications.

Duneier, Mitchell. 1994. *Slim's Table: Race, Respectability and Masculinity.* Chicago: University of Chicago Press.

——. 1999. *Sidewalk.* New York: Farrar, Straus, and Giroux.

——. 2001. "On the Evolution of *Sidewalk.*" In *Contemporary Field Research,* 2nd ed., ed. Robert M. Emerson, 167–187. Waveland Heights, IL: Waveland Press.

——. 2002. "What Kind of Combat Sport is Sociology?" *The American Journal of Sociology* 107 (May): 1551–1576.

Easterday, Lois, Diana Papademas, Laura Schorr, and Catherine Valentine. 1977. "The Making of the Female Researcher: Role Problems in Field Work." *Urban Life* 6:333–348.

Ebaugh, Helen Rose Fuchs. 1977. *Out of the Cloister: A Study of Organizational Dilemmas.* Austin: University of Texas Press.

Eisner, Elliot, W., and Peshkin, Alan, eds. 1990. *Qualitative Inquiry in Education: The Continuing Debate.* New York: Teachers College Press.

Elliott, Carl. 2000. "A New Way to Be Mad." *The Atlantic Monthly* (December): 73–84.

Ellis, Carolyn. 1995a. "Emotional and Ethical Quagmires in Returning to the Field." *Journal of Contemporary Ethnography* 24:68–98.

——. 1995b. *Final Negotiations: A Story of Love, Loss, and Chronic Illness.* Philadelphia: Temple University Press.

Ellis, Carolyn, and Arthur P. Bochner. 1996. *Composing Ethnography: Alternative Forms of Qualitative Writing.* Walnut Creek, CA: Alta Mira Press.

——. 2000. "Autoethnography, Personal Narrative, Reflexivity: Researcher as Subject." In *Handbook of Qualitative Research,* 2nd ed., ed. Norman K. Denzin and Yvonna S. Lincoln, 733–768. Thousand Oaks, CA: Sage Publications.

Emerson, Robert M. 1989. "Tenability and Troubles: The Construction of Accommodative Relations by Psychiatric Emergency Teams." In *Perspectives on Social Problems: A Research Annual* vol. 1., ed. Gale Miller and James A. Holstein, 215–237. Greenwich, CT: JAI Press.

——. 2001. "Fieldwork Practice: Issues in Participant Observation." In *Contemporary Field Research,* 2nd ed., ed. Robert M. Emerson, 113–151. Prospect Heights, IL: Waveland Press.

——. 2001a. "The Face of Contemporary Ethnography." In *Contemporary Field Research.* 2nd ed., ed. Robert M. Emerson, 27–53. Prospect Heights, IL: Waveland Press.

——. 2001b. "Preface." In *Contemporary Field Research,* 2nd ed., ed. Robert M. Emerson, vii–xi. Prospect Heights, IL: Waveland Press.

——. 2001c. "Producing Ethnographies: Theory, Evidence, and Representation." In *Contemporary Field Research,* 2nd ed., ed. Robert M. Emerson, 281–316. Prospect Heights, IL: Waveland Press.

——. 2001d. "Introduction: The Development of Ethnographic Field Research." In *Contemporary Field Research,* 2nd ed., ed. Robert M. Emerson, 1–26. Prospect Heights, IL: Waveland Press.

Emerson, Robert M., Rachel I. Fretz, and Linda L. Shaw. 1995. *Writing Ethnographic Fieldnotes.* Chicago: University of Chicago Press.

Emerson, Robert M., and Melvin Pollner. 1976. "Dirty Work Designations: Their Features and Consequences in a Psychiatric Setting." *Social Problems* 23:243–255.

——. 2001. "Constructing Participant/Observation Relations." In *Contemporary Field Research*, 2nd ed., ed. Robert M. Emerson, 239–259. Prospect Heights, IL: Waveland Press.

Erikson, Ken, and Donald Stull. 1998. *Doing Team Ethnography: Warnings and Advice.* Thousand Oaks, CA: Sage Publications.

Esterberg, Kristin. 1997. *Lesbian and Bisexual Identities: Constructing Communities, Constructing Selves.* Philadelphia: Temple University Press.

——. 2002. *Qualitative Methods in Social Research.* Boston: McGraw-Hill.

Fantasia, Rick. 1988. *Cultures of Solidarity: Consciousness, Action, and Contemporary American Workers.* Berkeley: University of California Press.

Fetterman, David M. 2001. *Foundations of Empowerment Evaluation.* Thousand Oaks, CA: Sage Publications.

Fine, Gary A., 1993. "10 Lies of Ethnography: Moral Dilemmas in Fieldwork." *Journal of Contemporary Ethnography* 22:267–294.

——. ed. 1995. *A Second Chicago School? The Development of a Postwar American Sociology.* Chicago: University of Chicago Press.

——. 1996. *Kitchens: The Culture of Restaurant Work.* Berkeley: University of California Press.

Forrest, Burke. 1986. "Apprentice-Participation: Methodology and the Study of Subjective Reality." *Urban Life* 14 (January): 431–453.

Foucault, Michel. 1977. *Discipline and Punish: The Birth of the Prison.* New York: Pantheon Books.

Friedman, David M. 2001. *A Mind of Its Own: A Cultural History of the Penis.* New York: Free Press.

Friedman, Judith. 2003. "How Visual Artifacts Preserve the Past." Paper presented to the International Visual Sociological Association meetings, Southampton, England. July.

Ganguly, Keya. 1992. "Migrant Identities: Personal Memory and the Construction of Selfhood." *Cultural Studies* 6 (1): 27–50.

Gardner, Carol Brooks. 1995. *Passing By: Gender and Public Harassment.* Berkeley: University of California Press.

Geertz, Clifford. 1973. *Interpretation of Cultures.* New York: Basic Books.

——. 1976. "From the Native's Point of View: On the Nature of Anthropological Understanding." In *Meaning in Anthropology*, ed. Keith H. Basso and Henry A. Selby, 221–237. Albuquerque, NM: University of New Mexico Press.

——. 1988. *Works and Lives: The Anthropologist as Author.* Stanford, CA: Stanford University Press.

——. 2001. "Thick Description: Toward an Interpretive Theory of Culture." *Contemporary Field Research*, ed. Robert M. Emerson, 55–75. Prospect Heights, IL: Waveland Press.

Gergen, Mary, and Kenneth Gergen. 2003. "Positive Aging." In *Ways of Aging*, ed. Jaber Gubrium and James Holstein, 203–224. Oxford: Blackwell Publishing.

Gibbs, Graham R. 2002. *Qualitative Data Analysis: Explorations With NVivo.* New York: McGraw-Hill.

Glaser, Barney, and Anselm Strauss. 1967. *The Discovery of Grounded Theory.* Chicago: Aldine Publishing Co.

Glassner, Barry. 2000. *The Culture of Fear: Why Americans Are Afraid of the Wrong Things*. New York: Basic Books.

Globerman, Judith. 2001. "The Unencumbered Child: Family Reputations and Responsibilites in the Care of Relatives With Alzheimer's Disease." In *Aging and Everday Life*, ed. Jaber Gubrium and James Holstein, 386–400. Oxford: Blackwell Publishing.

Goffman, Erving. 1959. *The Presentation of Self in Everyday Life*. Garden City, NY: Doubleday.

——. 1961. *Asylums: Essays on the Social Situation of Patients and Other Inmates*. Garden City, NY: Doubleday.

——. 1963a. *Behavior in Public Places: Notes on the Social Organization of Gatherings*. New York: Free Press of Glencoe.

——. 1963b. *Stigma: Notes on the Management of Spoiled Identity*. Englewood Cliffs, NJ.: Prentice-Hall.

——. 1967. *Interaction Ritual: Essays on Face-to-Face Behavior*. Garden City, NY: Anchor Books.

——. 1979. *Gender Advertisements*. Boston: Harvard University Press.

Goode, Erich. 1999. "Sex With Informants as Deviant Behavior: An Account and Commentary." *Deviant Behavior* 20: 301–324.

——. 2002. "Sexual Involvement and Social Research in a Fat Civil Rights Organization." *Qualitative Sociology* 25 (4) (Winter): 501–534.

Gordon, David F. 1987. "Getting Close by Staying Distant: Fieldwork With Proselytizing Groups." *Qualitative Sociology* 10 (Fall): 267–287.

Greenblat, Cathy S. 2003. "Tales of the Asilo." Paper presented to the International Visual Sociological Association meetings, Southampton, England. July.

——. 2004. *Alive With Alzheimer's*. Chicago and London: University of Chicago Press.

Greene, Jennifer C. 1994. "Qualitative Program Evaluation: Practice and Promise." In *Handbook of Qualitative Research*, ed. Norman K. Denzin and Yvonna S. Lincoln, 530–544. Thousand Oaks, CA: Sage Publications.

Gubrium, Jaber F. 1975. *Living and Dying at Murray Manor*. New York: St. Martins.

Gubrium, Jaber F., and James A. Holstein. 1995. *The Active Interview*. Thousand Oaks, CA: Sage Publications.

——. 1997. *The New Language of Qualitative Method*. New York: Oxford University Press.

——. 2002. "From the Individual Interview to the Interview Society." In *Handbook of Research Interviewing: Context and Method*, ed. Jaber F. Gubruim and James A. Holstein, 3–32. Thousand Oaks, CA: Sage Publications.

Gusfield, Joseph R. 1976. "The Literary Rhetoric of Science: Comedy and Pathos in Drinking Driver Research." *American Sociological Review* 41: 16–34.

Hackney, Jennifer. 1996. "Stairway to Heaven: Religious Expressions in an Overeaters Anonymous Group." Paper presented to the American Sociological Association, New York.

Halbert, Shawn C. 2003. "Rhythm and Reminiscence: Popular Music, Nostalgia, and the Storied Self." Senior thesis, Sociology, University of Houston.

Hammersley, Martyn. 2001. "Ethnography and Realism." In *Contemporary Field Research*, 2nd ed., ed. Robert M. Emerson, 102–151. Prospect Heights, IL: Waveland Press.

Harkness, Geoffrey. 2003. "Living on the Fringe: How Pawn Shops Keep Poor People Poor." Masters thesis, Sociology, University of Kansas.

Harkess, Shirley, and Carol Warren. 1993. "The Social Relations of Intensive Interviewing: Constellations of Strangeness and Science." *Sociological Methods and Research* 21 (3): 317–339.

Harper, Douglas. 1982. *Good Company.* Chicago: University of Chicago Press.

——. 1994. "On the Authority of the Image: Visual Methods at the Crossroads." In *The Handbook of Qualitative Research,* ed. Norman K. Denzin and Yvonna S. Lincoln, 403–412. Thousand Oaks, CA: Sage Publications.

——. 2001. *Changing Works: Visions of a Lost Agriculture.* Chicago: University of Chicago Press.

——. 2002. "Reimagining Visual Methods: Galileo to Necromancer." In *Handbook of Qualitative Research,* 2nd ed., ed. Norman K. Denzin and Yvonna S. Lincoln, 717–732. Thousand Oaks, CA: Sage Publications.

Heap, Chad. 2003. "The City as a Sexual Laboratory: The Queer Heritage of the Chicago School." *Qualitative Sociology* 26 (Winter): 457–487.

Hessler, Richard M., Jane Downing, Cathleen Beltz, Angela Pelliccio, Mark Powell, and Whitley Vale. 2003. "Qualitative Research on Adolescent Risk Using E-Mail: A Methodological Assessment." *Qualitative Sociology* 26 (Spring): 111–124.

Hill, Shirley A. 1994. *Managing Sickle Cell Disease in Low-Income Families.* Philadelphia: Temple University Press.

Holstein, James A. 1987. "Mental Illness Assumptions in Civil Commitment Proceedings." *Journal of Contemporary Ethnography* 16:147–175.

Holstein, James A., and Jaber F. Gubrium. 1995. *The Active Interview.* Thousand Oaks, CA: Sage Publications.

Hondagneu-Sotelo, Pierrette. 1994. *Gendered Transitions: Mexican Experiences of Immigration.* Berkeley: University of California Press.

Hopper, Columbus B., and Johnny Moore. 1990. "Women in Outlaw Motorcycle Gangs." *Journal of Contemporary Ethnography* 18 (January): 363–387.

Humphreys, Laud. 1970. *Tea Room Trade: Impersonal Sex in Public Places.* Chicago: Aldine.

Hunt, Jennifer. 1984. "The Development of Rapport Through the Negotiation of Gender in Field Work Among Police." *Human Organization* 43:283–296.

ILI. 2001. Tribal Language Field Survey Project Reports. Unpublished reports of the Indigenous Language Institute, Santa Fe, New Mexico.

Irving, Leslie. 1999. *Codependent Forever More: The Invention of Self in a Twelve Step Group.* Chicago: University of Chicago Press.

Jack-Roller, The, and Jon Snodgrass. 1982. *The Jack-Roller at Seventy.* Lexington, MA: Lexington Books.

Jackson, Janet E. 1990. "I Am a Fieldnote: Fieldnotes as a Symbol of Professional Identity." In *Fieldnotes: The Making of Anthropology,* ed. R. Sanjek, 3–33. Ithaca, NY: Cornell University Press.

Johnson, John M. 1975. *Doing Field Research.* New York: Macmillian Publishing Co.

Johnson, John. 1983. "Trust and Personal Involvement in Fieldwork." In *Contemporary Field Research,* ed. R. M. Emerson, 203–215. Prospect Heights, IL: Waveland Press.

Johnson, Richard. 2002. "The Sale Barn." Unpublished manuscript, University of Kansas.

Jones, James H. 1993. *Bad Blood: The Tuskegee Syphilis Experiment*. New York: The Free Press.

Jules-Rosette, Bennetta. 1975. *Vision and Realities: Aspects of Ritual and Conversion in an African Church*. Ithaca, NY: Cornell University Press.

Karas, Jennifer, and Tracy X. Karner. 2004. "Understanding the Diabetic Body-Self." Paper presented at the American Sociological Association meetings, San Francisco.

Karner, Tracy X. 1991. "Ideology and Nationalism: The Finnish Move to Independence, 1809–1918." *Ethnic and Racial Studies* 14 (2): 152–169.

———. 1994. "Masculinity, Trauma, and Identity: Life Narratives of Vietnam Veterans With Post Traumatic Stress Disorder." PhD diss., Univ. of Kansas.

———. 1995. "Medicalizing Masculinity: Post Traumatic Stress Disorder in Vietnam Veterans." *Masculinities* 3 (4): 23–65.

———. 1998a. "Professional Caring: Homecare Workers as Fictive-Kin." *Journal of Aging Studies* 12 (1): 69–82.

———. 1998b. "Retelling Selves Through Visual Narratives: The Reciprocity of Culture and Identity." In *Communication and Cognition*, ed. Michael S. Ball, 3 (2/3): 145–60.

———. 1999. "Demonstrated Lessons: Case Management Strategies for Serving Ethnically Diverse Families." *Geriatric Care Management Journal* 9 (2): 9–12.

———. 2001. "Caring for an Aging Society: Cohort Values and Eldercare Services." *Journal of Aging and Social Policy* 13 (1): 15–36.

Karner, Tracy X., and Donna Bobbit-Zeher. 2003. "Losing Self: Reflections on Dementia by Family Caregivers." Paper presented at the Stone-Couch Symbolic Interactionism Meetings, Phoenix, AZ.

Karner, Tracy X., and L. C. Hall. 2002. "Successful Strategies for Serving Diverse Populations." In *A New Look at Community Respite Programs: Utilization, Satisfaction, and Development*, ed. R. Montgomery, 107–132. Binghamton, NY: Haworth Press.

Karner, Tracy X., Rhonda Montgomery, Debra Dobbs, and Cara Wittmaier. 1998. "Increasing Staff Satisfaction: The Impact of Special Care Units and Family Involvement." *Journal of Gerontological Nursing* 24 (2): 39–44.

Karner, Tracy X., and Carol A. B. Warren. 1995. "The Dangerous Listener: Unforeseen Perils in Intensive Interviewing." *The Clinical Sociology Review* 13: 80–105.

Katz, Jack. 1972. *Experimentation With Human Beings*. New York: Russell Sage.

———. 2001. "From How to Why: On Luminous Description and Causal Inference in Ethnography, Part 1." *Ethnography* 2 (4): 443–473.

———. 2002. "From How to Why: On Luminous Description and Causal Inference in Ethnography, Part 2" *Ethnography* 3 (1): 63–90.

Kemmis, Stephen, and Robin McTaggart. 2000. "Participatory Action Research." In *Handbook of Qualitative Research*, 2nd ed., ed. Norman K. Denzin and Yvonna S. Lincoln, 567–606. Thousand Oaks, CA: Sage Publications.

Kilbourne, Jean. 2000. *Can't Buy Me Love: How Advertising Changes the Way We Think and Feel*. Carmichael, CA: Touchstone Books.

Kirk, Jerome, and Marc L. Miller. 1986. *Reliability and Validity in Qualitative Research*. Beverly Hills, CA: Sage Publications.

Kivett, Doug, and Carol A. B. Warren. 2002. "Social Control in a Group Home for Delinquent Boys." *Journal of Contemporary Sociology* 31 (Summer): 3–32.

Kleinman, Sherryl, and Martha A. Copp. 1993. *Emotions and Fieldwork*. Thousand Oaks, CA: Sage Publications.

Kneeland, Timothy, and Carol A. B. Warren. (2002). *Pushbutton Psychiatry: A History of Electroshock in America*. Westport, CT: Praeger.

Kondo, Dorrine K. 2001. "How the Problem of Crafting Selves Emerged." In *Contemporary Field Research*, 2nd ed., ed. Robert M. Emerson, 188–202. Prospect Heights, IL: Waveland Press.

Kosloski, Karl, Rhonda Montgomery, and Tracy X. Karner. 1999. "Differences in the Perceived Need for Assistive Services by Culturally Diverse Caregivers of Dementia Patients." *Journal of Applied Gerontology* (July): 239–256.

Kotarba, Joseph A. 1991. "Postmodernism, Ethnography, and Culture." *Studies in Symbolic Interaction* 12:45–52.

Krase, Jerry. 2002. "Park Slope, Brooklyn: In the Aftermath of the Destruction of the World Trade Center." Fall 2001 and Spring 2002 (Photoessay). *http://www.brooklynsoc.org/WTC/KraseWTC/index.shtml*.

Krieger, Susan. 1983. *The Mirror Dance: Identity in a Women's Community*. Philadelphia: Temple University Press.

———. 1991. *Social Science and the Self: Personal Essays on an Art Form*. New Brunswick, NJ: Rutgers University Press.

Kumin, Beatrice. 2003. "Brazilian Indians and Their Visual Representation in Different Media and Contexts in the 19th Century," Paper presented at the International Visual Sociological Association meetings, Southampton, England. July.

Kusenbach, Margarethe. 2003. "Street-Phenomenology: The Go-Along as Ethnographic Research Tool." *Ethnography* 4 (3): 455–485.

Kvale, Steinar. 1996. *InterViews: An Introduction to Qualitative Research Interviewing*. Thousand Oaks, CA: Sage Publications.

LeCompte, Margaret D., and Gary A. Dworkin. (1991). *Giving Up on School: Teacher Burnout and Student Dropout*. Newbury Park, CA: Corwin.

Lembcke, Jerry. 2000. *The Spitting Image: Myth, Memory, and the Legacy of Vietnam*. New York: New York University Press.

Leo, Richard A. 1995. "Trial and Tribulations: Courts, Ethnography, and the Need for an Evidentiary Privilege for Academic Researchers." *The American Sociologist* 26:113–134.

———. 2001. "No Trials but Tribulations: Courts, Ethnography, and the Need for an Evidentiary Privilege for Academic Researchers. "In *Contemporary Field Research*, 2nd ed., ed. Robert M. Emerson, 260–279. Prospect Heights, IL: Waveland Press.

Levi, Ken. 1981. "Becoming a Hit Man: Neutralization in a Very Deviant Career." *Urban Life* 10 (April): 47–63.

Lidz, Charles W., Alan Meisel, Eviatar Zerubavel, Mary Carter, Regina M. Sestak, and Loren H. Roth. 1984. *Informed Consent: A Study of Decisionmaking in Psychiatry*. New York: The Guilford Press.

Liebow, Elliott. 1967. *Tally's Corner: A Study of Negro Streetcorner Men*. Boston: Little Brown.

———. 1993. *Tell Them Who I Am: The Lives of Homeless Women*. New York: Penguin.

Lincoln, Yvonna, and Egon G. Guba. (1985). *Naturalistic Inquiry.* Newbury Park, CA: Sage Publications.

Littrell, W. Boyd. 1979. *Bureaucratic Justice: Police, Prosecutors, and Plea Bargaining.* Beverly Hills, CA: Sage Publications.

Lofland, John. 1966. *Doomsday Cult.* Englewood Cliffs, NJ: Prentice-Hall.

——. 1970. "Interactionist Imagery and Analytic Interruptus." In *Human Nature and Collective Behavior: Papers in Honor of Herbert Blumer,* ed. T. Shibutani, 35–45. New Brunswick, NJ: Transaction Books.

Lofland, John, and Lyn Lofland. 1995. *Analyzing Social Settings: A Guide to Qualitative Observations and Analysis.* Belmont, CA: Wadsworth.

Lofland, Lyn. 1973. *A World of Strangers.* New York: Basic Books.

——. 1998. *The Public Realm.* New York: Aldine de Gruyter.

Loseke, Donileen. 1992. *The Battered Woman and Shelters.* Albany, NY: SUNY Press.

Luff, Donna. 1999. "Doing Social Research—Issues and Dilemmas." *Sociology* 333:678–703.

Lyman, Karen. 1993. *Day In, Day Out With Alzheimer's.* Philadelphia: Temple University Press.

Maines, Douglas R. 1998. "Review of Fields of Play: Constructing an Academic Life." *Social Forces* 77 (1): 388–390.

Mann, Chris, and Fiona Stewart. 2002. "Internet Interviewing." In *Handbook of Interview Research,* ed. Jaber F. Gubrium and James A. Holstein, 603–628. Thousand Oaks, CA: Sage Publications.

Marcus, George E. 1986. "Ethnography in the Modern World System." In *Writing Culture: The Poetics and Politics of Ethnography,* ed. James Clifford and George E. Marcus, 165–193. Berkeley: University of California Press.

Margolis, Eric. 1988. "Mining Photographs: Unearthing the Meanings of Historical Photos." *Radical History Review* 40:32–48.

——. 1994. "Video Ethnography." *Jump Cut* 39:122–131.

——. 2000. "Class Pictures: Representations of Race, Gender, and Ability in a Century of School Photography." *Educational Policy Analysis Archives* 8 (31) online, *http://epaa.asu.edu/epaa/v8n31.*

——.2001. *The Hidden Curriculum in Higher Education.* New York: Routledge Falmer.

Marullo, Sam. 1998. "Bringing Home Diversity: A Service-Learning Approach to Teaching Race and Ethnic Studies." *Teaching Sociology* 26 (4): 331–340.

Mauthner, Natasha S., and Andrea Doucet. 2003. "Reflexive Accounts and Accounts of Reflexivity in Qualitative Data Analysis." *Sociology* 37 (3): 413–431.

McCracken, Grant. 1988. *The Long Interview.* Thousand Oaks, CA: Sage Publications.

Mead, George H. 1934. *Mind, Self, and Society.* Chicago: University of Chicago Press.

Michette, Alan, and Slawka Pfauntsch. 1996. *X-rays: The First Hundred Years.* New York: John Wiley & Sons.

Miczo, Nathan. 2003. "Beyond the 'Fetishism of Words': Considerations on the Use of Interview to Gather Chronic Illness Narratives." *Qualitative Health Research* 13 (4): 469–490.

Miles, Matthew, and A. Michael Huberman. 1994. *Qualitative Data Analysis: An Expanded Sourcebook.* Thousand Oaks, CA: Sage Publications.

Milgram, Stanley. 1963. "Behavioral Study of Obedience." *Journal of Abnormal and Social Psychology* 67:371–378.

Miller, Gale, and James Holstein. 1996. *Dispute Domains and Welfare Claims.* Greenwich, CT: JAI Press.

Milligan, Megan. 2003. "The House Told Me: Historic Preservation and Dwelling as Social Actor." Paper presented to the American Sociological Association, Atlanta, GA. August.

Mishler, Elliott G. 1986. *Research Interviewing: Context and Narrative.* Cambridge, MA: Harvard University Press.

Mitchell, Richard G., Jr. 2002. *Dancing at Armageddon: Survivalism and Chaos in Modern Times.* Chicago: University of Chicago Press.

Montgomery, Rhonda, Karl Kosloski, and Tracy X. Karner. 1996. "Integrating Support Services for Alzheimer's Families in Managed Care Systems." HRSA-Bureau of Primary Health Care.

Montgomery, Rhonda, Tracy X. Karner, and Karl Kosloski. 2003. "Analyzing the Success of a National Demonstration to Create State Responsibility for Long Term Care." *Journal of Aging and Social Policy* 14 (3–4): 119–139.

Montgomery, Rhonda, Tracy X. Karner, Karl Kosloski, and Jay Schaefer. 2002. "Initial Findings From the Evaluation of the Alzheimer's Disease Demonstration Grant to States Program." *Home Health Care Quarterly* 21 (3–4): 5–32. Reprinted in *A New Look at Community Respite Programs: Utilization, Satisfaction, and Development,* ed. R. Montgomery. Binghamton, NY: Haworth Press.

Morgan, David. 2002. "Focus Group Interviewing." In *Handbook of Interview Research,* ed. Jaber F. Gubrium and James A. Holstein, 141–159. Thousand Oaks, CA: Sage Publications.

Morganroth, Gullette M. 2003. "From Life Storytelling to Age Autobiography." *Journal of Aging Studies* 17 (1): 101–111.

Naples, Nancy A. 1996. "A Feminist Revisiting of the Insider/Outsider Debate: The 'Outsider Phenomenon' in Rural Iowa." *Qualitative Sociology* 19 (1): 83–106.

Narayan, Kirin, and Kenneth M. George. 2002. "Personal and Folk Narratives as Cultural Representations." In *Handbook of Research Interviewing: Context and Method,* ed. Jaber F. Gubruim and James A. Holstein, 815–832. Thousand Oaks, CA: Sage Publications.

Newton, Esther. 1972. *Mother Camp: Female Impersonators in America.* Englewood Cliffs, NJ: Prentice-Hall.

Noblit, George W., and Janie M. Burcart. 1975. "Ethics, Powerless Peoples, and Methodologies for the Study of Trouble." *Humboldt Journal of Social Relations* 2 (2): 20–25.

Oakley, Ann. 1981. "Interviewing Women: A Contradiction in Terms?" In *Doing Feminist Research,* ed. H. Roberts, 30–61. London: Routledge and Kegan Paul.

Obbo, Christine. 1990. "Adventures With Fieldnotes." In *Fieldnotes: The Makings of Anthropology,* ed. Roger Sanjek, 290–302. Ithaca, NY: Cornell University Press.

O'Connell Davidson, Julia, and Derek Layder. 1994. *Methods, Sex and Madness.* London: Routledge.

Palmer, Vivian. 1928. *Field Studies in Sociology: A Student's Manual.* Chicago: University of Chicago Press.

Paterniti, Debora A. 2003. "Claiming an Identity in a Nursing Home." In *Ways of Aging*, ed. Jaber Gubrium and James Holstein, 58–74. Oxford: Blackwell Publishing.

Penn, Helen. 1997. *Comparing Nurseries: Staff and Children in Italy, Spain, and the UK*. London: Paul Chapman Publications.

Personal Narratives Group. 1989. *Interpreting Women's Lives: Feminist Theory and Personal Narratives*. Bloomington and Indianapolis: Indiana University Press.

Peshkin, Alan. 1984. "Odd Man Out: The Participant Observer in an Absolutist Setting." *Sociology of Education* 57:254–264.

Peter, Lizette. 2003. "A Naturalistic Study of the Cherokee Language Immersion Preschool Project." PhD diss., Univ. of Kansas.

Platt, Jennifer. 2002. "The History of the Interview." In *Handbook of Interview Research*, ed. Jaber F. Gubrium and James A. Holstein, 33–54. Thousand Oaks, CA: Sage Publications.

Poland, Blake D. 2002. "Transcription Quality." In *Handbook of Interview Research*, ed. Jaber F. Gubrium and James A. Holstein, 629–650. Thousand Oaks, CA: Sage Publications.

Pratt, Mary Louise. 1986. "Fieldwork in Common Places." In *Writing Culture: The Poetics and Politics of Ethnography*, ed. James Clifford and George E. Marcus, 98–121. Berkeley: University of California Press.

Prosser, Jon. 1998. "The Status of Image Based Research." In *Image Based Research: A Sourcebook for Qualitative Researchers*, ed. Jon Prosser, 97–110. London: Falmer Press.

Prosser, Jon, and Dona Schwartz. 1998. "Photographs Within the Sociological Research Process." In *Image Based Research: A Sourcebook for Qualitative Researchers*, ed. Jon Prosser, 115–129. London: Falmer Press.

Punch, Maurice. 1994. "Politics and Ethics in Qualitative Research." In *The Handbook of Qualitative Research*, ed. Norman K. Denzin and Yvonna S. Lincoln, 83–97. Thousand Oaks, CA: Sage Publications.

Radley, Alan, and Diane Taylor. 2003. "Images of Recovery: A Photo-Elicitation Study on the Hospital Ward." *Qualitative Health Research* 13 (1): 77–99.

Rae, Ruth. 2003. "Visual Images of Meaning: Photographic Explorations of Homes and Gardens." Paper presented to the International Visual Sociological Association meetings, Southampton, England. July.

Reinharz, Shulamit, and Susan E. Chase. 2002. "Interviewing Women." In *Handbook of Interview Research*, ed. Jaber F. Gubrium and James A. Holstein, 221–238. Thousand Oaks, CA: Sage Publications.

Reiss, Albert J. 1979. "Governmental Regulation of Scientific Inquiry: Some Paradoxical Consequences." In *Deviance and Decency: The Ethics of Research With Human Subjects*, ed. Carl B. Klockars and Finbarr W. O'Connor, 61–95 Beverly Hills, CA: Sage Publications.

Rhoads, Richard A. 2003. "Traversing the Great Divide: Writing the Self Into Qualitative Research and Narrative." In *Studies in Symbolic Interaction* 26, ed. Norman K. Denzin, 235–259. Oxford: JAI Press.

Rhodes, Lorna A. 1995. *Emptying Beds: The Work of an Emergency Psychiatric Unit* (Comparative Studies of Health Systems and Medical Care, No. 27). Berkeley: University of California Press.

Richardson, Laurel. 1985. *The New Other Woman: Contemporary Single Women in Affairs With Married Men*. New York: Free Press.

———. 1990. *Writing Strategies: Reaching Diverse Audiences*. Newbury Park, CA: Sage Publications.

———. 1994. "Writing: A Method of Inquiry." In *Handbook of Qualitative Research*, ed. Norman K. Denzin and Yvonna S. Lincoln, 516–529. Thousand Oaks, CA: Sage Publications.

Riemer, Jeffrey W. 1979. *Hard Hats: The Work World of Construction Workers.* Beverly Hills: Sage Publications.

Riessman, Catherine K. 1992. "Making Sense of Marital Violence: One Woman's Narrative." In *Storied Lives*, ed. George Rosenwald and Richard Ochberg, 231–249. New Haven and New York: Yale University Press.

Robbins, Thomas, Dick Anthony, and Thomas E. Curtis. 1973. "The Limits of Symbolic Realism: Problems of Empathetic Field Observation in a Sectarian Context." *Journal for the Scientific Study of Religion* 12:259–271.

Robinson, Christine. 2003. "'The Web of Talk': Social Control and the Production of a Lesbian Community." PhD diss., Univ. of Kansas.

Rochford, E. Burke. 1985. *Hare Krishna in America.* New Brunswick, NJ: Rutgers University Press.

Rosenwald, George C., and Richard L. Ochberg. 1992. "Introduction: Life Stories, Cultural Politics, and Self Understanding." In *Storied Lives*, ed. George Rosenwald and Richard Ochberg, 1–18. New Haven and New York: Yale University Press.

Roth, Julius A. 1966. "Hired Hand Research." *The American Sociologist* 1:190–196.

Rubin, Irene, and Herbert J. Rubin. 1995. *Qualitative Interviewing: The Art of Hearing Data.* Thousand Oaks, CA: Sage Publications.

Rubin, Lillian B. 1976. *Worlds of Pain: Life in the Working-Class Family.* New York: Basic Books.

Sanchez-Jankowski, Martin. 1990. *Islands in the Street: Gangs in American Urban Society.* Berkeley: University of California Press.

Sanders, Clinton R. 1998. "Animal Passions: The Emotional Experience of Doing Ethnography in Animal-Human Interaction Settings." In *Doing Ethnographic Research: Fieldwork Settings*, ed. S. Grills, 184–198. Thousand Oaks, CA: Sage Publications.

———. 2003. "Actions Speak Louder Than Words: Close Relationships Between Humans and Nonhuman Animals." *Symbolic Interaction* 26 (3): 405–426.

Sanjek, Roger. 1990. "Fire, Loss, and the Sorcerer's Apprentice." In *Fieldnotes: The Makings of Anthropology*, ed. R. Sanjek, 34–44. Ithaca, NY: Cornell University Press.

Scarce, Rik. 1994. "(No) Trial (but) Tribulation: When Courts and Ethnography Conflict." *Journal of Contemporary Ethnography* 23:123–149.

Schratz, Michael, ed. 1993. *Qualitative Voices in Educational Research.* Washington, DC: Falmer Press.

Shaw, Clifford R. 1966. *The Jack-Roller: A Delinquent Boy's Own Story,* 2nd ed. Chicago: University of Chicago Press.

Shoemaker, Helen J. 1991. "Self-Construction in a Small Group Setting: Journal Narratives." *Small Group Research* 22 (3): 339–359.

Shostak, Marjorie. 1981. *Nisa: The Life and Words of a !Kung Woman.* London: Penguin.

Shuy, Roger. 2002. "In-Person Versus Telephone Interviewing." In *Handbook of Interview Research*, ed. Jaber F. Gubrium and James A. Holstein, 537–556. Thousand Oaks, CA: Sage Publications.

Silver, David. 2004. "Internet/Cyberculture/Digital Culture/New Media/ Fill-in-the-Blank Studies." *New Media and Society* 6 (1): 55–64.

Simmel, Georg. 1950. *The Sociology of Georg Simmel*, ed. and trans. K. H. Wolff. New York: Free Press.

Smith, Dorothy E. 1987. *The Everyday World as Problematic*. Toronto: University of Toronto Press.

Smith, Richard C. 2002. "Analytic Strategies for Oral History Interviews." In *Handbook of Research Interviewing: Context and Method*, ed. Jaber F. Gubruim and James A. Holstein, 711–732. Thousand Oaks, CA: Sage.

Sniezek, Tamara, 2002. "On Wedding and Becoming a Couple." Paper presented at a Conference on Fieldwork in Contemporary Society, UCLA, May 16–17.

Spindler, George. 1988. *Doing the Ethnography of Schooling: Educational Anthropology in Action*. Prospect Heights, IL: Waveland Press.

Spradley, James P. 1979. *The Ethnographic Interview*. New York: Holt, Rinehart, and Winston.

Spradley, James P., and Brenda J. Mann. 1975. *The Cocktail Waitress: Woman's Work in a Man's World*. New York: Alfred A. Knopf.

Stacey, Judith. 1998. *Brave New Families: Stories of Domestic Upheaval in Late-Twentieth-Century America*. Berkeley: University of California Press.

Staggenborg, Suzanne. 1988. "'Hired Hand Research' Revisited." *The American Sociologist* 19 (3): 260–269.

Suchman, Lucy, and Brigitte Jordan. 1990. "Interactional Troubles in Face-to-Face Survey Interviews." *Journal of the American Statistical Association* 85:232–250.

Sudnow, David. 1967. *Passing On*. Englewood Cliffs, NJ: Prentice-Hall.

Taylor, Stephen J. 1987. "Observing Abuse: Professional Ethics and Personal Morality in Field Research." *Qualitative Sociology* 10 (Fall): 288–302.

——. 1991. "'Leaving the Field' Research, Relationships, and Responsibilities." In *Experiencing Fieldwork: An Inside View of Qualitative Research*, ed. William B. Shaffir and Robert A. Stebbins, 238–247. Newbury Park, CA: Sage Publications.

Thomas, William I, and Florian Znaniecki. 1958. *The Polish Peasant in Europe and America (1918–1920)*. New York: Dover Publications.

Thompson, Paul. 1988. *The Voice of the Past*. Oxford University Press.

Thorne, Barrie. 1971. "Resisting the Draft: An Ethnography of the Draft Resistance Movement." PhD diss., Brandeis Univ.

——. 1980. "'You Still Takin' Notes?' Fieldwork and Problems of Informed Consent." *Social Problems* 27:284–297.

——. 1983. "Political Activist as Participant Observer: Conflicts of Commitment in a Study of the Draft Resistance Movement of the 1960s." In *Contemporary Field Research*, ed. Robert M. Emerson, 216–234. Prospect Heights, IL: Waveland Press.

Vail, D. Angus. 2001. "Researching From Afar: Distance, Ethnography, and Testing the Edge." *Journal of Contemporary Ethnography* 30 (6): 704–725.

——. 2002. "On Presenting the Tattooed Self." Paper presented at a Conference on Fieldwork in Contemporary Society, UCLA, May 16–17.

Van Maanen, John. 1983. "The Moral Fix: On the Ethics of Fieldwork." In *Contemporary Field Research*, ed. R. M. Emerson, 269–287. Boston: Little, Brown.

——. 1988. *Tales of the Field: On Writing Ethnography*. Chicago: University of Chicago Press.

Vaughan, Diane. 1990. *Uncoupling: Turning Points in Intimate Relationships.* New York: Vintage.

Wacquant, Loic. 2002. "Scrutinizing the Street: Poverty, Morality, and the Pitfalls of Urban Ethnography." *The American Journal of Sociology* 107 (May): 1468–1532.

Waid, L. D., and L. D. Frazier. 2003. "Cultural Differences in Possible Selves During Later Life." *Journal of Aging Studies* 17 (3): 251–268.

Wakeford, Nina, and Kris Cohen. 2003. "Photoblogging: Digital Photography and Sociology as Strange Chronicles." Paper presented to the International Visual Sociological Association meetings, Southampton, England. July.

Wang Caroline, Mary Ann Burris. 1994. "Empowerment Through Photovoice: Portraits of Participation." *Health Education Quarterly* 21 (2): 171–186.

Wang Caroline, Mary Ann Burris, and Yanping P. Xiang. 1996. "Chinese Village Women as Visual Anthropologists: A Participatory Approach to Reaching Policymakers." *Social Science and Medicine,* 42 (10): 1391–1400.

Warren, Carol A. B. 1972. *Identity and Community in the Gay World.* New York: Wiley-Interscience.

——. 1982. *The Court of Last Resort: Mental Illness and the Law.* Chicago: University of Chicago Press.

——. 1983. "The Politics of Trouble in an Adolescent Psychiatric Hospital." *Urban Life* 12:327–348.

——. 1987. *Madwives: Schizophrenic Women in the 1950s.* Rutgers, NJ: Rutgers University Press.

——. 1996. "Older Women, Younger Men: Self and Stigma in Age-Discrepant Relationships." *Clinical Sociology Review* (Fall): 62–86.

——. 1998. "Aging and Identity in Premodern Times." *Research on Aging* 20 (January): 11–35.

——. 2000. "Writing the Other, Inscribing the Self." *Qualitative Sociology* 23: 183–199.

——. 2001. "Gender and Fieldwork Relations." In *Contemporary Field Research* 2nd ed., ed. Robert M. Emerson, 203–223. Prospect Heights, IL: Waveland Press.

——. 2002. "Qualitative Interviewing." In *Handbook of Interview Research: Context and Method*, ed. Jaber F. Gubrium and James A. Holstein, 83–101. Thousand Oaks, CA: Sage Publications.

——. 2003. "Sex and Gender in the 1970s." *Qualitative Sociology* 26 (Winter): 499–513.

Warren, Carol A. B., and Jennifer K. Hackney. 2000. *Gender Issues in Ethnography,* 2nd ed. Thousand Oaks, CA: Sage Publications.

Warren, Carol A. B., and Tracy X. Karner. 1990. "Permissions and the Social Context." *The American Sociologist.* (Summer): 116–135.

Wax, Rosalie H. 1979. "Gender and Age in Fieldwork and Fieldwork Education: No Good Thing Is Done by Any Man Alone." *Social Problems* 26:509–522.

——. 1983. "The Ambiguities of Fieldwork." In *Contemporary Field Research,* ed. Robert M. Emerson, 191–202. Prospect Heights, IL: Waveland Press.

Weiss, Robert S. 1994. *Learning From Strangers: The Art and Method of Qualitative Interview Studies.* New York: Free Press.

White, Shirley. 2003. *Participatory Video: Images That Transform and Empower,* Thousand Oaks, CA: Sage Publications.

Whyte, William F. 1943. *Street Corner Society.* Chicago: University of Chicago Press.

——. 1984. *Learning From the Field: A Guide From Experience.* Newbury Park, CA: Sage Publications.

——. 1992. "In Defense of Street Corner Society." *Journal of Contemporary Ethnography* 21:5–68.

Wight, David. 1994. "Boys' Thoughts About Sex in a Working-Class Locality of Glasgow." *Sociological Review* 42:702–737.

Williams, Terry, Eloise Dunlap, Bruce D. Johnson, and Ansley Hamid. 1992. "Personal Safety in Dangerous Places." *Journal of Contemporary Ethnography* 21 (3) (Oct.): 343–374.

Winlow, Simon, Dick Hobbs, Stuart Lister, and Philip Hadfield. 2001. "Get Ready to Duck: Bouncers and the Realities of Ethnographic Research on Violent Groups." *British Journal of Criminology* 41:536–548.

Wirth-Cauchon, Janet. 2000. *Women and Borderline Personality Disorder: Symptoms and Stories.* New Brunswick, NJ: Rutgers University Press.

Worth, Sol, and John Adair. 1972. *Through Navajo Eyes: Explorations in Film Communication and Anthropology.* Bloomington: Indiana University Press.

Wright, R. Dean. 2001. "Tramp Training: Constructing a Service Learning Program in Homeless Intervention." In *Applying Sociology: Making a Better World,* ed. William Du Bois and R. Dean Wright, 201–212. Needham Heights, MA: Allyn & Bacon.

Yalom, Marilyn. 1997. *A History of the Breast.* New York: Alfred A. Knopf.

Young, Pauline. 1935. *Interviewing in Social Work.* New York: McGraw-Hill.

Zhan, Heying. 2000. "The Inverted Pyramid: Familial Eldercare in China." PhD diss., Univ. of Kansas.

Ziller, Robert C. 1990. *Photographing the Self: Methods for Personal Orientations.* Newbury Park, CA: Sage Publications.

Zinn, Maxine Baca. 1979. "Insider Field Research in Minority Communities." *Social Problems* 27 (2): 159–166.

Zola, Irving K. 1982. *Missing Pieces: A Chronicle of Living With Disability.* Philadelphia: Temple University Press. ❖

# Index